Preface

Nelson GCSE Modular Science is an extensive and topical series which fully supports the requirements of the Edexcel Science (B) Modular GCSE courses. Book 1 of the series is designed to deliver the Single Award (B) component.

Book 1 is organised into six modules and one coursework section. Within each module, each sub-topic is individually treated, so that all aspects are covered comprehensively and informatively. The special features included within each sub-topic are...

- Learning Outcomes, outlining the knowledge and understanding you can expect to accumulate by working through each of the topics.
- Key Words, emphasising in bold text the most important scientific terms for you to remember.
- Key Facts, summarizing the essential content of the topic and working as a useful revision aid.
- End of Topic Questions, strengthening your knowledge and understanding, and extending some of the scientific concepts. Where appropriate, answers to these questions can be found in the corresponding Teacher Support File, and at www.modularscience.co.uk

In addition, each module contains...

- Science Today articles – You will find that throughout the book, the content of each Module attempts to place Science in a real-life context. In addition, look out for the individual Science Today articles, which entertainingly explore some of the hottest and most interesting issues in modern science.
- Exam Questions – Answers to these can be found in the corresponding teacher support materials
- A Glossary – Here you will find straightforward definitions for the Key Words highlighted in the main text.

Practical work is a core part of any modern science course, as it enables you to put theory into practice, in an often enjoyable and memorable context. It also helps you to understand the impact and importance of Science in today's world. These are the reasons that practical work features so heavily in GCSE, and since it involves so much time and effort, it should be assessed to see how you perform. The unique coursework section at the rear of this book will therefore be of invaluable assistance in helping you to maximise your coursework results. The requirements of all four skill areas are clearly expressed, and there is ample advice on what is needed at each mark level in each skill area. You will find many examples of students' work - at various levels of achievement - punctuated by questions and observations and a commentary on each piece of work. Note that students' Sc1 activities are provided in the Teacher Support File, and at www.modularscience.co.uk

We hope that this book will give you all the information and support you need to do well in your assessments and examinations at GCSE. We hope too that it will help you develop a fascination for Science that will serve you well, long after your studies are over.

Paul Collison
David Horrocks
David Kirkby
Averil MacDonald

Contents

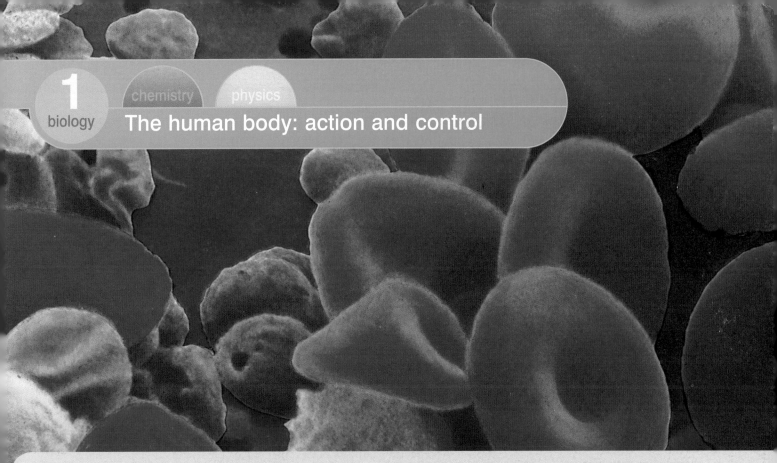

The human body: action and control

Everyone hopes to live a long, healthy life. Perhaps the most surprising thing is that so many people do. In this module you will learn about how your body manages to survive against all the odds.

The environment outside your body is hostile, but somehow you cope. You may occasionally catch a cold, but you fight off the illness and get better. If you could not fight the disease, it would kill you. The temperature outside your body can vary widely and suddenly, but the temperature inside remains the same. If you could not control your body temperature, your body would not function and you would die.

This module starts by looking at the main body functions. It explores some of the ways you are organised to manage the changes taking place in your body all the time. When things are going well, your body works like a well-oiled machine. But more than that, your body can grow and repair itself. Some machine!

The module also considers various chemical drugs and the effects, both good and bad, that they may have on your body. By understanding how your body works, you will be in a better position to make informed choices about your lifestyle and how to look after yourself.

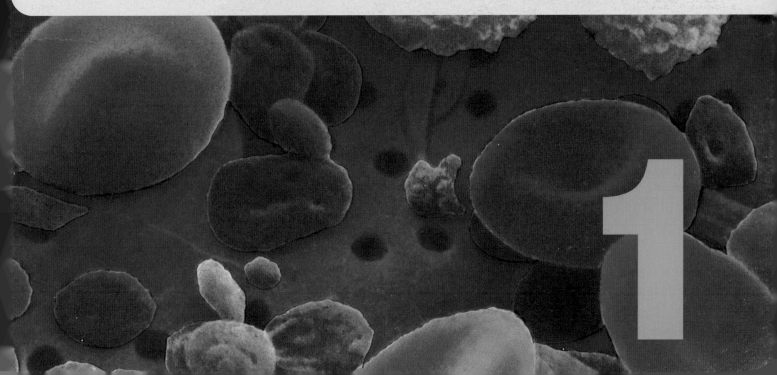

1

After completing the work in this topic you will be able to:

- describe the structure and function of the digestive system
- explain the action of enzymes and bile in the digestion process

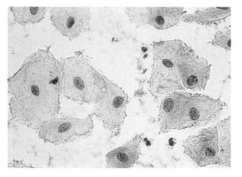

Figure 1.1 Cheek epithelial cells from inside a human mouth.

Getting started...

All living things have certain basic activities or processes in common.

Movement: Animals slither, roll, crawl, walk, run, jump, swim and fly. They can move all or part of their bodies. Plant shoots can bend. Their leaves can turn towards light and their roots can turn towards water.

Respiration: Activity uses up energy. Energy is released from food during the process of respiration.

Sensitivity: Living organisms can detect changes in their environment. This is called sensitivity. Animals can listen, smell and watch for signs of danger. They can also touch and taste. Plant shoots are sensitive to the direction of light and gravity.

Growth: All organisms grow for at least part of their lives. Animals stop growing when they reach their adult size. Plants grow throughout their lives.

Reproduction: Only living organisms produce offspring. This is called reproduction. Animals lay eggs or have babies. Plants produce seeds.

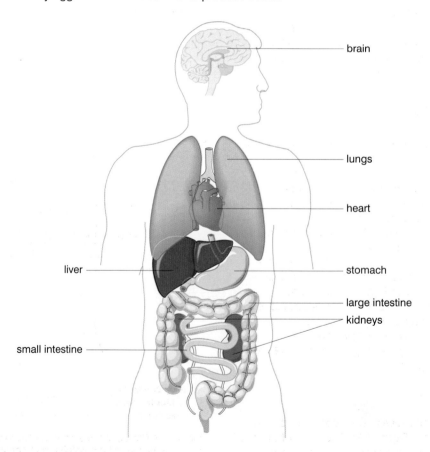

Figure 1.2 The major organs of the body. The kidneys lie behind the intestines.

Excretion: Activity produces waste products. Excretion is the removal of waste products from the body.

Nutrition: Food is needed for energy, growth, repair and replacement of tissues, and to help living things stay healthy and free from disease. Plants make their own food using energy from sunlight. Animals eat plants or other animals.

Know your parts…

The human body contains many important organs which support these processes. Figure 1.2 shows the position of the major organs.

The food you eat, such as bread, rice, meat, fish and vegetables, contains molecules of starch, protein and fat. These molecules are too large to be used in the cells in your body. They are broken down into smaller molecules during the process of **digestion**. The smaller molecules are then **absorbed**. Vitamins, minerals and water are already small enough to be absorbed. After absorption, the molecules from a chunk of cheese can become more molecules in a part of you!

Food is broken down in the digestive system by **enzymes**. It is then absorbed into the bloodstream.

A word about enzymes…

Enzymes are proteins that are involved in all the chemical processes in living things. Enzymes are catalysts. They speed up chemical reactions without being changed themselves. Enzymes can:

- build up lots of small molecules into a large molecule, for example turning thousands of glucose molecules into a starch molecule
- turn one type of molecule into another type
- break down large molecules into smaller molecules, for example turning a starch molecule into thousands of glucose molecules.

The names of enzymes usually end in the letters -ase, for example carbohydrase and lipase. There are thousands of different enzymes at work in your cells. You need this many because each enzyme is specialised for one reaction. For example, carbohydrase only works on carbohydrates and protease only works on protein.

Digestive organs…

The digestive system contains several organs (Figure 1.3). Each part of this food processing system has one or more functions (Table 1.1).

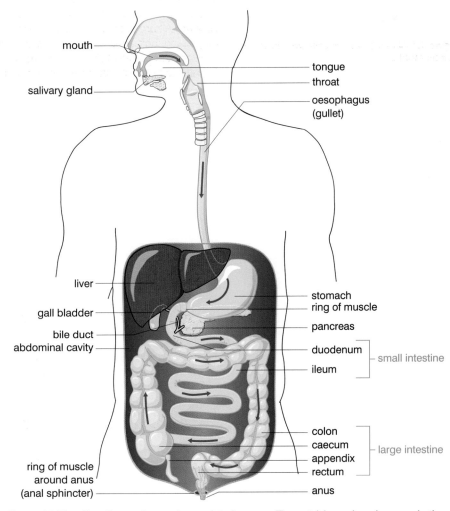

Figure 1.3 The digestive system and associated organs. The gut (shown in pale green in the diagram) is a long tube which runs from the mouth to the anus. It has specialised parts. The arrows show the direction of movement of food in the gut.

The human body: action and control   7

Part	Functions
salivary glands	production of saliva, which contains carbohydrase; mucus in saliva softens and lubricates food making it slip easily down the throat
oesophagus (gullet)	tube connecting the mouth to the stomach
stomach	bag with strong muscles; the muscles contract and relax to mix food with gastric juice and acid produced by the stomach wall; the acid kills bacteria in the food; gastric juice contains protease which requires acid conditions to work
liver	organ that produces bile – a green fluid that helps in the digestive process
gall bladder	bag which stores bile
pancreas	gland which produces pancreatic juice containing protease, carbohydrase and lipase; these enzymes require alkaline conditions to work
small intestine	long tube; it has millions of villi which give it a very large surface area; digested food is absorbed into the blood here
large intestine	tube which absorbs water into the blood and forms undigested food into a nearly solid waste called faeces

Table 1.1 The functions of the digestive system.

Moving it along…

After it has been swallowed, food is squeezed on its way. Your gut has circular muscles in its walls, which contract behind food and relax in front of it. The slow cycle of contraction and relaxation squeezes the food along. This process is called **peristalsis** (Figure 1.4).

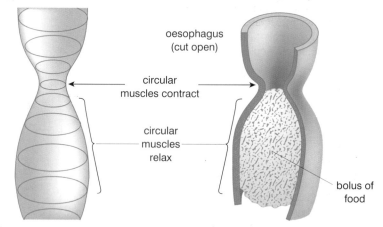

Figure 1.4 Food is squeezed along the gut by waves of muscular contraction called peristalsis.

The process of digestion

A large food molecule is made up of lots of smaller molecules. For example, starch is made up of thousands of glucose molecules. The smaller molecules are chemically bonded together. These bonds must be broken apart to release the smaller molecules. A large molecule is **insoluble** (will not dissolve in water) and is simply too big to pass through the intestine wall and into the blood. The small molecules are **soluble** (will dissolve in water) and can be absorbed into the blood (Figure 1.5). There is a different enzyme to break down each different type of food.

Large insoluble molecule	Enzyme	Small soluble molecule
carbohydrate	carbohydrase	glucose
protein	protease	amino acids
fat	lipase	fatty acids and glycerol

Table 1.2 The main types of digestive enzyme.

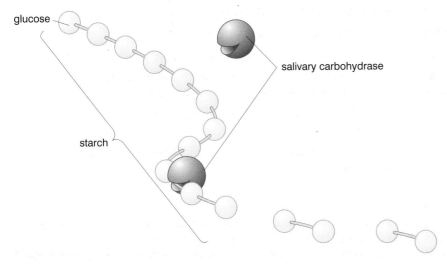

Figure 1.5 The action of salivary carbohydrase on starch. Starch is a large insoluble molecule made up of small glucose molecules. Salivary carbohydrase starts the process of starch digestion, producing small double sugar molecules.

In the stomach...

Each enzyme works best at a particular pH. The protease made by the stomach works best in acid conditions. Gastric juice, produced by the stomach, contains hydrochloric acid, giving protease the right pH to work. The acid also kills any bacteria that may have been swallowed. Food spends up to four hours in the stomach, before being squeezed out into the small intestine.

Bile salts...

Bile is made in the liver. It is an alkaline fluid that neutralises stomach acid and provides the best pH for the enzymes in the small intestine to work. Bile is not an enzyme; it contains bile salts, which **emulsify** fats. Emulsification is different from digestion. It turns drops of fat into tiny droplets (Figure 1.6). Each droplet has a relatively large surface area for the enzyme lipase to act on, so speeding up the breakdown of fats into fatty acids and glycerol by lipase.

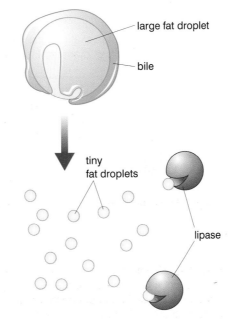

Figure 1.6 Bile emulsifies fats. Emulsification speeds up the digestion of fats by the enzyme lipase.

Key Facts

- The digestive system breaks down food and absorbs it into the bloodstream.
- Specialised parts of the digestive system have particular functions.
- Food is passed through the digestive system by muscular action called peristalsis.
- Digestion involves the breakdown of large food molecules into small soluble molecules, which can then be absorbed.
- Digestion is brought about by enzymes.
- Digestion in the small intestine is aided by bile.
- Villi in the small intestine have thin walls and provide a large surface area to assist with absorption of molecules into the surrounding blood capillaries.

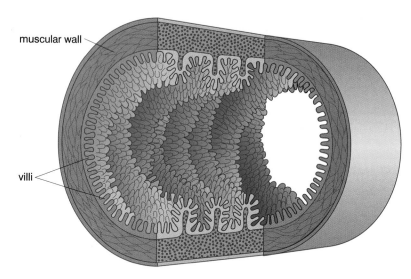

Figure 1.7 A cross-section through the small intestine showing the villi. Villi increase the surface area for absorbing the products of digestion.

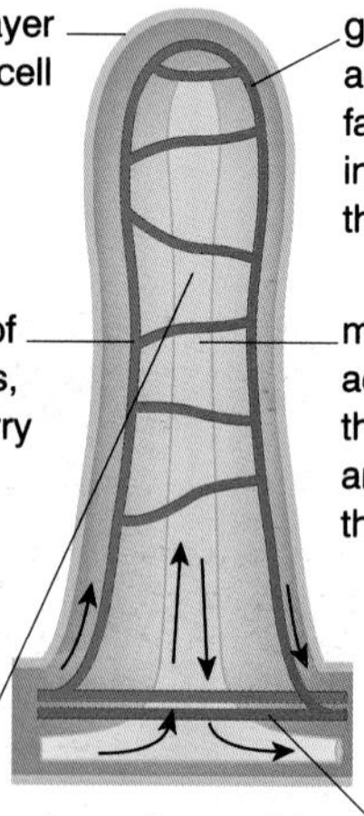

muscular wall

villi

surface layer only one cell thick

glucose, amino acids, and some fatty acids pass into the blood in the capillaries

network of capillaries, which carry blood

most of the fatty acids pass into the lacteal and are carried in the lymph

lymph vessel carrying digested food to the blood

blood vessel carrying digested food to the liver

Figure 1.8 A cross-section through a villus.

Absorption…

Your small intestine is a narrow tube approximately 6 m long where most of the digested food is absorbed into the blood and taken to your body. Inside the small intestine are millions of tiny finger-like projections called **villi** (Figure 1.7). Absorption takes place through the thin-walled villi into blood capillaries. The villi provide a huge surface area. This is important because, in order to absorb food, each molecule has to come into contact with the surface of your intestine. The bigger the surface area, the better the absorption.

Inside a villus…

Figure 1.8 shows a cross-section through a villus. The surface layer of the villus is only one cell thick. This allows digested food to pass through easily.

Questions

1 What are the two functions of the digestive system?

2 Why is it necessary to digest food such as bread?

3 Where in the digestive system are the following large molecules digested?
   a) carbohydrate
   b) protein
   c) fat

4 Explain the importance of bile in the digestion of food.

5 The disease dysentery is caused by bacteria that prevent the large intestine from absorbing water. Give one symptom you might expect with this disease.

6 People who suffer from the disease called lactose intolerance are not able to digest the sugar lactose. Do some research to discover:
   a) the cause of the problem
   b) the symptoms of lactose intolerance
   c) possible treatments that may be given to sufferers

…more at www.m…

After completing the work in this topic you will be able to:

* understand the function of each of the following parts of the blood: plasma, white blood cells, red blood cells and platelets

Figure 1.9 a) Whole blood and b) centrifuged blood, showing the clear plasma and the part containing the cells and platelets.

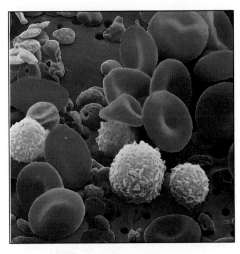

Figure 1.10 Electronmicrograph of human blood showing the different types of blood cells and the platelets that float in the plasma.

There are nearly 5 litres of blood (half a bucket) racing through your body. When blood is separated in a machine called a centrifuge, two main parts can be seen (Figure 1.9). The part that looks like a yellow watery liquid is called **plasma**. The function of plasma is to carry soluble substances, such as glucose, amino acids and carbon dioxide, around the body. When the second part is studied under the microscope, different structures can be seen (Figures 1.10 and 1.11). It contains two main types of cell: **red blood cells** and **white blood cells**.

Red blood cells carry oxygen around your body. Each red blood cell is packed with a protein called haemoglobin. The haemoglobin picks up oxygen from the lungs and drops off oxygen in the respiring tissues (Figure 1.12). Red blood cells are very small. There are about 5 million in each cubic millimetre of blood. White blood cells defend your body against infection. Blood also contains **platelets**, which play a part in the clotting of blood.

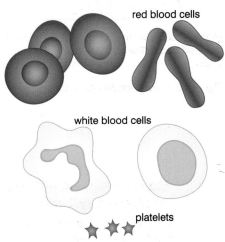

Figure 1.11 The different types of cells and the platelets seen in a blood smear under a light microscope.

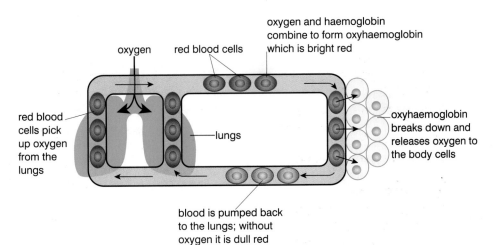

Figure 1.12 Haemoglobin is able to pick up oxygen from the lungs and release it to the tissues of the body.

Figure 1.13 Sneezing spreads disease. The droplets of mucus in a sneeze allow micro-organisms to spread from person to person.

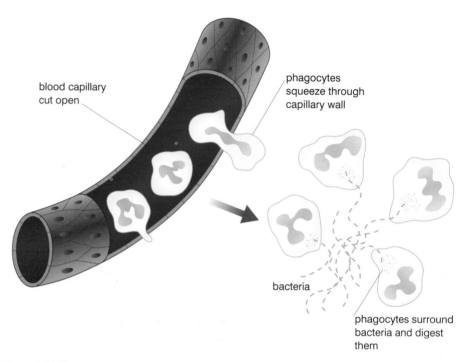

blood capillary cut open

phagocytes squeeze through capillary wall

bacteria

phagocytes surround bacteria and digest them

Figure 1.14 Phagocytes can squeeze through thin-walled capillaries to reach bacteria.

Fighting disease…

Infectious diseases such as colds and tuberculosis are caused by micro-organisms. They can be spread from person to person (Figure 1.13).

White blood cells fight infection in your body. There are two main types of white blood cell: **phagocytes** and **lymphocytes.** Phagocytes are able to squeeze through the walls of tiny blood vessels called capillaries to reach wounds (Figure 1.14). Phagocytes **ingest** (take in) invading micro-organisms, such as bacteria. When the micro-organisms are trapped inside the phagocyte, they are digested and destroyed (Figures 1.15 and 1.15).

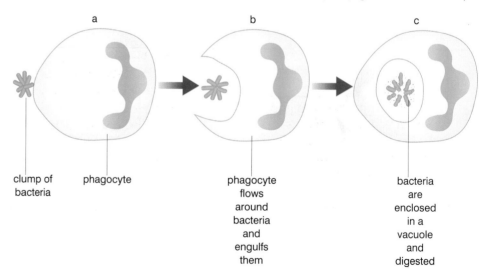

a

b

c

clump of bacteria

phagocyte

phagocyte flows around bacteria and engulfs them

bacteria are enclosed in a vacuole and digested

Figure 1.15 a) A phagocyte detects a clump of invading bacteria. b) The phagocyte ingests the bacteria. c) The bacteria are destroyed and digested by enzymes produced in the phagocyte.

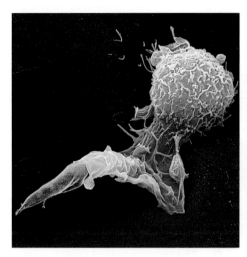

Figure 1.16 Electronmicrograph of a phagocyte engulfing a micro-organism.

Figure 1.17 Electronmicrograph of a blood clot showing the mesh of fibrin and the red blood cells trapped in it.

Lymphocytes are white blood cells that produce special proteins called **antibodies**. Antibodies attach to micro-organisms. This makes it more likely that the invader will be recognised by a phagocyte and ingested.

Blood clotting...

A small cut in your skin is quickly blocked by a blood clot. The clot prevents you from bleeding to death and stops micro-organisms entering your body. It is the platelets that help blood to clot. Damage to tissues causes the platelets to burst and release chemicals that produce thin fibres of **fibrin**. The fibrin forms a meshwork, trapping blood cells (Figure 1.17). As the mesh dries, the fibrin hardens and a scab is formed. New skin grows under the scab.

Questions

1   Copy and complete:
    Blood is a mixture of ...., red blood cells, ... blood cells and platelets. Plasma carries .... substances. Red blood cells carry .... Defence against infection is performed by the .... Platelets are responsible for helping blood to .... at the site of a wound.

2   Describe how the two different types of white blood cell fight infection.

3   Explain why it is important for a scab to form at a cut.

4   Describe the role of platelets in forming a clot.

Learning outcomes

After completing the work in this topic you will be able to:

* explain how information passes through the nervous system
* recall how you see

Did you know?

The flow of air is greater into one nostril than the other owing to a swelling that alternates back and forth every few hours. The difference in airflow results in the brain receiving two slightly different sets of information about a smell. It's a bit like smelling in stereo! (*The Telegraph*, 25 November 1999).

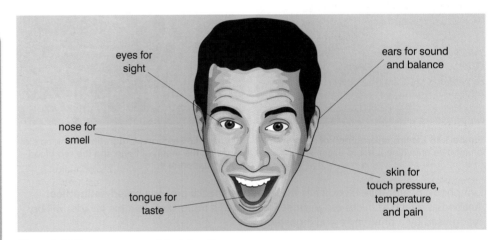

Figure 1.18 Sense organs and their functions.

You can see a flash of lightning and hear a roll of thunder. Your body can detect changes in your environment. Each change is called a **stimulus**. Your body is sensitive to a variety of stimuli. Specialised nerve endings called **receptors** are required to detect a stimulus. Receptors are often part of a **sense organ** (Figure 1.18). For example, the receptors that are sensitive to light are the cells in the retina at the back of the eye. Information from a sense organ is passed to the brain for processing. It is the brain that produces a sensation (sight, hearing, feeling, smell, taste).

The nervous system

The nervous system controls the body. It detects stimuli and co-ordinates the body's response. It ensures that all parts of the body act together. The nervous system has two parts (Figure 1.19):

* the central nervous system: the brain and spinal cord
* the peripheral nervous system: nerves connecting the central nervous system to the rest of the body

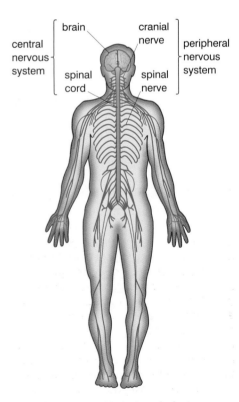

Figure 1.19 The human nervous system is divided into the central nervous system and the peripheral nervous system.

Nerves...

A **nerve** is composed of a bundle of **nerve fibres**, rather like the wires in an electric cable (Figure 1.20). A nerve fibre is the elongated part of a specialised cell called a **neurone**. A nerve fibre can be up to a metre long. Electrical signals called **impulses** travel along nerve fibres. Impulses only travel in one direction. Two important types of neurone are the **sensory** and **motor** neurones (Figure 1.21). A sensory neurone carries an impulse from a sense organ (when it detects a stimulus) to the central nervous system; a motor neurone carries impulses from the central nervous system to a muscle or gland (where there is an effect).

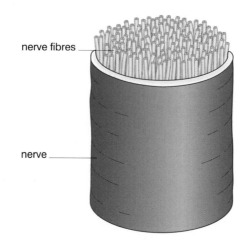

nerve fibres

nerve

Figure 1.20 Nerves are composed of bundles of nerve fibres.

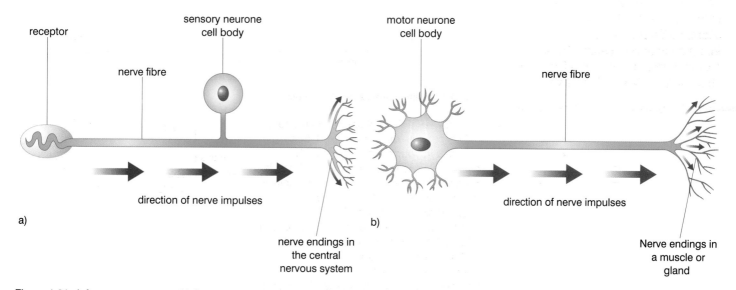

receptor

sensory neurone cell body

nerve fibre

direction of nerve impulses

a)

nerve endings in the central nervous system

motor neurone cell body

nerve fibre

direction of nerve impulses

b)

Nerve endings in a muscle or gland

Figure 1.21 a) A sensory neurone. b) A motor neurone.

Voluntary and involuntary...

Some parts of your nervous system are organised to allow you to make decisions and take actions based on thought, learning and reasoning, for example when you pick up a glass of water. Such an action is **voluntary**. It is under your conscious control.

Sometimes a much more rapid response is needed. This often happens when your body needs protecting, for example when you touch something hot. The action is both rapid and **involuntary**. It is called a **reflex action** and it is not under your conscious control (Figure1.22).

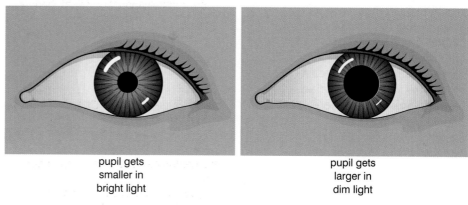

pupil gets smaller in bright light

pupil gets larger in dim light

Figure 1.22 An example of a reflex action is the iris reflex. The pupils get smaller in bright light to protect the retina from too much light. They get larger in dim light.

The human body: action and control 15

The nerves involved in a reflex action form a **reflex arc**. A reflex arc is made up of different types of neurone, each one separated by a tiny gap called a **synapse**. In Figure 1.23 the stimulus is a pinprick. It is detected by a pain receptor. This causes impulses to pass along sensory neurones to the central nervous system. Neurones do not touch each other but are always separated by a synapse. In the central nervous system, impulses are passed from sensory neurones to motor neurones via relay neurones. Motor neurones then transmit impulses to an effector, which carries out a response. In this case, a muscle contracts and the finger is pulled away.

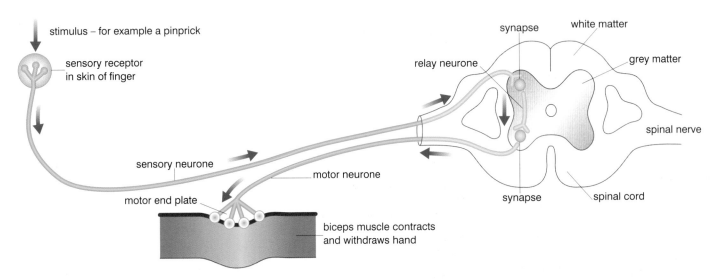

stimulus – for example a pinprick

sensory receptor in skin of finger

sensory neurone

motor neurone

motor end plate

biceps muscle contracts and withdraws hand

synapse

white matter

relay neurone

grey matter

spinal nerve

synapse

spinal cord

Figure 1.23 A simple reflex arc.

Synapses...

An impulse is an electrical signal that passes along the entire length of a neurone. When an impulse arrives at a synapse, it causes the release of a chemical **transmitter**, which diffuses across the **synaptic cleft** and binds onto the receiving neurone (Figure 1.24).

direction of impulse

synaptic cleft

transmitting neurone

impulse continues

▲ chemical transmitter

receiving neurone

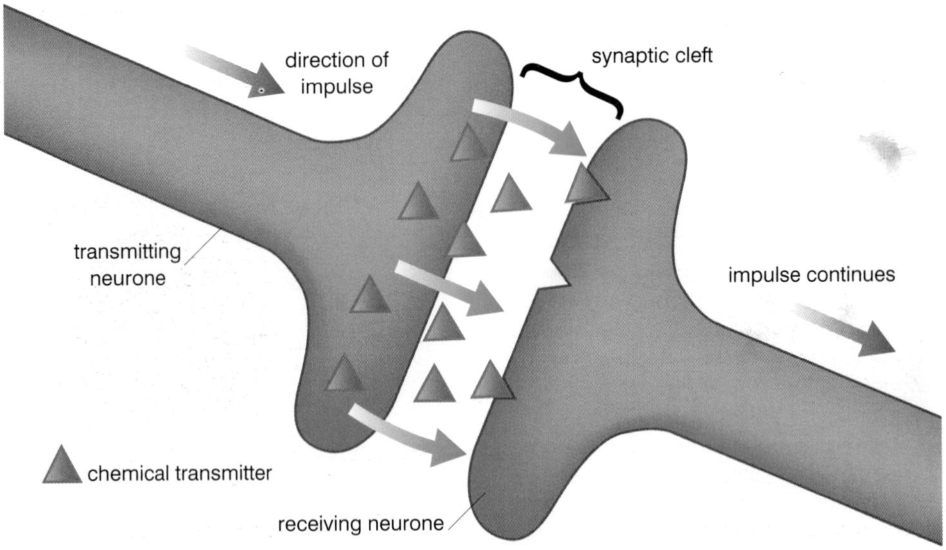

Figure 1.24 The process of transmission across a synapse. The transmitting neurone releases a chemical transmitter, which diffuses across the synaptic cleft. The transmitter binds to the membrane of the receiving neurone, which then produces its own impulse.

Did you know?

Blushing is an automatic reflex action. A nerve from the brain causes tiny blood vessels near the skin surface in the face to dilate. This results in increased blood flow to the skin and so the face looks red. Some people blush very easily, causing them distress. An operation (currently costing over £4000) cuts the nerve, stopping the blushing response.

When the receiving neurone is stimulated, the impulse continues along the pathway. There are at least 50 different types of chemical transmitter in the brain. The combination of these different transmitters and the fact that each one of the 1 000 000 000 neurones in the brain may be connected to 25 000 other neurones gives you an idea of how complex the brain is.

Many chemical compounds, such as nicotine, caffeine and amphetamines, either act in the same way as transmitters or block their effects. By doing this, they affect the way the brain functions.

The eye at work

The eye is an organ adapted to sense light (Figure 1.25). The amount of light entering the eye must be carefully controlled. This is important because if too much light were to enter the eye, the retina could be damaged.

Light passes through the **pupil**. The diameter of the pupil is controlled by the **iris**. The iris is a ring of two sets of muscle. When one set of muscle contracts, the pupil gets narrow. If the other set contracts, the pupil widens.

This automatic response of the eye to varying light intensity is another example of a reflex action. In this case it is called the **iris reflex**. The retina at the back of the eye detects light. Information about the intensity of the light is carried to the brain along the optic nerve in the form of electrical impulses. The brain reacts by sending impulses along motor nerves to the iris, causing just the right amount of contraction to adjust the pupil size (Figure 1.26).

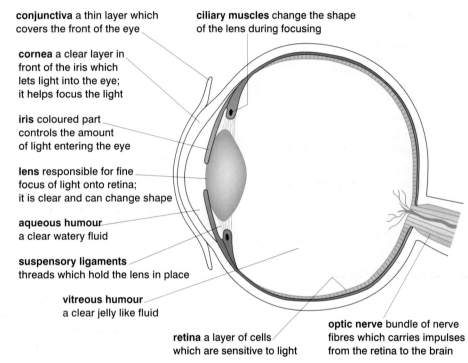

conjunctiva a thin layer which covers the front of the eye

cornea a clear layer in front of the iris which lets light into the eye; it helps focus the light

iris coloured part controls the amount of light entering the eye

lens responsible for fine focus of light onto retina; it is clear and can change shape

aqueous humour a clear watery fluid

suspensory ligaments threads which hold the lens in place

vitreous humour a clear jelly like fluid

ciliary muscles change the shape of the lens during focusing

retina a layer of cells which are sensitive to light

optic nerve bundle of nerve fibres which carries impulses from the retina to the brain

Figure 1.25 The structure and function of the different parts of the eye.

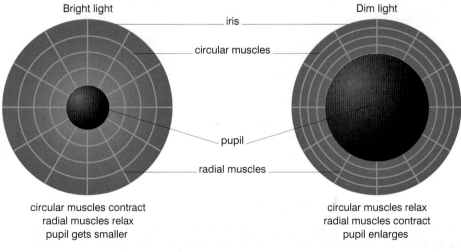

Bright light

iris

circular muscles

pupil

radial muscles

Dim light

circular muscles contract
radial muscles relax
pupil gets smaller

circular muscles relax
radial muscles contract
pupil enlarges

Figure 1.26 The iris reflex.

Seeing things…

Light is necessary to see. Figure 1.27 shows how the eye works.
1 Light rays falling on an object are reflected and some of these reflected rays fall on the eye.
2 The light rays are **refracted** (bent) as they pass through the **cornea**, the **aqueous humour** and the **lens** in the eye.
3 An upside-down image is formed on the **retina**.
4 Impulses from the retina pass along the **optic nerve** and enter the brain. The brain decodes the information, giving you a picture of the object, which is the correct way up and in colour.

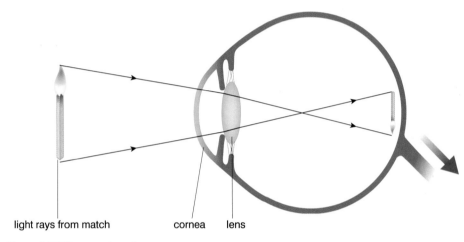

light rays from match   cornea   lens

Figure 1.27 The eye at work.

Focusing…

To be able to see clearly, your eyes must be able to focus light from objects at different distances. The cornea is rigid and cannot change shape. It refracts light strongly but can only form a blurred image on the retina.
Fine focusing to produce a sharp image is provided by the lens, which can change shape. A fat lens refracts light more than a thin lens. The lens is attached by the **suspensory ligaments** to a ring of muscles called the **ciliary body**.

Near objects…

Light rays from near objects have to be refracted strongly. A fat lens is needed (Figure 1.28). When the ciliary muscles in the ciliary body contract, the ring gets smaller causing the suspensory ligaments to slacken. This allows the lens to become fatter (more curved).

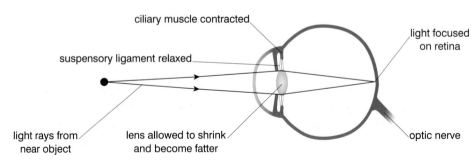

ciliary muscle contracted

light focused on retina

suspensory ligament relaxed

light rays from near object   lens allowed to shrink and become fatter   optic nerve

Figure 1.28 The eye focusing on a near object.

Far away objects…

Light rays from distant objects do not have to be refracted so much. A thin lens is needed (Figure 1.29). When the ciliary body relaxes, the ring of ciliary muscles gets larger, pulling the suspensory ligaments taut. This makes the lens thinner (less curved).

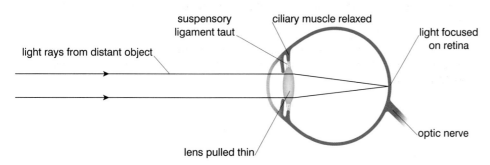

Figure 129 The eye focusing on a far object.

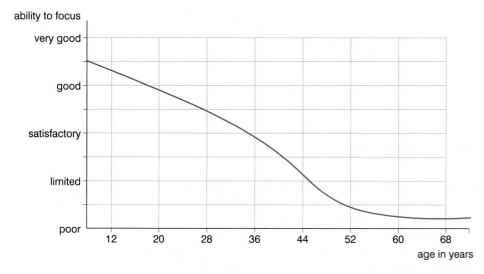

Figure 1.30 Graph to show how the ability of the eyes to focus decreases with age.

Questions

1   Name the two parts of the nervous system.

2   Define these terms: nerve, nerve fibre and neurone.

3   State the function of a) a sensory neurone, and b) a motor neurone.

4   State the sequence of events that occurs when an impulse arrives at a synapse.

5   Which tree parts of the eye shown in Figure 1.24 are able to refract light rays?

Learning outcome

After completing the work in this topic you will be able to:

• describe the effects of various drugs on the working of the body

What are drugs?

A drug is any substance that alters the way living things work. Some drugs are important as medicines to treat sick people. Antibiotics, which attack bacteria, have saved the lives of millions of people. Heroin relieves pain in people with serious illnesses.

Drug **abuse** occurs when drugs are used for non-medical purposes. Drug abuse kills millions of people each year and is a growing problem. Some drugs are **addictive**. This means that the person using the drug is physically dependent on it. Taking the drug away causes **withdrawal symptoms**, such as dizziness, vomiting and hallucinations. The body also develops a tolerance to the drug so the addict needs to increase the dose to get the same effect.

Did you know?

Drug abusers who inject substances into their blood often share hypodermic needles. The needles may be contaminated with a virus such as the HIV virus, which causes AIDS, or the hepatitis B virus. The abuser may become infected as a result.

Solvents…

Solvents are liquids that dissolve things. Some solvents give off fumes. If the fumes are breathed in, they can affect the brain, causing a light-headed feeling and hallucinations (Figure 1.31). Solvents are sedatives; they slow down the body's reactions. They can damage the brain, the heart, the kidneys, the liver and the lungs. Abusers may become unconscious, vomit and then suffocate.

"Figure 1.31 Solvent abuse.

Alcohol…

Alcoholic drinks contain alcohol (ethanol), which affects the brain. Alcohol is also a sedative. A small amount may make the drinker feel more confident and relaxed. However, alcohol slows the reactions, judgement suffers and the ability to concentrate is reduced (Figure 1.32). The body starts to lose control over co-ordination, causing dizziness, slurred speech and difficulty walking. A drunk may become argumentative and aggressive. Eventually, unconsciousness and possibly death can occur. Drinking alcohol affects the ability to drive. People should never drink and drive.

People who are addicted to alcohol are known as alcoholics. Alcohol abuse damages the brain, the heart, the stomach and the liver. Alcohol poisons the liver resulting in a disease called cirrhosis.

Figure 1.32 The effects of alcohol.

Amount of alcohol in blood mg/litre

1 unit of alcohol =

Units of alcohol		Effects
1 bottle spirits	550	Death possible
$\frac{3}{4}$ bottle spirits	400	sleepiness coma
12 units	6 pints beer / 12 whiskies — 200	unsteady walk double vision
10 units	5 pints beer / 10 whiskies — 150	slurred speech loss of self-control
5 units	2½ pints beer / 5 whiskies — 80	judgement affected, warm feeling
2 units	1 pint beer / 2 whiskies / 2 glasses wine — 30	

1 measure whisky
1 glass sherry
½ glass wine
½ pint beer

Tobacco...

During the next hour, 16 people in Britain will die from diseases caused by smoking. Tobacco smoke contains over 4000 chemicals. Many of them are poisons:

- Nicotine is an addictive stimulant. It damages the heart, blood vessels and nerves.
- Carbon monoxide lowers the ability of blood to carry oxygen.
- Tar collects in the lungs. It causes cancer.
  Smoking causes heart disease, and cancers of the mouth, throat, lungs and bladder. Other lung diseases, such as emphysema and bronchitis, are also caused by smoking (Figure 1.33).

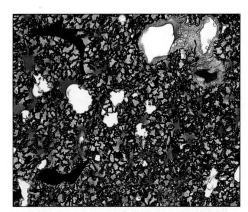 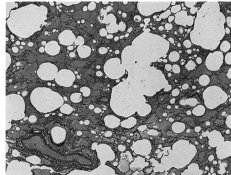

Figure 1.33 a) Healthy lung tissue. b) Diseased tissue from the lung of a person suffering from emphysema.

Effects of drugs

Stimulants speed up the brain and make you feel more alert. Caffeine (found in tea and coffee), ecstasy, nicotine and amphetamines are stimulants.

Sedatives slow down the brain and make you feel sleepy. Barbiturates are powerful sedatives which slow the heartbeat and breathing rate. Abuse can lead to unconsciousness and death.

Hallucinogens are drugs that cause hallucinations. A person taking a hallucinogenic drug may hear voices or see faces when there is no one there. LSD (lysergic acid diethylamide) is a hallucinogenic drug.

Painkillers suppress the parts of the brain that give us the feeling of pain. Examples include aspirin, paracetamol and morphine or heroin. Paracetamol is useful for treating mild pain, particularly in young children, since it is available as a syrup. However, overdose of paracetamol causes liver damage and death. Morphine is given to ease pain in terminally ill patients. Overdose causes heart failure and death.

Key Facts

- Drugs are substances that alter the way the body works.
- Some drugs are stimulants, others are depressants.
- Painkillers are drugs that suppress the sensation of pain.
- Some drugs are very useful as medicines.
- Drug abuse produces harmful effects.
- Some drugs are addictive.

Questions

1 Copy and complete:
   Drugs are substances that alter the way the body works. Depressants slow down reactions. Two examples of depressants are .... and .... Other drugs, such as nicotine and caffeine, act as ...., speeding up the brain.

   Useful drugs taken as medicines include antibiotics and .... Unfortunately, even useful drugs can be abused, producing harmful effects. Some drugs are very addictive. Lack of the drug may cause an addict to experience .... symptoms.

2 Draw a poster explaining the dangers of smoking.

3 Draw an outline of the body and label each part that is affected by alcohol.

4 Explain why people should not drive after drinking alcohol.

modularscience.co.uk

... more at www.modularscience.co.uk

The human body: action and control

Hormones...

Hormones are chemicals that bring about gradual changes in the body. Special glands produce hormones, which then travel in the blood. There are many different hormones (Figure 1.34). Each hormone has a particular function.

Some hormones control the rate at which your body grows. Other hormones trigger processes that control reproduction. Hormones are involved in keeping the right balance of chemicals in the body. The hormone **ADH** (anti-diuretic hormone) controls the water content of the blood. Insulin is a hormone that controls blood sugar levels.

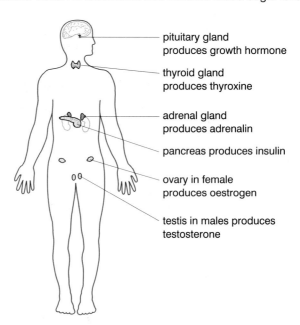

pituitary gland
produces growth hormone

thyroid gland
produces thyroxine

adrenal gland
produces adrenalin

pancreas produces insulin

ovary in female
produces oestrogen

testis in males produces
testosterone

Figure 1.34 The major hormone-producing glands of the body.

Homeostasis...

The maintenance of a constant internal environment in the body is called **homeostasis**. Despite big changes in the environment outside, your internal environment remains fairly constant. For example, if you drink a bottle of cola, your blood glucose level soon rises because a large amount of sugar is quickly absorbed in the intestine. However, your body responds rapidly to bring the blood glucose level back to normal. This is homeostasis at work.

Your body cells are bathed in a fluid formed from blood plasma, called **tissue fluid**. It supplies everything your cells need, such as water, nutrients, hormones and oxygen, delivered at a constant temperature of 37˚C. In turn, your cells produce waste products such as carbon dioxide. These waste products enter the tissue fluid and are absorbed into the blood (Figure 1.35).

As a result of homeostasis, conditions in the tissue fluid remain favourable for the correct working of your cells, no matter what your body is doing or where it is doing it! The control of blood glucose levels is one example of homeostasis. Another example is the control of water.

Water balance…

The different ways in which you take in and lose water are shown in Figure 1.36. You will see that, on average, daily input is balanced by daily output. If you take in a lot of liquid, urine output rises. You may have noticed that during hot weather you tend to sweat more, but you produce less urine than during cold weather. Fine control on water balance is one function of the kidneys.

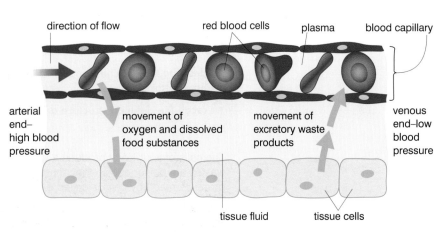

Figure 1.35 The formation and return of tissue fluid. At the arterial end of a capillary, fluid is forced out of the blood through the thin-walled leaky capillaries. At the venous end, fluid is absorbed through the capillary walls and back into the blood.

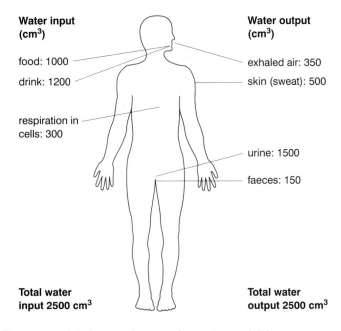

Water input (cm³)

food: 1000
drink: 1200

respiration in cells: 300

Total water input 2500 cm³

Water output (cm³)

exhaled air: 350
skin (sweat): 500

urine: 1500
faeces: 150

Total water output 2500 cm³

Figure 1.36 The average daily input and output of water in an adult human.

Key Facts

- Homeostasis is the maintenance of a constant internal environment.
- Control of the water content of blood and control of body temperature are examples of homeostasis.
- Body cells are bathed in a fluid which is mostly composed of water.
- Water is taken in with food and drinks and is lost in exhaled air, urine, sweat and faeces.

Questions

1 Define the term homeostasis.

2 Explain the importance of homeostasis.

3 What does tissue fluid contain that is useful for cells?

4 From which part of the blood is tissue fluid formed?

… more at www.moduscience.co.uk

Excretion

The cells of your body produce a variety of waste substances, including **urea**. These wastes are poisonous so they must be removed. The removal from your body of waste products made by cells is called **excretion**. To dispose of urea, your kidneys produce urine.

Kidney function…

The blood circulating around your body passes through your kidneys many times each day (Figure 1.37). Every 24 hours, nearly 2000 litres of blood flows through your kidneys – equivalent to about four full baths! Blood is filtered in the kidneys and urea is removed, together with varying amounts of water, to form urine.

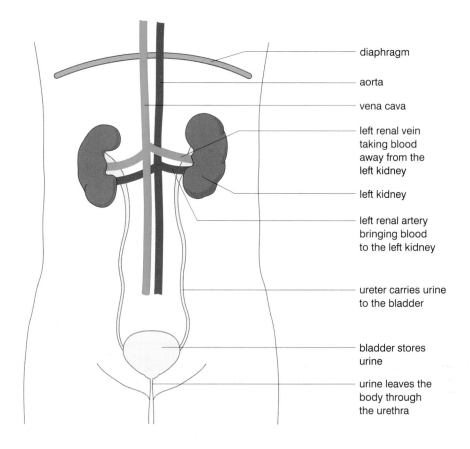

diaphragm

aorta

vena cava

left renal vein taking blood away from the left kidney

left kidney

left renal artery bringing blood to the left kidney

ureter carries urine to the bladder

bladder stores urine

urine leaves the body through the urethra

Figure 1.37 The position of the kidneys, showing the blood supply and the bladder. The kidneys constantly filter blood to remove waste substances.

What is urea?

The digestion of proteins produces amino acids. Excess amino acids cannot be stored in the body. The liver produces urea from the breakdown of amino acids. This waste product would be harmful if it were to accumulate in the body. Urea is released into the blood from the liver and travels to the kidneys.

The kidneys

Each of the two kidneys contains over a million tiny filtering units called **nephrons** (Figure 1.38).

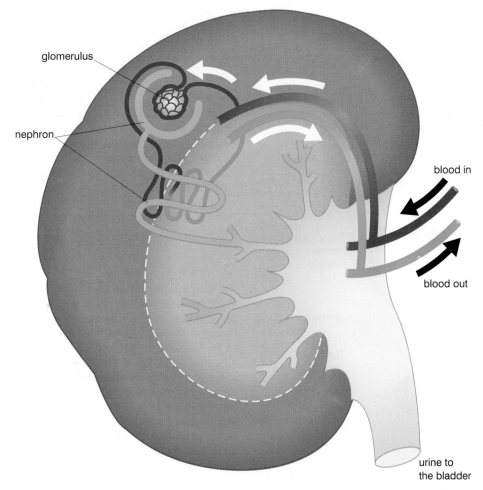

Figure 1.38 The kidney in section, with one nephron greatly enlarged. The renal artery carries blood with a high concentration of urea and variable concentrations of water and salts to the kidney. The renal vein carries blood with a low concentration of urea and balanced concentrations of water and salts from the kidney.

The nephron...

The renal artery branches many times, so only a small blood vessel (an arteriole) enters a nephron. This blood vessel then branches further to form a bunch of thin-walled capillaries, called a **glomerulus**. The glomerulus is located inside **Bowman's capsule**. The capillaries then unite again to form one blood vessel, which leaves Bowman's capsule.

The outgoing blood vessel splits up into a network of capillaries. These wrap around the tube that makes up the rest of the nephron (Figure 1.39). Each nephron 'cleans' the blood that enters it (Figure 1.40).

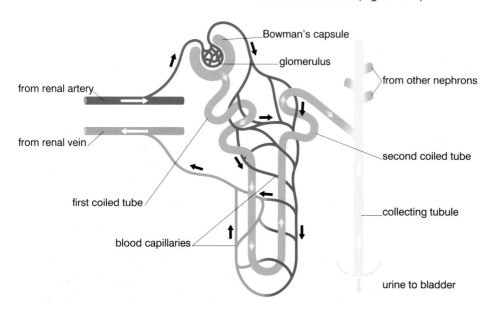

Figure 1.39 The structure of a nephron.

1 blood flows into the glomerulus

2 blood filtered at high pressure into the cavity of Bowman's capsule; water, urea, salts and glucose enter the capsule; blood cells and proteins stay in the blood

4 useful substances such as glucose are taken back into the blood from the nephron tube

5 cleaned blood flows to renal vein and out of the kidney

6 urine containing water and urea flows to the bladder

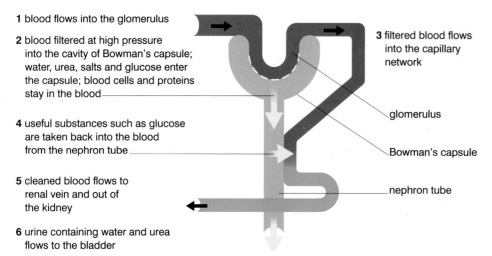

Figure 1.40 The nephron at work.

Ultrafiltration…

Blood entering the glomerulus is under high pressure. This is because the vessel that carries blood away from the glomerulus is narrower than the vessel carrying blood to it. The pressure forces the fluid part of the blood through the walls of the capillaries, and into Bowman's capsule. This high-pressure filtration of small molecules and ions is called **ultrafiltration**.

Reabsorption…

When the waste substances are forced out of the blood and into the nephron tube, useful substances such as glucose are forced out too, and are in danger of being lost in the urine. However, as the filtered fluid trickles through the remainder of the nephron, all the glucose and some of the water and salts are **reabsorbed** back into the blood.

Urine production…

The fluid that remains in the nephron after the process of selective reabsorption is called **urine**. Urine is a solution of water, urea and some salts. The urine passes out of the kidney, through the **ureter**. This is a tube that carries urine to a storage bag called the **bladder**. At intervals, when it is convenient, urine is released from the bladder to the outside through the **urethra**. This process of urination removes the waste urea, together with excess water and salts, from our bodies.

Controlling water…

On a hot day, sweat production increases. Water loss through the skin increases so it is important to reduce water loss in urine. The amount of water in urine is controlled by ADH (anti-diuretic hormone).

ADH acts to reduce urine volume. It is produced by a gland in the brain called the pituitary. A group of cells just above the pituitary monitors the water content of blood plasma. If the water content is low, the cells instruct the pituitary to produce more ADH. If the water content is high, the pituitary is instructed to produce less ADH.

ADH acts on the nephrons (especially the second coiled tube and the **collecting tubules**) by making their walls more 'leaky'. As a result, more water leaves these tubes and can be reabsorbed into the blood. Therefore, high ADH output results in low urine volume and low ADH output results in high urine volume (Figure 1.41).

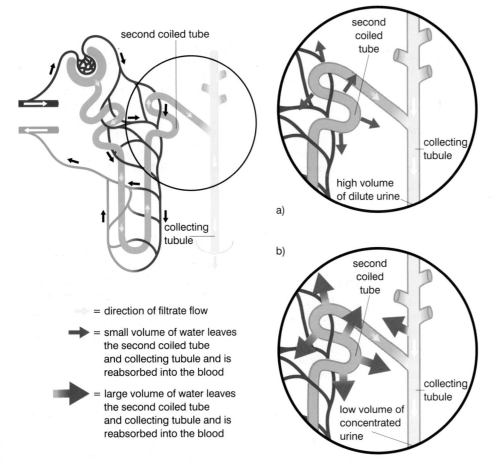

a)

b)

→ = direction of filtrate flow

➡ = small volume of water leaves the second coiled tube and collecting tubule and is reabsorbed into the blood

➡ = large volume of water leaves the second coiled tube and collecting tubule and is reabsorbed into the blood

Figure 1.41 The action of the hormone ADH. a) When a person is well hydrated, the ADH output is low. The second coiled tube and the collecting tubule are not very leaky. A relatively small amount of water leaves the fluid in the nephron and is reabsorbed into the blood. The result is a relatively large amount of dilute urine. b) When a person becomes dehydrated, the ADH output is high. The second coiled tube and the collecting tubule become more leaky. A relatively large amount of water leaves the fluid in the nephron and is reabsorbed into the blood. The result is a relatively small amount of concentrated urine.

Key Facts

- Excretion is the removal from the body of waste products made by the cells.
- The kidneys produce urine, which contains water and a waste called urea.
- Urea is made in the liver from excess amino acids.
- Kidneys contain structures called nephrons.
- High-pressure filtration (ultrafiltration) and reabsorption take place in the nephrons. These processes produce urine.
- Urine passes from each kidney through a ureter to the bladder.
- Urine leaves the body through the urethra.
- The fine control of the water content of the blood takes place in the kidneys due to the action of ADH.

Questions

1 Define the term excretion.

2 What is urea and where is it made?

3 Glucose and urea are both filtered out of the blood in the glomerulus. Explain why glucose does not normally appear in the urine.

4 Why are blood cells and proteins not found in urine?

5 Describe the action of ADH.

6 You usually produce less ADH in winter than in summer. Explain.

The human body: action and control

Did you know?

The temperature of brain tissue varies by less than 0.1°C. So much for describing someone as being 'hot headed'!

Skin has an important protective role, acting as a barrier against infection and preventing water loss from the body. The outer protective layer is made of dead cells, which flake off continually, carrying micro-organisms with them. The dead cells are replaced by new cells from beneath (Figure 1.42).

Your hair protects your head from the harmful effects of the sun's rays. Oil glands produce an oily fluid that spreads over your skin surface to help keep it supple, soft and waterproof. It also helps to slow the growth of micro-organisms, helping to protect you from disease.

The skin is also an important sense organ. In the living layers of the skin there are touch and pain receptors close to the surface. When these receptors are stimulated, they send impulses along sensory neurones to the central nervous system.

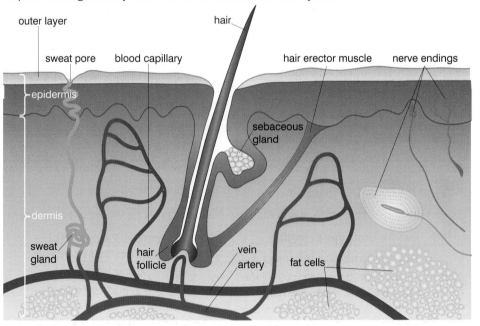

Figure 1.42 A cross-section through human skin.

Body temperature

During the course of one day, you are likely to lose nearly a litre of water through your skin as sweat. If you get hot, you will lose a lot more. A hard work-out in a gym could cause you to lose over a litre of sweat in an hour (Figure 1.43).

Figure 1.45 shows a section through human skin. Sweat is a weak salty solution. It is made in the sweat glands; it seeps through the pores of the skin and spreads over the skin surface. As the water in sweat **evaporates**, heat energy from your body is transferred to the environment and your skin cools down (Figure 1.44). If sweat is allowed to run off your body, or is rubbed off with a towel, its cooling effect is lost. Overuse of an antiperspirant also interferes with this natural cooling process. When you are cold, sweat production stops and you may start to shiver. Then the muscles in the skin produce a rapid cycle of contraction and relaxation. As the muscles do work, they release heat energy, and you warm up.

Sweating and shivering are partners in a temperature control system that helps to keep your body temperature at about 37°C, even though the temperature around you varies a great deal.

Temperature control is called **thermoregulation**. It is another example of homeostasis. You are likely to die if your body temperature rises above 44°C.

To help thermoregulation in hot climates or during strenuous exercise, it is important to drink plenty of water to allow sweating to continue.

Older people in winter and people exposed to extremely cold conditions may not be able to stop their body temperature from falling dangerously low. Natural thermoregulation can no longer cope. This condition is known as **hypothermia**. A body temperature of less than 32°C is usually fatal.

Figure 1.43 As water evaporates from the surface of the skin, heat energy is lost.

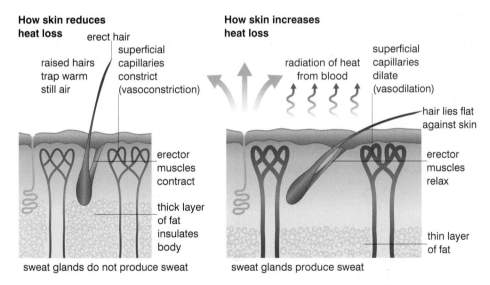

How skin reduces heat loss

- erect hair
- superficial capillaries constrict (vasoconstriction)
- raised hairs trap warm still air
- erector muscles contract
- thick layer of fat insulates body

sweat glands do not produce sweat

How skin increases heat loss

- radiation of heat from blood
- superficial capillaries dilate (vasodilation)
- hair lies flat against skin
- erector muscles relax
- thin layer of fat

sweat glands produce sweat

Figure 1.44 Cross-section of the skin to show how heat loss can be a) reduced and b) increased.

Control of thermoregulation…

A small part of the brain called the **hypothalamus** controls thermoregulation. This thermoregulatory centre continuously monitors blood temperature and receives information in the form of impulses from temperature sensors in the skin. It adjusts sweat output and activates the shivering response. It also controls the amount of blood flow near the skin surface. As a result, heat loss by radiation and convection may be either decreased or increased (Figure 1.44).

Did you know?

It is recommended that you should drink eight glasses of water a day, as part of a balanced diet. If you feel thirsty, you are already becoming dehydrated. Drinking an equivalent volume of coffee or tea is not so effective, since both these drinks act as diuretics – that is they make you produce more urine. As a result, there is less water in the blood to replace water lost in sweat.

The human body: action and control

Vasodilation…

When your body temperature rises and you need to cool down, the blood vessels near the surface of your skin **dilate** to allow increased blood flow (Figure 1.45). You lose extra heat through your skin, which may appear reddish or flushed.

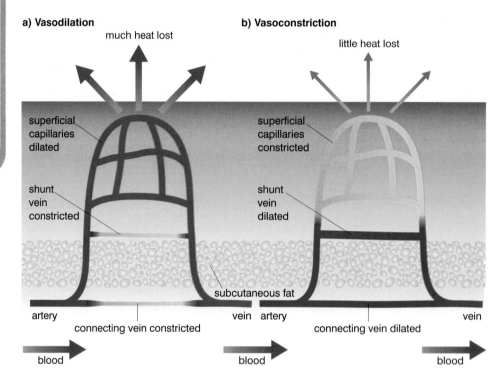

Figure 1.45 a) Vasodilation and b) vasoconstriction control the flow of blood through the skin. They have opposite effects but they work together to help maintain a constant body temperature.

Vasoconstriction…

When your body temperature falls and you need to warm up, the blood vessels near the surface of your skin **constrict**, so reducing the flow of blood, and reducing heat loss. Your skin may appear paler than usual.

Temperature regulation…

Birds and mammals are able to keep a fairly constant internal body temperature. They are called **homoiotherms**. Other animals are less able to control their internal temperature. They are called **poikilotherms**. Figure 1.46 shows the internal body temperature of a person and a lizard exposed to the same external temperatures during a day in the desert. The human is homoiothermic and is less dependent on the temperature of the environment than the lizard, which is poikilothermic.

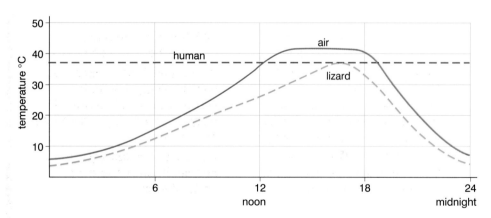

Figure 1.46 Changes in the internal body temperature of a human and a lizard during a day in the desert.

Enzyme action…

The chemical processes that take place in the body make up the **metabolism**. The rate at which these processes take place is dependent on enzymes (p.7). Enzymes speed up the rate of metabolism.

The activity of enzymes is very sensitive to temperature (Figure 1.47). For example the rate at which the body digests food or contracts muscles depends on how fast the necessary enzymes are working. Most human enzymes work fastest at about 37°C. This is called the **optimum temperature**. In birds, the optimum temperature is 40°C. At temperatures above or below the optimum, enzyme action is slower, so metabolism is slower and the animal is less active.

Efficient thermoregulation in homoiotherms helps to account for the ability of birds and mammals to colonise some of the more extreme climates in the world.

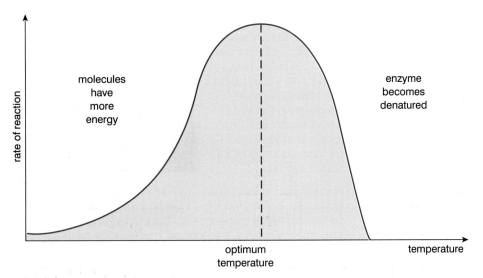

Figure 1.47 The rate of enzyme activity depends on temperature. The rate is fastest at the optimum temperature. At temperatures above the optimum, the shape of the enzyme is damaged. It becomes denatured and cannot work.

Key Facts

- The skin forms a barrier to the environment, protecting the body from disease.
- Oil produced by oil glands prevents the skin from drying out and cracking.
- Sweat is made in sweat glands. As it evaporates, it cools the skin.
- Humans can maintain a constant body temperature by sweating, shivering, vasodilation and vasoconstriction.
- Temperature control (thermoregulation) allows activity to remain high despite changes in external temperature.
- Thermoregulation is under the control of the thermoregulatory centre in the hypothalamus.
- A constant body temperature is important for maintaining a high level of enzyme activity.

Questions

1 Copy and complete:
   The outer layer of the skin is made of flat cells, which are …………… and help to …………… the body. Underneath this layer, the skin acts as a sense ……………
   If you get hot, you produce more sweat, which cools the body as it …………… If you get cold, you may start to ……………, warming your body. These two processes help you to keep a constant body temperature.

2 On a very hot day, your face may appear flushed or reddish. Explain the process that brings this about and its importance.

3 What changes take place in the skin when you get cold?

4 Which part of the brain monitors body temperature?

5 Reptiles such as snakes may be very sluggish in cold weather. Explain in terms of enzyme action why this should be the case.

6 What major advantage do homoiotherms have over poikilotherms?

A window on plantlife

Science Today

Could washing and cleaning windows soon become a thing of the past? Perhaps it could, if new technology under development to help glass and other smooth surfaces clean themselves is successful. The secret to a lazy life for window cleaners lies in very thin film layers that can be stuck to the surface of the glass. The films are transparent, so the window remains clear, but they are strong, scratch resistant and have special properties.

Special, but not unique. In fact, nature has been making special layers that are self-cleaning for thousands of years – on the leaves of the Japanese lotus plant. Lotus leaves keep themselves spotless because they are covered in tiny projections, coated with water-repellent wax. These numerous spikes stop water spreading out as a thin film on these leaves, so it rolls around as droplets, removing dirt and grime as it goes. Chemists and engineers have attempted to copy this 'lotus-effect' for decades.

Scientists at the University in Tokyo, Japan have now succeeded in developing artificial, water-repellent films that can keep themselves almost as clean as lotus leaves do. They hope that fitting these films to glass and screens could help keep everything from shop windows to car windscreens spotless.

The new films copy lotus leaves in more ways than one. The ability of lotus leaves to repel water depends as much on their bumpy surfaces as on their waxy coating. Roughness reduces the ability of water to spread out, so droplets snag and gather up into almost spherical beads. Such surfaces have very high 'contact angles' (a measure of the tendency for liquids to spread over or wet the surface). By making the artificial film just as

bumpy, the Japanese scientists encourage water to form droplets, which remove dirt as they roll off.

It is not quite as simple as that however. The new films also need the ability to break down grime that may still build up. Lotus leaves do not suffer from these troublesome stains because they constantly make new waxy material to cover their surfaces. Artificial films cannot do this, but the scientists have found a chemical answer to the problem. They mix tiny amounts of a chemical called titanium-oxide into the film. When exposed to ultraviolet light (an important component of sunlight), the titanium oxide reacts with the dirt, breaking it down into small enough pieces to be washed away by the water droplets.

Some scientists say that these self-cleaning materials will be too expensive to ever make it on to the domestic marketplace. They suggest that they will only be used for specialist applications such as protecting satellite dishes. But the British company Pilkington Glass disagrees. In fact, the company has now launched what it says is the world's first self-cleaning glass, designed to be used in external windows.

The new glass also relies on a special film. The overall thickness of the film, which has several distinct chemical layers, is about 50 nm (50 millionths of a millimetre).

The film is patented, so Pilkington have not yet released much information about what it is made of. But it seems to work in a different way to the one developed in Japan. The company says that it actually attracts water, causing it to flow over the surface of the glass. This ensures that loose particles of dust and dirt are washed away when it rains. This film also reacts under ultraviolet light, oxidising dirt and organic deposits and breaking their adherence to the surface of the glass.

After an initial 'running-in' period of a few days, (the time in which the coating needs to become activated), the UV radiation absorbed during daylight hours is enough to ensure that the necessary chemical reactions continue through the night.

If you leave a piece of raw meat outside during warm summer weather, you will most likely find that, within a few days, the meat will be crawling with young fly larvae (maggots), feeding hungrily and growing fast on the protein-rich food (Figures 1.48 and 1.49).

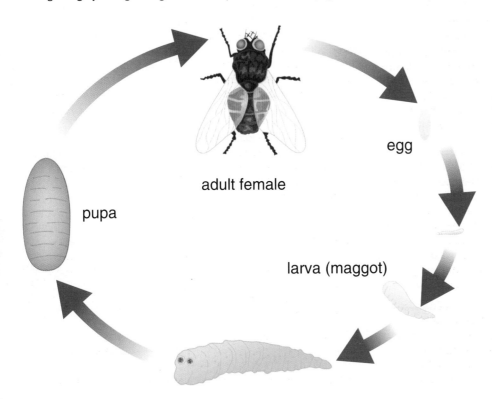

adult female

egg

larva (maggot)

pupa

Figure 1.48 The life cycle of a fly.

Figure 1.49 Fly larvae are commonly known as maggots.

William Baer was a surgeon for the American forces in France during the First World War (1914–1918). One day, he treated two soldiers who had been lying terribly injured in a battlefield for a week. During the war, many soldiers died following bacterial infection of their wounds rather than from the wound itself (Figure 1.50). However, these two soldiers had survived. What had saved them was that their open wounds were crawling with blowfly maggots.

Baer first removed the maggots and cleaned up the wounds. To his surprise, he discovered that, far from being infected, the flesh around the wounds was healthy and beginning to mend. He reasoned that, in some way, the maggots were preventing infection by bacteria. After the war, Baer set up a children's hospital in America and used maggot therapy successfully in 89 cases to help

Figure 1.50 A First World War battlefield.

The human body: action and control   33

speed up recovery following surgery. In those days, before antibiotics, infection of open wounds by bacteria was a major risk. Baer used his work to try to find out how the maggots prevented infection. This is what he did. First, he cleaned up the wound to remove bacteria. He also cut out dead or infected tissue. He did not use chemical antiseptics to treat the wound because the use of antiseptics would have confused the results.

Next, the wound was packed with plain, sterile cloth for 48 hours until the bleeding stopped. The cloth was then removed and the open wound was packed with maggots. Later he observed that maggots move away from bright light. He used this observation to help in the recovery process by placing strong lamps above the maggots in the wound. This encouraged the maggots to move down deep into the wound, so they were more effective.

Fresh batches of maggots were applied regularly since they stop feeding after a few days. Baer found that, in children, the wound had healed after a period of 6–7 weeks, but in adults it took longer. He noted that the wound became strongly alkaline, which seemed to prevent bacterial growth. He thought that there was some biological reaction at work, but he was unable to isolate the biological chemical responsible.

Maggot therapy was successful, but expensive, and with the introduction of antibacterial drugs, maggots dropped out of favour in the 1930s. However, research went on trying to find an active antibacterial compound in maggot tissues. In 1957, long after Baer's death, such a compound was reported to have been found. In 1976, maggots were again used successfully, this time in a patient where antibiotic drugs had failed to stop infection.

Questions

1 Explain how skin protects us from bacterial infection.

2 Explain how the body defends itself once bacteria have invaded.

3 Why was Baer surprised to discover that the wounds of the soldiers were clean and healthy?

4 In Baer's research at the children's hospital, he did not use chemical antiseptics to treat the wounds. Explain why not using antiseptics was important for his experimental methods.

5 Baer found that it was important that the maggots had plenty of air. Explain the biology behind this point.

6 a) What observation about the behaviour of maggots was put to good use by Baer?

   b) Suggest why such behaviour in maggots is important for their survival.

7 Why did the maggots have to be replaced every few days?

8 Suggest why healing was faster in children than in adults.

9 Suggest why the alkaline conditions in the wound may have stopped bacterial growth.

10 The first report of an antibacterial compound in maggot tissues was published in a highly respected science journal called *Nature*. This journal is published once a week and is taken by many scientists all over the world.

   a) Why is it important for scientists to publish their findings?

   b) What four factors make *Nature* particularly useful for scientists who wish to present their findings?

11 Many bacteria are now resistant to antibiotics. Infection rates following surgery are now rising for the first time in over 50 years. Maggot therapy is now a routine procedure in some hospitals. How would you react if you were offered maggot therapy?

1. (a)   Complete the table using words from the box. The first one has been done for you.

brain   heart   kidney   liver   lung

Function	Organ
coordination	brain
gas exchange	
pump blood	

(2)

(b)   The diagram shows some human organs.

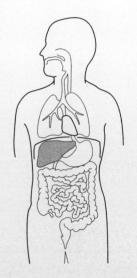

Label and name ONE organ in the digestive system.   (2)
(Total 4 marks)

Edexcel GCSE Double Award (Modular) 1531 June 1999, Paper 1, no.1

2.   A group of students went walking in the hills. When they stopped to rest, one boy felt very cold and began to shiver. His friend suggested he should curl up in a ball shape.

(a)   Suggest why curling up in a ball shape helps to reduce heat loss from his body.   (1)

(b)   If his body temperature drops by 5 °C, he will suffer from hypothermia.

(i) Give ONE risk of hypothermia.

(ii) How does shivering help to keep his body warm?   (2)

(c)   The diagram below shows a section of human skin.

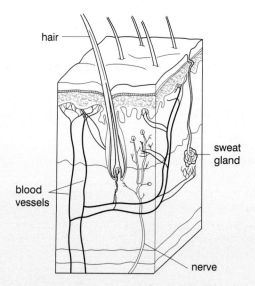

(With acknowledgements to 'Science at Work – How living things work' (1992)
ed G. Snape & D. Rowlands, publ. by Addison Wesley Longman)

Choose TWO of the labelled parts and explain how each one helps to reduce heat loss from the body.

Part of skin ...

This helps to reduce heat loss by ...   (4)

(Total 8 marks)

Edexcel GCSE Double Award (Modular) 1531 June 1999, Paper 1, no.1

Glossary 1

Absorb	To take in a substance so that it becomes part of the organism.
Abuse	Using drugs for non-medical reasons. Drug abuse kills millions of people each year.
Addictive	A drug is addictive if a person taking it becomes physically dependent on it, finding it very hard to stop taking the drug.
ADH	Anti-diuretic hormone. The hormone that controls the amount of water in the blood.
Antibody	A special protein that attacks and helps destroy micro-organisms. The body produces different types of antibodies adapted to different types of micro-organism.
Aqueous humour	A transparent fluid containing salts, sugars and proteins in the front of the eye that refracts light and maintains the shape of the eyeball.
Bladder	The bag where urine is stored until it is convenient for it to be released from the body.
Bowman's capsule	The capsule that contains the glomerulus in the kidneys.
Cell	This is the basic 'building block' from which all living things are formed. Different plant or animal tissues are formed from different types of cell.
Cornea	The thick, transparent, protective layer at the front of the eye.
Digestion	The process of breaking down food into molecules that can be absorbed by the body.
Emulsify	To break fat down into tiny droplets, so that it is easier to digest.
Enzyme	One of a group of proteins that help speed up the rate of chemical reactions in an organism.
Evaporation	The process of water in sweat changing to water vapour. As it does so it uses some body heat, so cooling the body.
Excretion	The process of removing metabolic waste products from the body.
Fibrin	Thin fibres that form a mesh to trap blood cells, so that a scab forms over a wound.
Function	The task performed by any particular type of cell. For example the function of cheek cells is to produce mucus.
Glomerulus	The bunch of thin walled capillaries found inside each nephron (filtering unit) in the kidneys.
Hallucinogen	A drug that causes hallucinations, making a person experience voices or faces that are not there.
Homeostasis	Maintaining a constant environment inside the body. The body responds to changes to return the internal environment to its optimum conditions.
Homoiotherm	Animals that maintain a constant internal body temperature.
Hypothalamus	The part of the brain that controls thermoregulation, the adjusting of the body's internal temperature to keep it constant.
Hypothermia	The condition in which the internal body temperature falls too low. It can be fatal.
Impulses	The electrical signals that carry information from the sensory organs to the brain and from the brain to the muscles.
Ingestion	The absorption, by cells or by an organism, of food or other substances, such as bacteria.
Insoluble	A molecule is insoluble if it will not dissolve in water and so cannot be absorbed into the blood.
Involuntary	An involuntary action is one that cannot be consciously controlled, such as snatching a hand away from something hot.
Iris	A ring of two sets of muscles that control the size of the pupil. One set contracts to make the pupil smaller, the other set contracts to make the pupil larger.
Iris reflex	The automatic response of the iris muscles to increase or decrease pupil size in different amounts of light.
Lens	A clear crystalline body that changes shape to refract the light to form a clearly focused image on the retina.
Lymphocytes	White blood cells that produce antibodies to fight infection.
Metabolism	The chemical processes that take place in cells in the body. The rate at which these processes take place is called the metabolic rate.
Motor neurone	A nerve cell that carries impulses from the central nervous system (brain and spinal chord) to a muscle or gland.
Nephron	One of the millions of tiny filtering units contained in the kidneys.
Nerve	An organ adapted to carry impulses from sensory organs to the brain, and from the brain to the muscles or glands.

Nerve fibre	The elongated part of the cells that make up the nerves.	Retina	The layer of light sensitive cells at the back of the eye that transmit an image to the brain via the optic nerve.
Neurone	The correct term for nerve cells that carry impulses through the body.	Sedative	A drug that slows down the brain, making a person feel sleepy.
Optic nerve	The nerve that carries impulses from the retina of the eye to the brain.	Sense organ	Organs that collect information about the environment and send it to the brain.
Optimum temperature	The temperature at which the enzymes controlling metabolism work best. In humans it is 37°C.	Sensory neurone	A nerve cell that carries impulses from a sense organ to the central nervous system (the brain and spinal cord).
Organ	A group of different tissues that work together to carry out a 'large scale' task such as pumping blood round the body.	Soluble	A molecule is soluble if it will dissolve in water, and so can be absorbed into the blood.
Organism	The scientific name used for any living thing. All plants and animals are organisms.	Stimulant	A drug that speeds up the brain, making a person feel more alert.
Organ system	A group of organs working together. For example the brain, spinal cord and the nerves form the nervous system.	Stimulus	A change in the environment that the body reacts to.
Pain killer	A drug that suppresses the part of the brain that makes us feel pain.	Synapse	The tiny gap between different types of neurone
Peristalsis	The process of muscular contraction and relaxation that squeezes food along the digestive tract.	Synaptic cleft	This allows a chemical signal released by one electrical impulse to diffuse across the synapse to the next neurone.
Phagocytes	White blood cells that can squeeze through capillary walls to reach wounds. They take in, digest and destroy micro-organisms, such as bacteria, that invade the body.	Thermoregulation	The process of the body controlling its internal temperature.
		Tissue	A collection of cells all joined together and all performing the same function or task.
Plasma	The yellow watery part of blood that carries soluble substances around the body.	Tissue fluid	The fluid, formed from blood plasma, that surrounds all body cells, supplies their needs and removes their waste products.
Platelets	Small fragments of cells that are important in helping blood to clot.	Transmitter	A chemical that is released when an electrical impulse travelling along a neurone reaches a synapse.
Poikilotherms	Animals that are unable to maintain a constant internal temperature.		
Pupil	The hole at the front of the eye that allows light to enter the eye.	Urea	A waste product produced in the liver by the breakdown of excess amino acids.
Receptor	Nerve endings that respond to changes in the environment. Receptors include cells in the retina of the eye, pain receptors in the skin and stretch receptors in muscles.	Ureter	The tube that carries urine from the kidney to the bladder, where it is stored.
		Urine	The solution of water, urea and some salts remaining in the kidneys after the blood has been filtered.
Red blood cells	The iron rich blood cells that absorb oxygen from the lungs and carry it around the body.	Villi	Tiny thin-walled finger-like projections that stick out from the wall of the small intestine and absorb molecules of food and water.
Reflex action	A very rapid, involuntary action, usually in response to a harmful stimulus, such as blinking when something would otherwise hit your eye.	Voluntary	A voluntary action is one that can be consciously controlled, such as picking up an object.
Reflex arc	This is the nerve pathway between the receptor that detects the stimulus and the effector that makes the blinking, coughing or other reflex action happen.	White blood cells	The blood cells that detect and fight any infection in the body.
Refraction	The changing direction (bending) of light rays as they pass from one material to another, for instance from air into the cornea of the eye.	Withdrawal symptoms	The unpleasant effects such as vomiting, dizziness and hallucinations suffered by a person addicted to a drug, when that drug is taken away.

2
biology

chemistry   physics

Inheritance and survival

The offspring produced by sexual reproduction are capable of growing into individuals that resemble, but are not identical to, their parents. They will inherit characteristics from both of their parents. This module looks at the principles governing inheritance and the study of genetics.

In recent years, the understanding of genetics has increased rapidly. The Human Genome Project has unravelled the whole of the human genetic code. The genetic make-up of organisms can be altered. Human genes have been put into bacteria and sheep, and jellyfish genes have been put into monkeys. Animals have been cloned and there is a debate about the ethics of producing 'designer babies'.

Some people find these developments worrying. Other people point to the advances that may become possible in the treatment of human diseases and improvements in agriculture. This module provides an introduction to these subjects, in what is possibly the most important area of development in science in recent years.

The module also looks at some of the ways in which living things are adapted to survive in their environment, and reviews ideas on evolution and natural selection. It then considers ways in which humans are causing harm to the environment and outlines some of the things that can be done to reduce the damage.

You started life as a single cell – a fertilised egg cell, or **zygote**. You were about the size of a full stop on this page and you looked like the cell in Figure 2.1. A zygote divides many times to form a ball of identical cells called an **embryo**. Soon some of the cells become specialised to carry out certain functions and are grouped into tissues of similar cells (Figure 2.2).

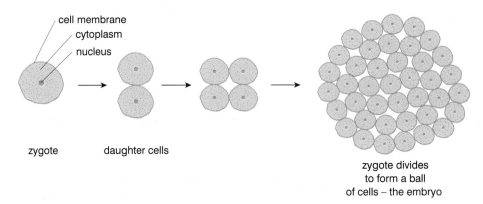

Figure 2.1 A human zygote divides to form a ball of cells, called the embryo.

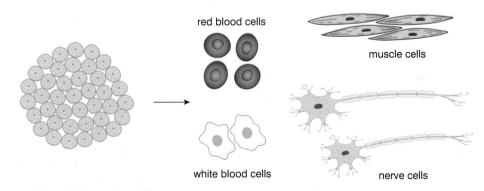

Figure 2.2 The cells in the embryo divide to form tissues of specialised cells.

Sperm and ova…

A **sperm** is a male sex cell (Figures 2.3 and 2.4). An **ovum** is a female sex cell (Figure 2.5). Sex cells are highly specialised. Sperm are specialised to swim to an ovum. A sperm is made up of a head, a middle piece and a tail. The head contains the nucleus. At the tip of the sperm are enzymes that dissolve the membrane of the ovum. The middle piece releases energy for the tail, which pushes the sperm along. The head of one sperm enters the ovum.

Did you know?

Sperm are tiny. In fact you would need to pack 100 000 of them together before you could see them. A sperm can swim at up to 240 mm an hour.

An ovum is much larger than a sperm. It is a round shape and has food stores in the cytoplasm. It cannot swim. The nucleus of the sperm and the nucleus of the ovum each contain a set of chromosomes, which carry the genes (p.49).

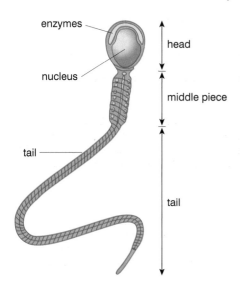

Figure 2.3 The structure of a human sperm.

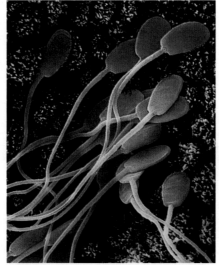

Figure 2.4 Electronmicrograph of human sperm.

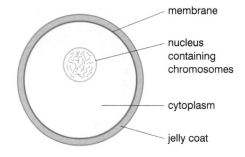

Figure 2.5 The structure of a human ovum. The diameter of an ovum is about one tenth of a millimetre.

Sex organs…

Sperm are produced in the testes in the male (Figure 2.6). The sperm tubes carry sperm in a liquid called **semen** to the penis. The liquid part of semen is made in the prostate gland.

Ova are produced in the ovaries in the female (Figure 2.7). **Ovulation** occurs when an ovum is released from an ovary. Ova move down the oviduct to the **uterus**, where a fertilised ovum develops into a baby. The cervix is a ring of muscle closing the lower end of the uterus.

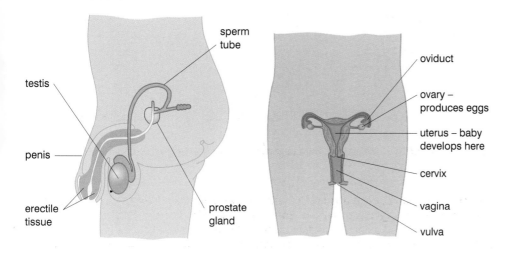

Figure 2.6 The male reproductive organs.

Figure 2.7 The female reproductive organs.

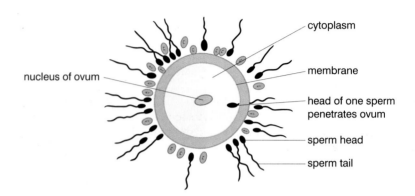

Figure 2.8 Fertilisation is the start of a new life. A sperm fuses with an ovum to form a zygote.

Starting a new life…

Fertilisation occurs when a sperm and an ovum join together to form a zygote. This is the start of a new life. Fertilisation takes place in an **oviduct** inside the female (Figure 2.8).

During sexual intercourse, up to 500 million sperm enter the vagina. Very few of these manage to swim as far as the oviduct and only one sperm enters the ovum. Fertilisation takes place and a new life is created. The zygote divides repeatedly and the resulting ball of cells, or embryo, **implants** in the lining of the uterus (Figure 2.9).

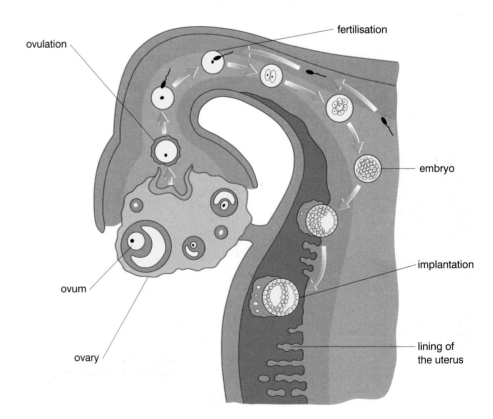

Figure 2.9 Ovulation, fertilisation and implantation.

Protection...

Following implantation, the cells of the embryo continue to divide rapidly. First of all tissues develop, and then organs. Further development takes place and by about eight weeks the embryo is recognisably a baby. From this stage until birth it is called a **fetus**.

The embryo develops a fluid-filled bag called the **amnion**. The amniotic fluid cushions the developing fetus against knocks, but allows it to move, grow and exercise its muscles (Figures 2.10 and 2.11).

The placenta...

Inside the mother, the fetus needs to breathe, feed and excrete. It is able to do this because of the development of a large disc-shaped organ called the **placenta**, which is attached to the wall of the uterus. The fetus is connected to the placenta by the **umbilical cord**. Blood from the mother and blood from the fetus enter the placenta, but the two blood supplies never mix. Thin membranes separate the fetal blood from the mother's blood. In the placenta, exchange of substances takes place. The fetal blood receives oxygen and food from the mother's blood. The mother's blood receives wastes such as carbon dioxide and urea from the fetal blood (Figures 2.12 and 2.13).

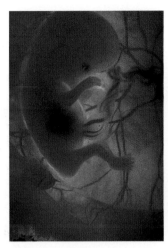

Figure 2.10 The embryo develops tissues and organs and becomes recognisably human at a stage known as the fetus. This fetus is 8–10 weeks old.

Figure 2.11 A fetus at 16–20 weeks.

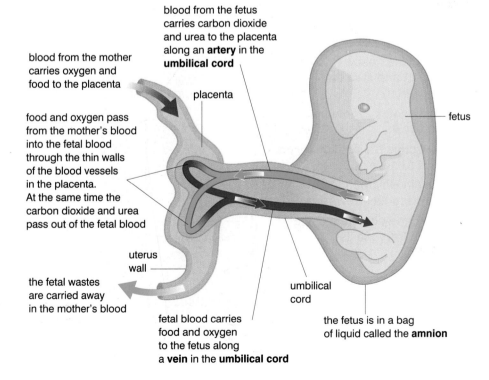

blood from the fetus carries carbon dioxide and urea to the placenta along an **artery** in the **umbilical cord**

blood from the mother carries oxygen and food to the placenta

placenta

food and oxygen pass from the mother's blood into the fetal blood through the thin walls of the blood vessels in the placenta. At the same time the carbon dioxide and urea pass out of the fetal blood

fetus

uterus wall

umbilical cord

the fetal wastes are carried away in the mother's blood

fetal blood carries food and oxygen to the fetus along a **vein** in the **umbilical cord**

the fetus is in a bag of liquid called the **amnion**

Figure 2.12 The needs of a growing baby are provided by the placenta.

Key Facts

- Sex cells are highly specialised.
- At fertilisation, a sperm and an ovum join to form a zygote.
- Fertilisation takes place in an oviduct.
- Cell division in the zygote produces an embryo.
- The embryo implants in the lining of the uterus.
- The amniotic fluid protects the embryo.
- The placenta allows oxygen and food from the mother to pass to the fetus. It also removes wastes.

At birth, the baby is separated from the placenta when the umbilical cord is cut. The baby starts to breathe air and excrete wastes without help from the mother. However, like all mammals, human babies depend on their mothers for food in the form of milk.

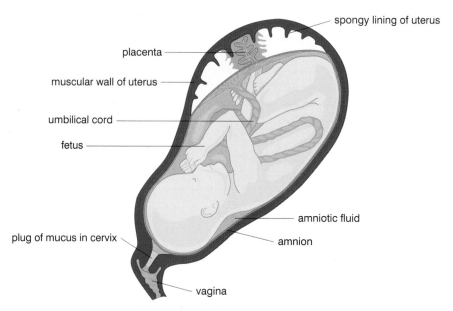

Figure 2.13 The fetus at a late stage of development.

Questions

1   Copy and complete:

A sperm may meet an ....in one of the two .... When the head of a sperm penetrates an ovum, fertilisation occurs. A fertilised ovum is called a .... The zygote is carried down the oviduct. It divides repeatedly to form a ball of cells which .... in the lining of the uterus.

2   Draw a sperm cell and an ovum. Label both cells with the membrane, nucleus and cytoplasm.

3   Draw a table to compare the structure of a sperm cell and an ovum.

4   What takes place i) in the oviduct and ii) in the lining of the uterus?

5   How does a zygote become an embryo?

6   How does the amnion help the fetus to develop?

7   Explain why the membranes of the placenta are very thin.

8   Copy and complete using words from the list:

muscles   carbon dioxide
cushions   oxygen
urea   placenta
implantation   food
fetus

Following .... in the lining of the uterus, the embryo develops into a ....The amnion allows the fetus to grow and exercise its .... It also .... the fetus from knocks. An organ of exchange called the .... develops to provide .... and .... from the mother's blood. The fetus is also able to get rid of wastes such as .... and ....through the placenta. These wastes are carried away in the mother's blood.

Sex hormones

Learning outcomes

After completing the work in this topic you will be able to:

- describe how the sex hormones affect men and women
- explain how infertility in women may be treated
- understand the role of the menstrual cycle

Sexual development in boys and girls is brought about by sex hormones. In boys, the hormone **testosterone**, produced by the testes, controls the production of sperm. In girls, the hormone **oestrogen**, produced by the ovaries, controls the production of ova. In addition, the sex hormones bring about **secondary sexual characteristics**. These are shown in Table 2.1. These changes take place at a stage in life called puberty. The age at which puberty starts varies. It usually occurs earlier in girls than in boys.

Boys	Girls
there is a growth spurt	there is a growth spurt
underarm and pubic hair grows	underarm and pubic hair grows
body and facial hair grows	the breasts (mammary glands) develop
the penis and testes increase in size	menstruation starts
the shoulders broaden	the hips broaden
the voice deepens	

Table 2.1 Secondary sexual characteristics.

The menstrual cycle…

During the course of each month, a cycle of changes takes place in a woman's body. These changes are called the menstrual cycle (Figure 2.14). They ensure that the uterus is prepared to receive an embryo.

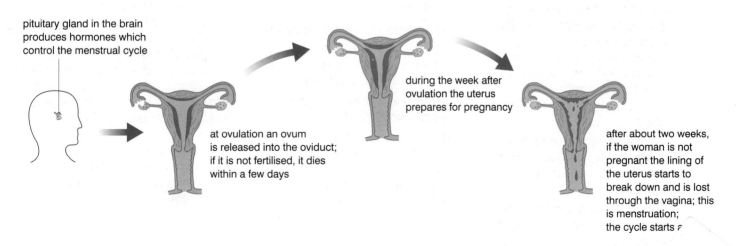

pituitary gland in the brain produces hormones which control the menstrual cycle

at ovulation an ovum is released into the oviduct; if it is not fertilised, it dies within a few days

during the week after ovulation the uterus prepares for pregnancy

after about two weeks, if the woman is not pregnant the lining of the uterus starts to break down and is lost through the vagina; this is menstruation; the cycle starts a

Figure 2.14 The menstrual cycle is controlled by hormones.

Inheritance an

Two hormones produced by the ovaries bring about the menstrual cycle. These hormones are oestrogen and **progesterone**. However, the pituitary gland in the brain is in overall control. It produces hormones that travel in the bloodstream to the ovaries, where they control the timing of oestrogen and progesterone production.

The lining of the uterus...

During the menstrual cycle, the lining of the uterus becomes thicker, spongy and well supplied with blood vessels. It is preparing to receive an embryo. Up to the point of ovulation, when an ovum is released from one of the two ovaries, growth of the uterus lining is controlled by oestrogen. After ovulation, progesterone controls the growth and development of the lining. Towards the end of the menstrual cycle, the production of progesterone falls. As a result, the lining of the uterus starts to break down (Figure 2.15).

However, if fertilisation occurs and an embryo implants in the lining of the uterus, it is important that the lining continues to develop to support the embryo. Following implantation, the ovaries continue to produce progesterone for several weeks. Later, the placenta takes on the role of progesterone production. The high level of progesterone in the blood halts production of the hormone from the pituitary gland that starts the menstrual cycle, so throughout pregnancy, menstruation stops.

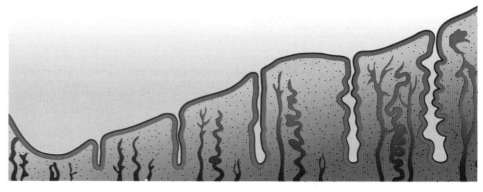

oestrogen   progesterone

lining of uterus

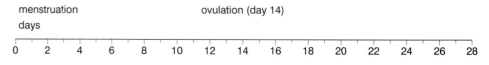

menstruation   ovulation (day 14)
days

0   2   4   6   8   10   12   14   16   18   20   22   24   26   28

Figure 2.15 The changes in the relative concentrations of oestrogen and progesterone in the blood and their effects on the lining of the uterus during the menstrual cycle.

Did you know?

Infertility is increasing. One in six couples in the UK are infertile. A possible cause is the increased use of so-called 'gender benders'. These are chemicals in everyday use that act like oestrogen. They include the plastic PVC and alkylphenols used in detergents, paints and cosmetics. Some may be entering drinking water. They are known to cause a complete sex change in some animals such as fish and alligators. Oestrogen-like chemicals used in female contraceptive pills have also entered our water supplies and may also be lowering male fertility.

Treating infertility…

Sometimes a man or a woman may be infertile, so the woman is unable to become pregnant. Couples in this position may seek medical help. In one form of female infertility, the menstrual cycle does not work properly because the pituitary gland fails to produce the controlling hormones. As a result, the woman does not ovulate. It is now possible to treat this form of infertility using a course of manufactured hormones (fertility drugs) similar in effect to those that are normally produced by the pituitary gland. If successful, the ovaries will produce oestrogen and progesterone as normal, and the woman will ovulate.

Key Facts

- Sex hormones cause sexual development and secondary sexual characteristics.
- The menstrual cycle prepares the uterus for pregnancy.
- The menstrual cycle is brought about by hormones made in the ovaries.
- The production of hormones in the ovaries is controlled by hormones produced in the pituitary gland.
- Ovulation takes place during the menstrual cycle.
- Changes in the levels of oestrogen and progesterone affect the lining of the uterus during the menstrual cycle.
- Manufactured hormones can be used to treat infertility.

Questions

1 Copy and complete using words from the list:

sexual   hips
puberty   voice
oestrogen

At a stage in life called …………… testosterone in boys and …………… in girls bring about the secondary …………… characteristics. These include a growth spurt and growth of underarm and pubic hair in both sexes.

In boys, there is a deepening of the …………… and broadening of the shoulders. In girls, the breasts develop and the …………… broaden.

2 What is the importance of the menstrual cycle?

3 How does the pituitary gland in the brain affect the menstrual cycle?

4 Give one cause of female infertility.

5 How may some forms of female infertility be treated?

6 Describe, in detail, the effects of oestrogen and progesterone during the menstrual cycle.

7 Why is it important that the level of progesterone should remain high during pregnancy?

… more at www.modularscience.co.uk

What causes variation?

Did you know?

In November 1999, a chromosome was 'sequenced' for the first time. A British team of scientists identified all the genes on chromosome number 22. This is one of the shortest chromosomes, but it has over 500 genes.

Figure 2.16 Despite some similarities, we are all different.

Figure 2.17 Inherited characteristics can be seen within families.

Look around at your friends. Compare characteristics such as the colour of their skin, eyes and hair (Figure 2.16). Everyone is an individual – even identical twins differ in some ways in their appearance. You can easily recognise the face of a friend in a crowd. In other words, there is a lot of variation.
Much of the variation is inherited from an individual's parents. You share some characteristics with each parent although you may look more like one parent than the other, and some people look strikingly like a grandparent (Figure 2.17). The study of inherited characteristics is called heredity. To understand heredity, we must first look at cells and chromosomes.

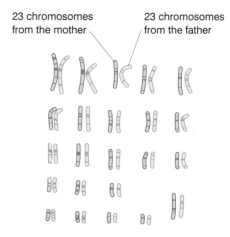

23 chromosomes from the mother

23 chromosomes from the father

Figure 2.18 Each human body cell has 23 pairs of chromosomes.

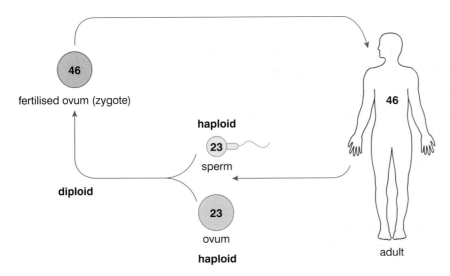

Figure 2.19 At fertilisation, the haploid sex cells join to produce a diploid zygote.

In the nucleus of every human body cell there are two sets of chromosomes. Each set contains 23 chromosomes, so there are 23 pairs of chromosomes, or 46 chromosomes in total. The total number of chromosomes in a body cell is called the **diploid** number. This varies from one species to another, but in humans the diploid number is 46 (Figure 2.18). Sperm and ova are the sex cells (or **gametes**). Each gamete contains one set of chromosomes. This is called the **haploid** number. The haploid number in humans is 23. When a sperm joins an ovum at fertilisation to form a zygote, the diploid number (46) is restored (Figure 2.19).

Chromosomes carry instructions for a particular characteristic, such as eye colour. Since you inherit one set of chromosomes from your father and one set from your mother, it follows that you have two sets of instructions.

Genes and alleles...

Chromosomes contain **genes**. Each chromosome may contain hundreds of genes (Figure 2.20). A gene controls a particular inherited characteristic. For example, there are genes that control the production of eye colour and hair colour.

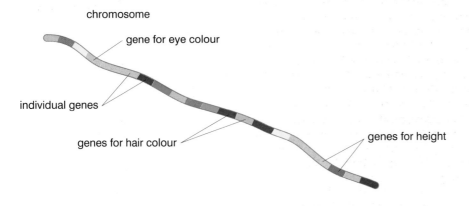

Figure 2.20 This diagram represents a single chromosome showing several labelled genes. A real chromosome contains hundreds of genes.

Key Facts

- Individuals inherit some characteristics from their father and some from their mother.
- Body cells are diploid.
- Gametes are haploid.
- At fertilisation, gametes combine to restore the diploid number in the zygote.
- A zygote has two sets of chromosomes — one set from the father and one set from the mother.
- Chromosomes carry information in the form of genes.
- A gene controls the production of a particular inherited characteristic.
- An allele is an alternative form of a gene.

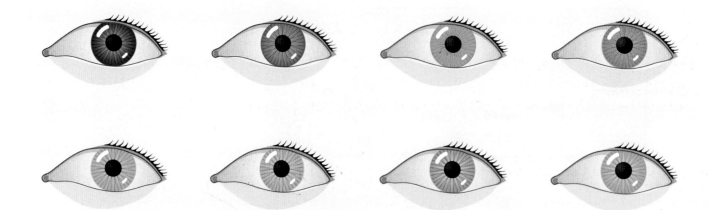

Figure 2.21 Alternative forms of genes (alleles) help to bring about variation.

When you look at eye colour, you notice that the colour of the iris varies considerably between individuals – from very dark brown to hazel, green or light blue. This is because there are alternative forms of the same gene. Alternative forms of a gene are called **alleles**. In the case of the gene controlling eye colour, there must be many alleles (Figure 2.21).

Look at Figure 2.18. If you were to take the chromosomes out of the cell and match up the pairs, you would find that, with one exception, each pair is identical in size and shape. The pairs are called **homologous** chromosomes. In a zygote, one chromosome from each homologous pair comes from the father and one comes from the mother. Each partner of a homologous pair carries the same genes in exactly the same place (**locus**). However, the alleles may be different (Figure 2.22).

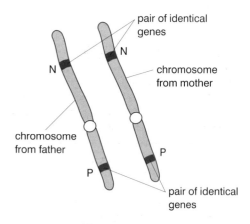

Figure 2.22 A homologous pair of chromosomes. In a zygote, one of the pair comes from the father and one from the mother. They carry identical genes. The alleles may be different.

Questions

1 Copy and complete using words from the list:

fertilisation zygote
parents diploid
haploid chromosomes

We are all individuals because we inherit some characteristics from both .... Our body cells have two sets of .... These are ....cells. Gametes have just one set of chromosomes.

They are .... cells. The diploid number is restored in the .... at ....

2 What is the function of a gene?

3 How does a gene differ from an allele?

Inheritance

Boy or girl?...

The pair of chromosomes that determine sex, the sex chromosomes, are not identical. Females actually have a homologous pair of sex chromosomes – the X chromosomes –but in males there is one X chromosome and one Y chromosome. The Y chromosome is shorter than the X chromosome and it carries fewer genes. However, the Y chromosome has at least one gene that brings about the production of male characteristics.

Figure 2.23 shows a complete set of paired chromosomes from a body cell of a female. Compare this with Figure 2.24, which shows the paired chromosomes from a body cell of a male. Notice how the homologous pairs are sorted and numbered by length. The sex chromosomes, however, are placed separately and given the number 23. The short Y chromosome in Figure 2.24 shows that this cell is from a male.

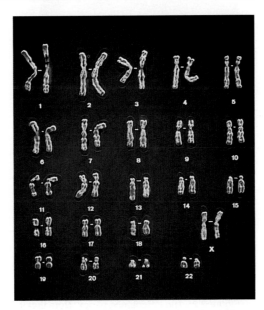

Figure 2.23 A complete set of chromosomes from a body cell of a human female.

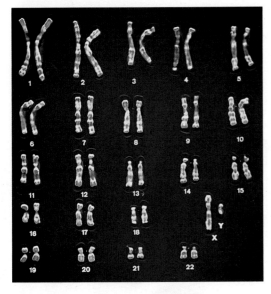

Figure 2.24 A complete set of chromosomes from a body cell of a human male.

Did you know?

Occasionally, males are born with an extra Y chromosome. Their genetic make-up is XYY instead of XY. It has been suggested that XYY males may be more aggressive than normal males. This suggestion has been used by defence lawyers acting for XYY males on trial for murder, to try to get a reduced sentence – or even an acquittal!

When a female produces ova, she passes on an X chromosome to all her offspring. When a male produces sperm, half will contain an X chromosome and half will contain a Y chromosome. This is how the sex of a baby is determined (Figure 2.25).
Another way of showing how sex is determined is to set out a diagram like the one in Figure 2.26.

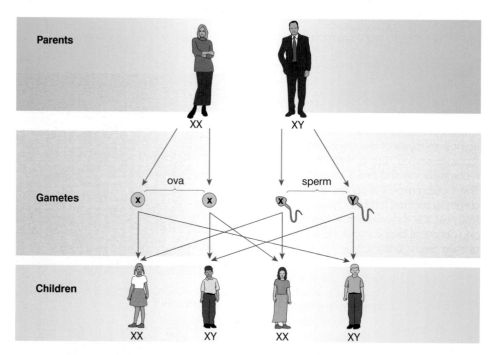

Figure 2.25 The inheritance of sex. Note that it is the male parent that determines the sex of the offspring.

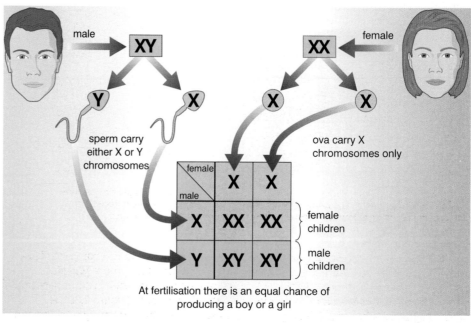

Figure 2.26 A Punnet square diagram to show the inheritance of sex.

Environmental influence...

Some characteristics are controlled only by genes. They are determined at fertilisation and will not change throughout life. One example is human blood groups. People belong to one of four blood groups, known as A, B, AB and O. No matter what you do in life, you cannot change your blood group. However, the environment can affect some characteristics. In these cases, what you do in your life can have a huge influence (Figures 2.27, 2.28 and 2.29).

Figure 2.27 Weight training stimulates muscle growth.

Figure 2.28 Overexposure to ultraviolet light can burn the skin.

Figure 2.29 These plants were grown at different light intensities. The plant on the left was grown at high light intensity and the plant on the right was grown at low light intensity.

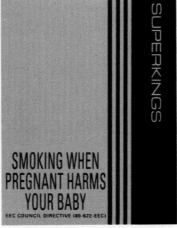

Figure 2.30 Some cigarette packets carry a health warning about the harm smoking can cause to an unborn child.

Similarly, during pregnancy, the lifestyle of a mother can affect the development of her baby by changing its environment. A healthy diet is important for proper growth. Smoking cigarettes and drinking alcohol during pregnancy can result in an underweight baby, with an increased risk of death during or shortly after birth (Figure 2.30). A pregnant woman who drinks heavily may produce a baby who is mentally retarded and has heart problems.

Clones…

Sexual reproduction involves the mixing of genetic information from two parents, producing offspring that are genetically varied. If a new offspring is produced from the body tissues of the parent, it is genetically identical to the parent, and is called a **clone**. Reproduction of this sort is without sex, and is called **asexual** (Figure 2.31).

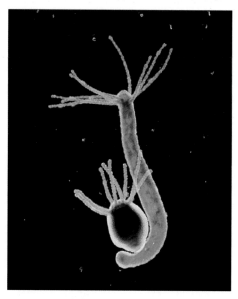

Figure 2.31 *Hydra* is an animal that can reproduce by budding a genetically identical copy of itself – a clone. The clone breaks off and lives an independent life.

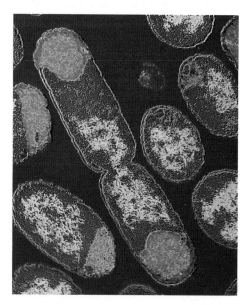

Figure 2.32 Binary fission in bacteria. Before each bacterium divides, it must grow to a certain size and copy its genes. Each daughter cell receives one full set of identical genes.

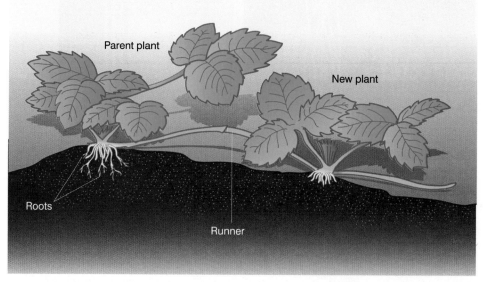

Figure 2.33 Asexual reproduction in strawberries. The new plants are genetically identical to the parent. Strawberry plants can reproduce both sexually (by producing seeds) and asexually by producing runners.

Did you know?

Clones have been produced of mice, sheep, cows and several other species by using adult cells taken from developed organs, such as ears and udders. These cells are the result of many repeated cell divisions and so are already quite 'old'. Clones produced by this method often show signs of premature ageing, such as developing tumours.

Cloning can be very useful to living things. If a parent has survived successfully in an environment and the offspring is genetically identical to the parent, then it too should be able to survive.

Bacteria are able to reproduce asexually simply by splitting into two. This is called **binary fission**. Before it divides, a bacterium must grow to a certain size and copy its genes. In ideal conditions, bacteria can divide every 20 minutes, so a colony can soon build up (Figure 2.32). This is why a bacterial infection can produce symptoms so quickly.

The disadvantage of producing genetically identical offspring is that the clone may not be able to survive in a changing environment, whereas variation in the offspring may be useful in changing conditions.

Many plants can reproduce both sexually and asexually, by producing seeds (Figure 2.33). Cloning some plants is quite easy. People often make copies of their favourite houseplants quickly and cheaply by taking cuttings (Figure 2.34).

Figure 2.34 These cuttings will produce identical features to those of the parent plant.

Key Facts

- The sex of an individual depends on the sex chromosomes.
- The environment can change some inherited characteristics.
- Lifestyle during pregnancy can affect the development of a fetus.
- Asexual reproduction results in offspring that are genetically identical to the parent.

Questions

1 Explain why it is the male that determines the sex of the offspring. You should include a genetic diagram in your answer.

2 List three of your own characteristics that have been affected by your environment.

3 Make a poster to explain the importance to a fetus of a healthy lifestyle for its mother. Work in a group to produce a co-ordinated advertising campaign promoting good health. When you have completed your poster work, give a group presentation.

4 What is a clone? Why are clones genetically identical?

5 Why may clones develop to look different from each other?

Learning outcomes

After completing the work in this topic you will be able to:

- recall that genes are made of DNA and are found in the chromosomes
- describe the structure and function of DNA

The genes on chromosomes are composed of a remarkable molecule called **DNA** – deoxyribonucleic acid. DNA has two functions: it forms the genetic code and it can copy itself exactly.

To understand these functions you need to understand the structure of DNA. A molecule of DNA is a very long thread, which is folded, twisted and tightly packed. It is held together by protein molecules to form a chromosome. If you were to unravel a chromosome you would see that DNA is made up of two parallel strands twisted together to form a **double helix** – a bit like the two handrails of a spiral staircase (Figure 2.35).

Did you know?

If all the DNA from just one of your cells was unravelled, it would measure about 200 cm in length. That's the height of a very tall person.

Figure 2.35 DNA is a double helix.

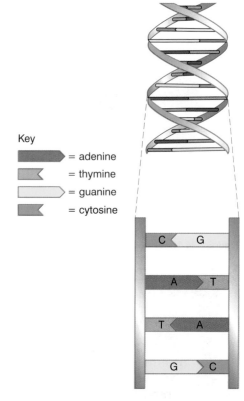

Key

= adenine

= thymine

= guanine

= cytosine

Figure 2.36 The structure of DNA showing the pairing between the four bases – adenine (A) with thymine (T) and cytosine (C) with guanine (G).

If you were to unwind a double helix, you would reveal a structure that looks like a ladder. The rungs of the ladder are composed of pairs of chemicals called **bases.** There are four different types of base: **adenine** (A), **thymine** (T), **cytosine** (C) and **guanine** (G). They link together to form **base pairs**. Because of their chemical structure, A always pairs with T, and C always pairs with G (Figure 2.36).

DNA replication…

Just before a cell divides, the DNA makes an exact copy, or replica of itself. This process is called **replication** (Figure 2.37).

Weak bonds between the linked base pairs break and the two strands separate. Each exposed single base then bonds with a new partner base (extra bases are already present in the nucleus). So, two new complete, identical molecules of DNA are formed. The DNA re-ravels to complete the production of the double helix.

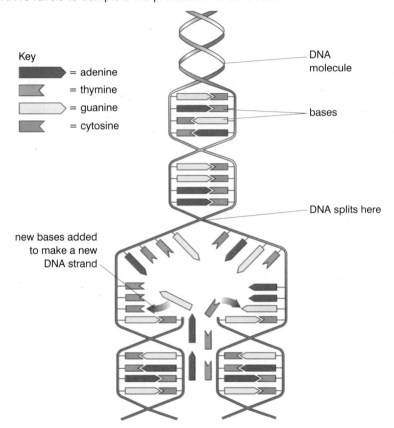

Key
= adenine
= thymine
= guanine
= cytosine

DNA molecule

bases

DNA splits here

new bases added to make a new DNA strand

Figure 2.37 Replication of DNA. The mechanism of replication is exact, producing two strands of DNA identical to the original strand.

Questions

1 Copy and complete:
   The genetic code is made up of just four chemicals. These chemicals are known as …………… The base adenine always links with …………… The other base combination is between …………… and …………….. The code is part of a long thread-like molecule called …………… This molecule is twisted into a spiral or double ………….. structure. DNA is able to copy itself exactly. This process is called …………… A gene is made of a length of ……………

2 Which important process takes place in the nucleus just before cell division?

Did you know?

Fifty million of your cells will have died in the time it takes you to read this sentence.

Cell division takes place throughout your life. There are two types of cell division. **Mitosis** takes place in all the tissues. **Meiosis** takes place only in the ovaries and testes.

Mitosis…

Tissue growth, repair and replacement require the production of genetically identical cells. Cell division of a diploid parent cell by mitosis results in two diploid **daughter cells**. Each daughter cell has the same two sets of chromosomes as its partner. The cells are genetically identical (Figure 2.38).

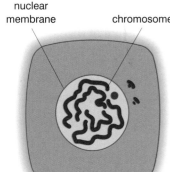

nuclear membrane   chromosome

sister chromatids

spindle fibres

1 This cell has a diploid number of four. There are two pairs of homologous chromosomes.

2 The chromosomes have replicated. Each chromosome consists of two identical sister chromatids.

3 The nuclear membrane breaks down. The chromosomes are arranged at the 'equator' of the cell by spindle fibres.

4 The sister chromatids are pulled to opposite poles of the cell by the spindle fibres.

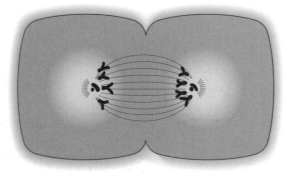

5 Each set of chromatids (now once again called chromosomes) becomes separated by new nuclear membranes. The cytoplasm begins to pinch inwards at the equator.

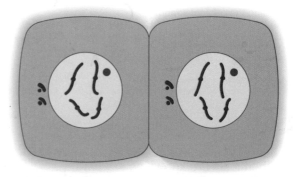

6 Two daughter cells are formed. Note that these two cells are genetically identical to each other and to the original cell.

Figure 2.38 The process of mitosis. This is the production of two diploid daughter cells, which are genetically identical to the original cell.

Meiosis…

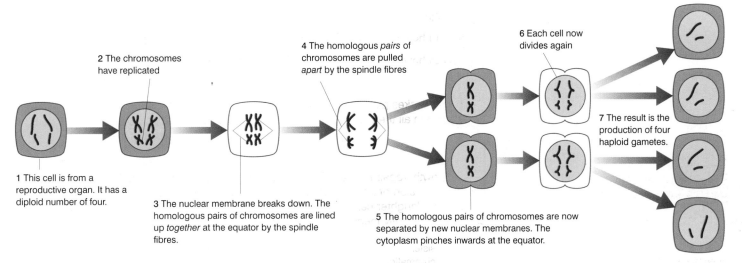

Figure 2.39 The process of meiosis. This is the production of haploid gametes, which are genetically unique.

The process of meiosis is different from the process of mitosis in three important ways. Cell division of a diploid parent cell by meiosis produces four daughter cells (the sex cells or gametes). The daughter cells are haploid and they show genetic variation (Figure 2.39).
Consider an organism with a diploid number of four. There are two homologous pairs of chromosomes; one pair is long and one pair is short. The outcome of meiosis in the parent cell is shown in Figure 2.40.

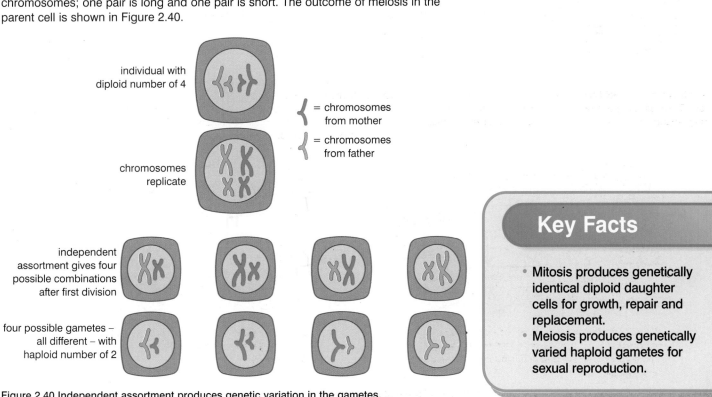

Figure 2.40 Independent assortment produces genetic variation in the gametes.

Key Facts

- Mitosis produces genetically identical diploid daughter cells for growth, repair and replacement.
- Meiosis produces genetically varied haploid gametes for sexual reproduction.

The paired homologous chromosomes line up in the middle of the cell and then separate. Each pair of homologous chromosomes lines up independently of the other pair. This is called **independent assortment**. It is a random or chance process. In this example there are four possible results. Each of the four gametes contains a single set of chromosomes, containing a complete set of genes, but a unique set of alleles. Human diploid cells contain 23 pairs of homologous chromosomes. The number of possible combinations of chromosomes in a human gamete is 8 388 608. This is one reason why each gamete is unique – and why you are unique too! Table 2.2 summarises the essential features of mitosis and meiosis.

Mitosis	Meiosis
daughter cells: two, diploid	daughter cells: four, haploid
genetically identical	genetically varied
function: growth, replacement, repair and asexual reproduction to produce clones	function: to produce gametes for sexual reproduction
occurs in body tissues	occurs in sex organs only

Table 2.2 Comparison of cell division in mitosis and meiosis.

Questions

1 What is the importance of replication in mitosis?

2 What is the function of cells produced by meiosis?

3 How do cells produced by mitosis differ from cells produced by meiosis?

... more at www.modularscience.co.uk

Learning outcomes

After completing the work in this topic you will be able to:

* describe the organisation of the genetic code
* understand some of the implications of the Human Genome Project
* recall that genes control the production of proteins
* explain that inheritance can be understood and predicted

The entire human genetic code (genome) consists of about 35 000 genes or separate instructions. Each gene instructs a cell to produce a particular protein. Small changes in a gene allow for different forms of a protein to be produced. These variations within a gene are the different alleles. For example, an eye colour gene provides a code for a protein involved in a sequence of chemical events that result in a particular iris colour. One allele of this gene may result in brown eyes, while another allele may cause a change in the sequence and result in blue eyes.

Did you know?

If you were to start reading your own genetic code today at a steady speaking rate, and were to keep going non-stop day and night, you would finish it close to your 25th birthday.

The map of life…

An international project involving several laboratories working together has recently completed the **Human Genome Project**. Scientists have succeeded in 'mapping' all the human genes – the human genome. The precise location of each of our genes on each of our 23 pairs of chromosomes is now known. Also, the function of some of those genes is now understood, for example the gene that codes for the production of insulin.

The implications of this knowledge for future generations may be enormous. For example:

* It may be possible to 'mend' faulty genes in zygotes or fetuses to prevent diseases such as cystic fibrosis.
* It may one day be possible to identify and alter genes involved in determining lifespan.
* Life insurance companies may require people to declare whether or not they are carrying faulty genes. Those at high risk of developing a genetic disease may have to pay higher premiums, or may be refused life insurance cover.
* It may be possible to select 'cosmetic' features for our children, such as eye, skin or hair colour.

We have produced the 'recipe' for human life. There is still much research to be done into how each gene works, but progress is rapid. All recipes can be altered, or 'modified' to bring about different results. Control over the uses to which the Human Genome Project will be put is a major challenge for the new century.

Genes and proteins…

Much of your soft tissue is made of protein. Your hair, nails and skin are almost entirely protein. Each different protein molecule has a fixed size, but there is a large range of sizes for protein molecules. Therefore, some genes are longer than others. Proteins are made up of long chains of amino acids. There are about 20 different amino acids. The structure of a protein depends on the number of amino acids in the chain, together with their precise sequence (Figure 2.41).

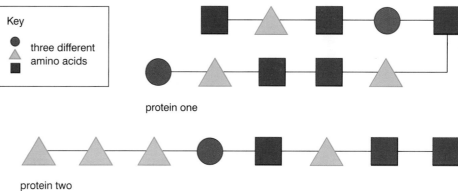

Key

● three different
▲ amino acids
■

protein one

protein two

Figure 2.41 Two possible proteins based on three different amino acids. These two proteins will have very different functions.

The genetic code in the DNA instructs cells to assemble the exact number and sequence of amino acids to produce a particular protein. For example, insulin is a small protein consisting of just 51 amino acids arranged in a precise order.

How does inheritance work?

At one time it was thought that inheritance was to do with mixing fluids from males and females to produce a blend of characteristics in the offspring. However, investigations by scientists have shown that:

* Genes are 'particles' (not fluids) that are passed on whole.
* Everyone has two genes for each characteristic, making two complete sets of genes in each body cell.
* One of these two genes is passed on to the offspring.
* There are alternative forms or alleles of genes.
* It is possible to inherit two identical alleles, or two different alleles for each gene.
* Alleles that are not identical are often either **dominant** or **recessive**.

Dominant and recessive alleles can be explained using eye colour as an example. In eye colour, brown is dominant to blue. In other words, the allele for brown eyes is dominant to the allele for blue. In Figures 2.42, 2.43 and 2.44 the allele for brown is B and the allele for blue is b.

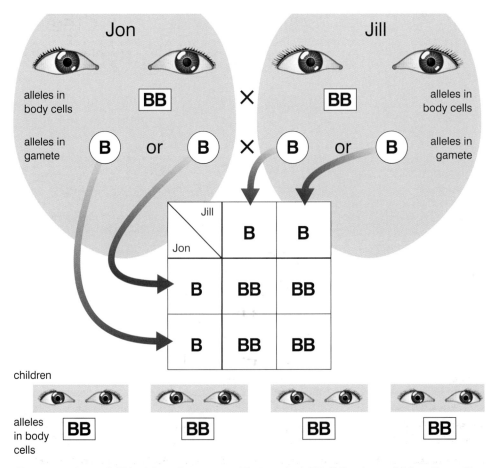

Figure 2.42 Jon and Jill both have brown eyes. They are both BB. If they have children, they will all be BB.

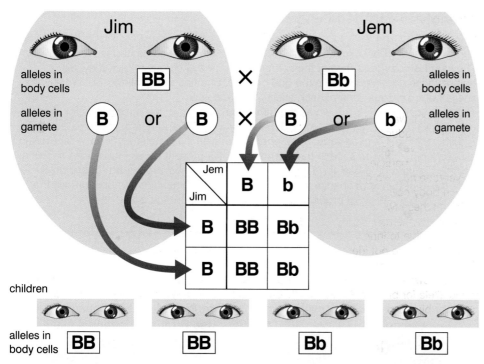

Figure 2.43 Jim and Jem also have brown eyes. Jim is BB. Jem has one dominant allele and one recessive allele. She is Bb. The dominant allele is expressed so she has brown eyes. All their children will have brown eyes.

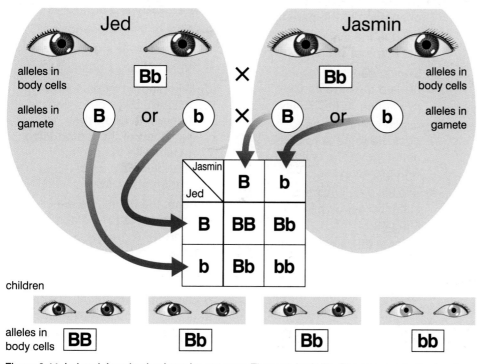

Figure 2.44 Jed and Jasmin also have brown eyes. They are both Bb. They have one dominant allele and one recessive allele. The dominant allele is expressed so they both have brown eyes. If they have children, one in four could have blue eyes.

Key Facts

- The four bases in DNA make up the genetic code.
- The function of a gene is to instruct a cell to produce a particular protein.
- An allele of a gene may instruct a cell to produce a different version of the protein.
- The Human Genome Project has identified the precise location of all the genes in the human genome.
- The implications of the knowledge revealed by the Human Genome Project are considerable.
- Protein structure dictates function.
- Alleles are often either dominant or recessive.
- The phenotype is the outward appearance of an individual.
- The genotype is the genetic make-up of an individual.
- An individual with two identical alleles is said to be homozygous for that gene.
- An individual with mixed alleles is said to be heterozygous for that gene.

Did you know?

In the 18th century, a popular theory about inheritance was that during sexual intercourse males put a whole, but very tiny, baby into the female. The female then grew it on until it was ready to come out!

Phenotype and genotype...

In Figures 2.42 and 2.43 Jon, Jill, Jim and Jem all have brown eyes. This is their outward appearance, or **phenotype**. Jon, Jill and Jim also carry the same alleles. They are BB. They are **homozygous** (two of the same alleles) for eye colour. In fact, they are homozygous dominant. Jem is the odd one out. She has mixed alleles Bb. We say that she is **heterozygous** (one of each allele) for eye colour.

The genetic make-up is known as the **genotype**. The genotype possibilities for eye colour are homozygous dominant BB, heterozygous Bb, and homozygous recessive bb. A dominant allele is expressed in the phenotype even if it is heterozygous. A recessive allele will only be expressed in the phenotype if it is present twice. Figure 2.44 shows a genetic diagram or 'cross' for a couple who are both heterozygous Bb for eye colour. Note the importance of chance in determining the outcome. You can only predict the chance, or probability, of producing a child with brown or blue eyes.

Questions

1   A strand of DNA in a gene contains the base sequence AATCGCGTA.

   a) What sequence of bases would you expect on the other strand?

   In another individual, the same piece of DNA has the sequence AATGGCGTA.

   b) What one change has occurred to the sequence?

2   What is the name given to an alternative form of a gene? How might this change affect the structure of the resulting protein?

3   Draw genetic diagrams, including Punnet squares, to show the possible outcomes of the following crosses:

   a) Two people with blue eyes.

   b) A person who is heterozygous for eye colour and one who is homozygous recessive for eye colour.

   c) A person who is homozygous dominant for eye colour and one who is homozygous recessive for eye colour.

4   Two people with brown eyes have five children. The first four children have brown eyes, but the fifth child has blue eyes.

   a) What is the eye colour phenotype of the parents?

   b) What is the eye colour genotype of each parent?

   c) Draw a genetic cross to explain the inheritance of eye colour in this family.

   d) Explain why it is not possible to be sure of the genotype of the children with brown eyes.

   e) Explain why it is possible to state the genotype of the fifth child.

   f) What is the likelihood of a sixth child having brown eyes?

5   Most people are able to roll their tongue into a U-shape. They are known as rollers. Some people, the non-rollers, are unable to do this. Rolling is controlled by a dominant allele. Use R for the dominant allele and r for the recessive allele to help you explain the answers to these questions. Mike is heterozygous for rolling. Molly can roll her tongue, but her mother, Mary is a non-roller.

   a) What is Mike's phenotype?

   b) What is Molly's genotype?

   c) What is Mary's genotype?

   d) Mike and Molly plan to have children. Draw out a genetic diagram to show the likelihood of them producing a child with the same phenotype as its grandmother, Mary.

6   In peas, the plants are either tall or short. Tall (T) is dominant to short (t). A grower crosses a tall pea plant with a short pea plant. She collects all the seeds. When these seeds are grown, there are 25 tall plants and 23 short plants. Explain these results fully to the grower.

Genetic modification...

Genetic modification means changing DNA in some way in order to produce a useful outcome.

An example of an early success in genetic modification is the use of bacteria to produce human insulin. To understand how this is achieved, it is necessary to remember that insulin is a protein. There is therefore a gene for insulin production.

The procedure involves inserting the gene for human insulin into the DNA of a bacterium. The bacterium then reproduces asexually for several generations.

Each time a bacterium divides, it replicates its own DNA and with it the inserted human gene (Figure 2.45). Soon there will be millions of cloned bacteria. In the bacteria, each copy of the insulin gene is switched on, resulting in a constant supply of pure human insulin (Figure 2.46).

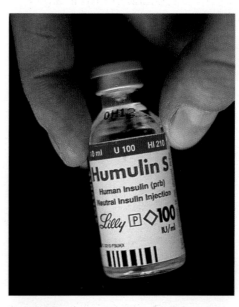

Figure 2.46 Human insulin made by genetic modification.

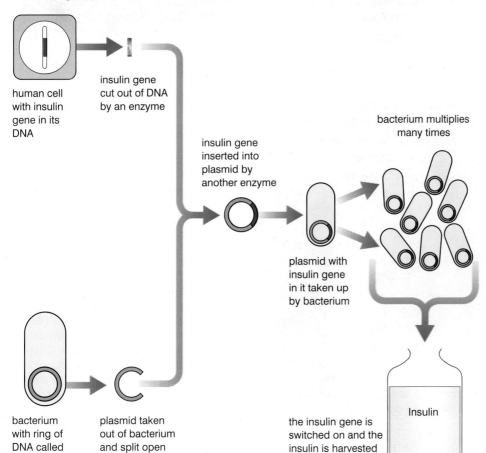

human cell with insulin gene in its DNA

insulin gene cut out of DNA by an enzyme

insulin gene inserted into plasmid by another enzyme

bacterium multiplies many times

plasmid with insulin gene in it taken up by bacterium

bacterium with ring of DNA called a plasmid

plasmid taken out of bacterium and split open by an enzyme

the insulin gene is switched on and the insulin is harvested

Insulin

Figure 2.45 The main steps in the production of human insulin using genetically modified bacteria.

Genetically modified crops...

Genetic modification has been used in agriculture to bring about changes to crop plants. These altered plants are genetically modified (GM) crops.

Some plants have been modified so that they produce their own insecticide to kill insect pests. Other crop plants have been modified to be resistant to herbicides (weedkillers). Insects can do a lot of damage to crops. In 1989, scientists discovered that the bacterium, *Bacillus thuringiensis*, produces a chemical which is toxic to the caterpillars that damage the leaves of tomato plants (Figures 2.47 and 2.48).

Figure 2.47 A genetically modified tomato plant containing a gene that produces a protein that is toxic to certain caterpillars.

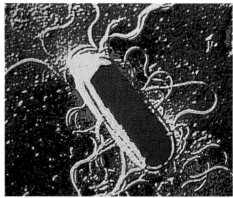

Figure 2.48 *Bacillus thuringiensis* is a bacterium from which a gene has been removed to make genetically modified tomato plants.

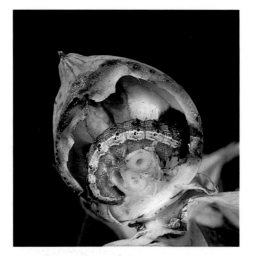

Figure 2.49 The bollworm is a serious pest in cotton crops.

Researchers then isolated, from the bacterium, the gene that is responsible for producing the toxin. They cut out the gene and inserted it into the tomato plant. The gene is active in the leaves of the GM plant and so the toxin is produced. When the caterpillars eat the leaves, they take in the toxin and die. The same process has been used successfully with GM maize to kill the corn borer larva and in cotton to kill the bollworm (Figure 2.49).

Farmers often use herbicides in their fields to kill weeds while their crop plants are growing. The problem is that the crops themselves may be damaged by the herbicide. Recent research has identified a gene in some plants that gives resistance to the herbicides used by farmers. Once again, the gene has been isolated, removed and transferred to the crop plants. Farmers can now use the herbicide to kill weeds without the risk of damaging the crop. This has been particularly successful with soya plants.

Ethical dilemmas...

In the UK, GM plants are at the trial stage only, but the products of GM crops have reached the market in, for example, tomato purée and soya. In other parts of the world, GM crops are already grown widely.

Did you know?

Scientists have produced hens' eggs containing drugs to treat cancer and other diseases, turning genetically modified chickens into cheap pharmaceutical factories (*New Scientist*, reported in *The Telegraph*, Feb 2000).

The potential benefits of GM crops are:
- The plant-produced insecticides mean less use of artificial chemicals and greater yields in crops.
- GM soya plants are resistant to the herbicide glyphosphate. This broad-spectrum herbicide kills many species of weeds but it also kills the normal type of soya. In the past, farmers had to use several different herbicides that do not damage soya to target specific weeds. Now farmers can spray glyphosphate, so less herbicide is needed.
- Current research areas for GM crops include disease resistance, improved food value, and the ability to survive drought, flood or frost.

However, many people are very concerned about this new technology. They point out the risks to the environment. Their arguments include:
- If crop plants are resistant to herbicides, more powerful chemicals will be used to kill weeds. These chemicals will kill more plants, as well as harmless insects and birds, than the herbicides that we now use.
- The chemicals will enter the soil, killing useful soil organisms such as the decomposers.
- The insecticides now produced by tomatoes, soya and cotton may pass through food chains and kill useful insects.
- The 'new' genes could escape from the crop plants during cross-pollination with weeds. If this were to happen, weeds would be resistant to herbicides and able to kill their own insect pests.
- The chemicals produced by GM crops, or those used to treat them, might enter the human food chain with unknown effects.

Key Facts

- Human insulin can be produced by bacteria, using genetic modification.
- Crop plants can be genetically modified.
- Genetic modification offers potential benefits but also potential problems.

Questions

1 In the production of human insulin by genetic modification, explain the necessity to produce large numbers of bacteria by asexual rather than sexual reproduction.

2 Conduct an attitude survey on recent developments in genetic modification. You should work in a group to design your survey. Decide who will be surveyed, for example Year 9, Year 12, staff, general public, males, females? Ask a small number of questions, no more than 10. Make sure that your questions can be analysed easily. To do this, design a survey that uses one or more of these styles of question:

- Questions producing yes or no answers. Questions of this type might include:

Do you agree with genetic modification? Would you eat genetically altered food?

- Correct or incorrect response questions. This type of questioning might include: Is Dolly a clone of a) a mouse b) a cow c) a sheep or d) a goat?

- Attitude scale type questions in which you ask for a response scaled from 1 to 5, as in: What do you think of the use of hens as pharmaceutical factories?

1 strongly agree
2 generally agree
3 no view
4 not really in favour
5 strongly disagree

When you have completed the survey, analyse your data and present your findings.

3 Work in a group and being as creative as possible, write down all the possible outcomes of our knowledge of the human genome, the map of human life. List those outcomes into three categories: most likely, quite likely and least likely. Using the same outcomes, list those that would be acceptable and those that would be unacceptable to the members of your group. What factors were important in guiding your decisions? Compare your account with those from other groups.

modularscience.co.uk

... more at www.

Twins versus clones

In 1997 scientists at the Roslin Institute in Scotland announced that they had cloned an adult sheep. They produced an animal, which they called Dolly, that was an exact copy of the sheep they used to create her. Since then, Dolly has become the most famous sheep in the world and her creation is included, alongside such events as landing on the moon, as one of the twentieth century's greatest scientific achievements.

Nature, however, produces such clones all the time. Identical twins are like clones because they have identical DNA. Identical twins start life as a single cell (the zygote) which then divides by mitosis and separates, so that in effect there are two zygotes. Nobody is quite sure why this happens but each twin then grows up looking alike, right down to hair and eye colour.

Of course, identical twins are not exact replicas of each other. They have different personalities, they like eating different foods and they also behave differently. This is because circumstances and environments help to shape all of us. In the same way, clones would not all think and behave the same as each other.

In fact, Dr Richard Seed, (an American scientist who wanted to set up a human cloning clinic in Chicago), was criticised by other scientists when he said that he wished he had obtained a sample of blood from Mother Theresa before she died. He was hoping that from this he could have created a replica saint. What sort of life would such a baby have, the scientists questioned, with people expecting it to grow up into a second Mother Theresa?

Dolly the Sheep was cloned using a scientific technique called nuclear transfer. Usually, embryos are formed from one sperm and one egg, each of which carry half the DNA needed to make new life. Nuclear transfer is different. The nucleus from the egg is removed and replaced with one from a cell taken from a fully grown adult. This creates an embryo, but one with all of its genetic instructions copied from just one source. So it grows up genetically identical to the adult it was cloned from.

Well, almost identical. There is one crucial difference between identical twins and clones. A key bit of DNA actually sits outside the nucleus in all cells, and is not removed from the egg before nuclear transfer takes place. This is called mitochondrial DNA and everyone inherits it from their mother. So men can't be cloned exactly unless an egg from an immediate female relative is used.

Dolly was not actually the first animal to be cloned, or in fact even the first sheep. Frogs have been copied before and sheep have been cloned using nuclei taken from embryo cells. Dolly was unique because she was cloned from cells taken from an adult sheep.

Scientists hope that cloning can help them to find new ways of treating diseases. Cloned sheep have been produced since Dolly, for instance, that produce expensive human medicines in their milk. In this case, the medicine gene is added to the nucleus DNA before it is implanted in the empty egg cell.

Cloning human cells in the laboratory could also produce tissue such as blood cells or skin for transplant.

But some people feel that the technology will inevitably lead to the cloning of a complete human being. Scientists in Rome are even offering to clone a baby for couples who cannot conceive children normally, if they are willing to pay for it. Many scientists feel this is a big mistake. Clones prepared from adult cells could be liable to premature ageing, they warn, because the DNA in our cells gets older and more worn out as we get older. The DNA could also be more susceptible to genetic mutation and therefore cancer.

Adaptation

2.09 biology

Learning outcomes

After completing the work in this topic you will be able to:

- describe how adaptations allow animals and plants to survive in particular environments
- understand that competition controls population size

Animals and plants are specialised, or **adapted**, to live in a particular environment. Mammals are adapted in various ways. They have a hairy skin to help keep them warm. Hair traps a layer of air, which insulates the body, reducing heat loss (Figure 2.50). The hair may also be coloured to give camouflage from predators or prey. Mammals living in cold climates may have small external ears to reduce the surface area exposed to heat loss by radiation. In warm climates, ear size is often larger to increase radiated heat loss.

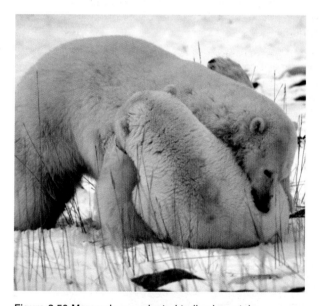

Figure 2.50 Mammals are adapted to live in certain environments.

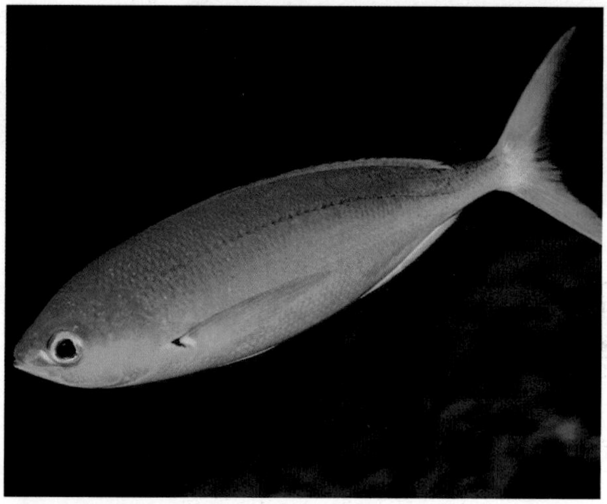

Figure 2.51 Fish are adapted to live in water.

Female mammals give birth to a small number of live young, which they feed on milk produced in mammary glands. The young are well developed at birth, increasing their chance of survival. Mammals breathe through lungs, which provide a large surface area for gas exchange. They can also maintain a relatively high constant body temperature, which allows them to survive in a changing environment.

Fish have a mucus-covered scaly skin. The slimy mucus, the overlapping scales and their streamlined body shape all help to reduce drag as the fish swims through water.

Female fish produce eggs, which are released into the water. The number of eggs released is often very large to compensate for heavy losses to predators. Fish breathe through gills, which are adapted to remove oxygen from water and to release carbon dioxide into water from the blood (Figure 2.51).

Figure 2.52 Cactus plants are adapted to live in hot, dry conditions.

Plant adaptations...

Plants have adaptations that enable them to survive in particular environments. The desert is an environment where rainfall is low and unpredictable. Desert-living cacti have an extensive root system to absorb water from deep underground. They have reduced leaves, often merely spines, and are covered with a thick, waxy cuticle to reduce water loss (Figure 2.52).

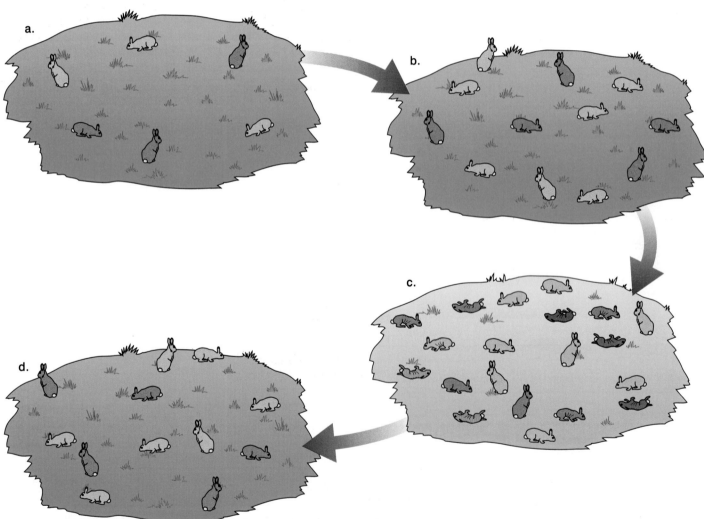

Figure 2.53 a) Six rabbits are placed on an unpopulated island. At first there is plenty of space and food. The rabbits are healthy. The size of the population increases rapidly. b) There is still enough space for each rabbit and the grass is able to grow back. The size of the population continues to increase. c) The rabbits have become overcrowded and the grass cannot grow fast enough to supply all the rabbits. Competition develops between the rabbits for space and food. The weak rabbits die from disease or starvation. The size of the population starts to fall. d) The size of the population falls back to a level that can be supported on the island. Over the following years, the numbers of rabbits may rise and fall (fluctuate) but the average number will stay the same.

Populations...

There are about 6000 million people in the world today. This is the human population. A population is the number of individuals of a particular species living in a certain space at one time. The size of a population can change.

Figure 2.53 shows a population of rabbits. This example shows some important points:

• Increasing numbers of individuals causes **pressure** on a population.
• Individuals in a population **compete** for resources, such as space and food.
• Competition between individuals controls population size.

As population size increases, poisonous wastes can build up. Infectious diseases can spread rapidly between members of a closely packed population. These factors also cause numbers to fall.

The rabbits in Figure 2.53 do not have any **predators**, such as foxes or birds of prey. Predators have an important role to play in controlling population size of **prey** animals, such as rabbits. The size of the predator population also fluctuates over a number of years, depending on the size of the prey population (Figure 2.54).

Key Facts

• Living things are adapted to live in a particular environment.
• Competition between individuals in a species controls population size.
• Predation controls population size.
• The predator and prey populations fluctuate over a period of years.

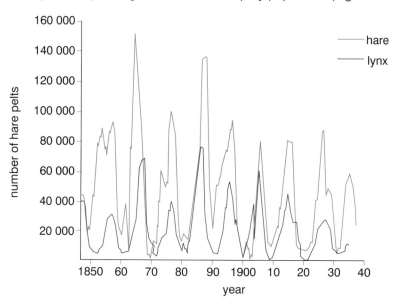

Figure 2.54 Changing numbers of snowshoe hares (shown as pelts) and lynx over a period of 90 years in Canada. The lynx is the main predator of the snowshoe hare. The numbers of the predator and prey seem to be linked.

Questions

1   Draw up a table to describe how mammals are adapted to live in air and fish are adapted to live in water. Include as many adaptations as you can think of but make sure that each one is found only in a mammal or fish.

2   Polar bears are predators living in the Arctic. How does their thick white fur help them to hunt successfully?

3   Define the term population.

4   List the resources that individuals compete for.

... more at www.modularscience.co.uk

Evolution

Learning outcomes

After completing the work in this topic you will be able to:

* explain how species may become extinct or new species can evolve by natural selection

* recall that fossils provide evidence for evolution

* describe how antibiotic resistance in bacteria and warfarin resistance in rats spread rapidly

* explain how selective breeding can be used to improve yields in agricultural production

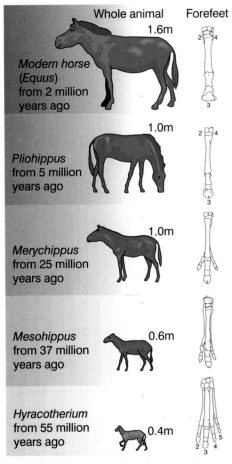

Figure 2.55 Evolution of forms leading to the modern horse based on the fossil evidence. The middle digit of the forefoot has grown longer, while the other digits have become shorter.

There has been life on Earth for at least 3500 million years. Throughout this time, different species of living organisms have come and gone. Evidence for this can be found in the fossil record. Species change, or evolve, over time in response to the changing environment. If new forms are better adapted to new conditions, they will survive and reproduce. The older forms that were suited to previous conditions die before they can reproduce.

How the horse got its legs…

The ancestor of the modern horse was the size of a small dog (Figure 2.55). It lived by nibbling shrubs and small trees growing in swamps. It had short legs, with toes that were splayed to spread out its weight so that it did not sink into the swamp. As the climate became warmer and drier, the swamps gave way to open grassland. Over generations, descendants of the original forms evolved adaptations enabling them to eat grass. They also became bigger with longer legs, enabling them to escape the newly evolving predators on the open plains.

Natural selection

In the 19th century, Charles Darwin put forward an explanation for how living organisms evolve. Alfred Russell Wallace was a naturalist living in the Far East. Working on his own he had developed ideas similar to those of Darwin. Their theory was based on what they called **natural selection**. The main points of their theory are:
* Living organisms are able to reproduce in large numbers.
* Over long periods of time, the size of a population remains fairly stable.
* Many individuals in a population must die before being able to reproduce.
* Living organisms show a lot of variation.
* Much of the variation is inherited.
* Some variants are better adapted to an environment than others and so survive to reproduce, while the rest die. We now say that individuals with the more advantageous alleles survive to pass on their characteristics.
* The entire species may evolve. Species that fail to evolve may become **extinct** (die out).

The peppered moth…

The peppered moth is often used as an example of how natural selection works. These moths rest on tree trunks during the day and are eaten by insect-eating birds. Two hundred years ago, most of the moths were a pale speckled colour. They were well camouflaged on the pale lichens that grew on the tree trunks. Occasionally, a dark form would appear as a result of a mutation. These were not well camouflaged and were easily spotted and eaten by birds. The pale form was better adapted (Figure 2.56). With industrialisation, the burning of fossil fuels in cities resulted in smoke pollution. The soot killed lichens and darkened tree trunks, so the dark form was better camouflaged and better adapted. The pale form was more likely to be spotted and eaten. As a result, the pale form became less common and the numbers of dark moths increased.

The Clean Air Act, which was introduced in the middle of the last century, helped to reduce air pollution. Lichens began to reappear and tree trunks became pale

Figure 2.56 The peppered moth. Depending on the colour of their background, camouflaged moths are more likely to be undetected by predators. These moths are better adapted. They will survive to pass on their genes to the next generation.

once again. The pale form of the peppered moth made something of a comeback in areas where it had become rare. It is an important principle of natural selection that, as a result of inherited variation, the species as a whole may be able to cope with the changing environment, even though individuals die. In this example, it is the proportion of pale and dark forms that changes, rather than the size of the peppered moth population.

Antibiotic resistance...

Antibiotics are drugs that act against bacteria, either by killing them directly or by stopping their growth. Since their introduction in the 1940s, antibiotics have saved the lives of millions of people who would otherwise have died from diseases caused by bacteria. Diseases such as diphtheria and TB were almost wiped out in the UK. Other diseases such as pneumonia were easily treated. There are over 70 different types of antibiotic, the most famous being penicillin.

In recent years, bacteria have been increasingly successful at fighting back. Many types of bacteria are now **resistant** to (not affected by) not just one antibiotic, but several. This is because of the small genetic differences between bacteria that arise as a result of mutations (see p.76). When a population of bacteria is dosed with an antibiotic, almost all may die, but a tiny proportion with a particular genetic make-up may survive.

As the bacterial population is now small, the survivors find themselves with much less competition for resources, and so thrive. Since some bacteria can reproduce asexually every 20 minutes, the population size quickly soars, and every bacterium is resistant. Natural selection has acted strongly and rapidly on the bacteria in order to ensure the survival of their population as a whole.

Mycobacterium tuberculosis holds the record for killing more people annually than any other living thing. This bacterium causes TB (Figure 2.57). Antibiotic-resistant forms of this bacterium are spreading rapidly, killing about half of the people they infect. Drug companies are working hard to find new antibiotics. Genetic research is trying to find out which genes in bacteria give them resistance to antibiotics. The aim is to find the gene and stop it working. The most likely outcome is that natural selection will ensure that bacteria will always be able to respond.

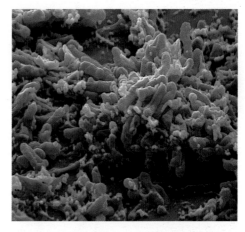

Figure 2.57 *Mycobacterium tuberculosis* – the bacterium that causes tuberculosis.

Warfarin resistance in rats...

Rats are serious pests. They can do a lot of damage, especially in agriculture, where they destroy about 20 percent of the world's food supply. They spread diseases, most famously the plague (Figure 2.58).

Figure 2.58 Rats are serious pests.

Inheritance and survival

A chemical called warfarin was found to be very effective at killing rats. It is an anti-coagulant (stops blood clotting). It is used in humans in small doses to treat patients who have had heart attacks. When warfarin was given to rats as bait, the chemical caused bleeding in the digestive system and most of the rats died. Once again, natural selection was at work. A small number of rats in the population had a slightly different genetic make-up, and as a result they were not affected by warfarin. Now, most rats are resistant to warfarin.

Selective breeding…

The principles of selecting plants or animals for breeding have been known for a very long time. In order to improve a certain quality in cattle, such as milk yield, a breeder will first identify the cows that produce the most milk. These will then be crossed with a bull whose previous female offspring have had large milk yields. Hopefully, some of the female offspring will grow up to be good milkers. The best of these will be selected and then crossed as before. This process will be repeated over several generations. Eventually a herd of cows is produced in which each cow produces a good milk yield (Figure 2.59). This is an example of **selective breeding**. Selective breeding has also been used to increase the number of offspring produced by sheep and improve yields in many crops, for example dwarf wheat.

Mutations…

A change to a gene is called a **mutation**. A mutation alters the genetic code, so can produce variation in individuals or their offspring. Ultraviolet light in sunlight, X-rays, ionising radiation such as gamma rays and chemical agents such as the tar in cigarettes can cause mutations. Mutations that occur in body cells cannot be passed on to offspring. Mutations that occur in gametes may be passed on.

Figure 2.59 Selective breeding can be used to develop certain desired qualities in plants and animals. The modern cow has been produced over many generations by selective breeding from wild cattle, such as those shown here.

Questions

1 How did the environment change during the evolution of the horse?

2 What advantages did short legs with splayed out digits provide for the ancestor of the modern horse?

3 Write a summary of the main points in the evolution of the horse.

4 What happens to species that fail to evolve to suit a changing environment?

5 Use the main points of the theory of natural selection to explain changes in the proportion of pale and dark forms in the population of peppered moths over the past 200 years.

6 Imagine that you are a cattle farmer. You have a herd of 10 bulls and 100 cows. You want to use selective breeding to produce a herd of cows that produce a lot of milk. What would you do?

7 Why are mutations important in evolution?

8 Why have bacteria evolved antibiotic resistance so rapidly?

9 X-rays are used to give doctors a picture of the inside of the body. Why is it necessary to protect the ovaries and testes from X-rays during medical examinations?

Pollution occurs when harmful substances are added to the environment. Everyone is responsible for producing waste substances. If these substances are not treated properly they can cause pollution. The increasing size of the human population is causing an increase in pollution. The burning of fossil fuels provides two examples.

Acid rain…

The burning of fossil fuels releases acidic gases into the atmosphere. **Acid rain** occurs when these acidic gases dissolve in rainwater (Figure 2.60).

smoke and acidic gases, including sulphur dioxide

acidic gases dissolve in rain water and cause damage to plants and animals when they fall as acid rain

burning fossil fuel releases harmful wastes into the air

Figure 2.60 The cause and effects of acid rain. Human activity often leads to pollution.

Key Facts

- Increasing population size leads to increasing pollution.
- Burning fossil fuels releases harmful gases into the air.
- Acidic gases combine with water vapour to form acid rain.
- Harmful substances occur in vehicle exhaust gases.
- Pollution from vehicle exhaust gases can be reduced.

Figure 2.61 Pollution from vehicle exhausts is particularly severe in cities.

Figure 2.63 Alcohol is an alternative fuel. It is cleaner than petrol.

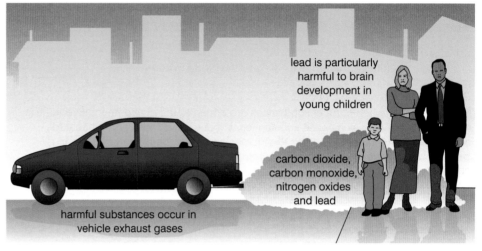

lead is particularly harmful to brain development in young children

carbon dioxide, carbon monoxide, nitrogen oxides and lead

harmful substances occur in vehicle exhaust gases

Figure 2.62 The combustion of conventional fuels in vehicles produces a cocktail of poisons.

Vehicle exhaust gases…

Fuels such as petrol and diesel contain impurities. In some cases, chemicals such as lead may be added to the fuel to help protect the engine from wear or to improve the performance of the vehicle. Combustion of these fuels produces atmospheric pollution (Figures 2.61 and 2.62). The problem is particularly bad in towns and cities. Suggestions to limit air pollution caused by vehicles include:

• Using alternative fuels, such as alcohol, which produce less pollution (Figure 2.63).
• Improving public transport to encourage people to leave their cars at home. Fewer car journeys result in less pollution. Alternatively, park-and-ride schemes provide car parks on the edge of towns, with buses to ferry people in and out.
• Creating traffic-free zones, especially in the centre of towns where pollution is worst.
• Lowering speed limits. Pollution increases with increasing speed.
• Increasing costs, including fuel tax and the cost of parking in town centres.

Industrialised countries in Europe and North America continue to produce increasing amounts of pollution. Other countries seeking to become more industrialised are adding to the problem.

Questions

1 Powdered limestone is sometimes added to lakes affected by acid rain.
   a) What is the purpose of doing this?
   b) Limestone has to be quarried from the ground. What environmental damage may result from quarrying?

2 Suggest how the amount of harmful acidic gases in the atmosphere may be reduced.

3 Imagine that you are responsible for reducing the amount of pollution from vehicle exhausts in Britain. Write a newspaper article detailing:

a) the measures that you intend to introduce
b) the benefits these measures will bring to the nation
c) exactly why these measures are needed

… more at www.modularscience.co.uk

At school, Charles Darwin was reported to be of below average ability. He hated lessons. His father sent him to Edinburgh University to study medicine, but he dropped out, partly because he felt faint at the sight of human blood. He went to Cambridge to study Greek and maths. He hated both. He scraped through his exams and prepared to become a vicar. His hobbies were hunting and shooting. His passion was the study of nature. He collected anything he could get his hands on, especially beetles. Each specimen was carefully recorded, labelled and described in detail. Then he had a bit of luck. At the age of 22, he was offered the post of naturalist on board *HMS Beagle*, sent by the Admiralty on a surveying trip around the world.

Figure 2.64 Charles Darwin, towards the end of his life

Charles was away for five years. During that time he made the observations and connections that led him to far-reaching conclusions. He saw the enormous variety of life. He described the way that one species gives way to another in different parts of the world. He realised that small changes in the form of one species gives a particular advantage or adaptation that helps survival (Figure 2.65). He also collected lots of fossils.

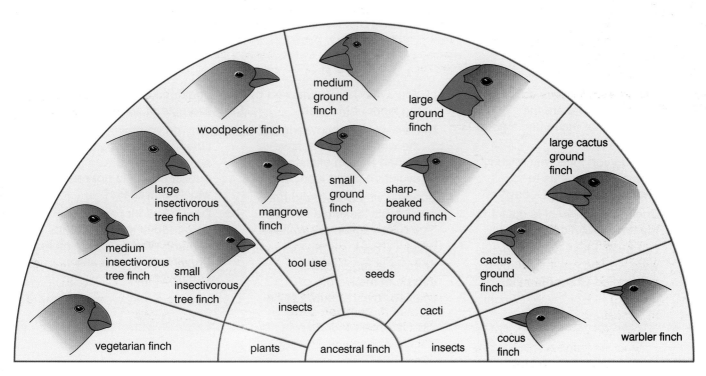

Figure 2.65 Darwin realised that the finches of the Galapagos Islands must have evolved from a common ancestor. As each population became increasingly well adapted to a particular diet, they evolved into separate species.

When Darwin returned from his voyage, he didn't publish his ideas. Then, over 20 years later, he had an unpleasant surprise in a letter he received from a naturalist called Alfred Russell Wallace. Wallace had developed the same ideas and wanted to publish them. This news stung Darwin into action and he rushed into publication.

Wallace knew of Darwin's long-term work and insisted that Darwin should take the greater credit. Darwin's book *On the Origin of Species* was published in 1859. It was a huge success. It sold out on the first day of publication.

In the book he set out his views (Figure 2.66). They were in startling contradiction to those held as true by most people at the time. The general view in Europe, based on a study of the Bible, was that God created the Earth, humans and all other living things just a few thousand years ago. Darwin reasoned that the Earth was formed probably many millions of years ago, that life originated in the distant past and that over long periods of time, species can change. They come and they go. Furthermore it is not God who picks which species will survive and which will become extinct, but rather what Darwin called natural selection. In other words, living things evolve in response to changes in their environment.

The logic of his argument also suggests the idea of common descent – that life arose probably once only. This means that humans are really just another animal and not a special creation. *On the Origin of Species* contains so much evidence and such a clearly set out, logical argument that evolution became established as an accepted theory.

Darwin's work lacked just one ingredient – the mechanism of how species change. However, the basic ideas on genetics were being worked out at exactly the same time by a man called Gregor Mendel. His work was unknown to Darwin because Mendel published his findings in 1866 only in a local magazine that was not sold widely.

Darwin's ideas on gradual evolution actually caused something of a revolution in the way we think about life. His ideas are still controversial. A recent poll showed that 100 000 000 Americans believe that humans were created by God within the last 10 000 years.

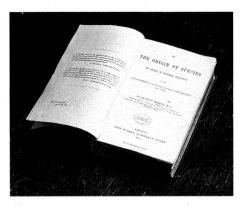

Figure 2.66 An extract from Darwin's original manuscript for *On the Origin of Species*.

Questions

1 Darwin was not very successful at school. What are the qualities that made him a good scientist?

2 Why do you think that a study of past life helps us to understand biology today?

3 Briefly explain what is meant by the term evolution.

4 Our basic ideas about genetics were worked out in 1866 by a man called Gregor Mendel.

a) Why was Darwin unaware of the work of Mendel?

b) How would a knowledge of the work of Mendel have helped Darwin explain how evolution might work?

5 Suggest why Darwin did not publish his ideas until he was 'stung into action' by Wallace.

6 Darwin's book *On the Origin of Species* is regarded as a classic in the history of science. What features of the book make it such a good example of science writing?

7 Why do you think that *On the Origin of Species* was such a success when it was first published but is not read widely nowadays?

8 Darwin's work caused a tremendous stir in the 19th century. Why do you think that Darwin's ideas are still controversial?

1.   The sex of a person is controlled by chromosomes X and Y.

(a)   Where are chromosomes X and Y found in a cell?

(b)   Complete the genetic diagram below to show how sex chromosomes are passed on from parents to their children.

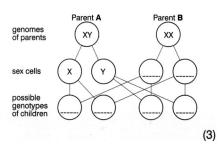

(3)

(c)   Mrs Smith is pregnant.

(i)   Which TWO sex chromosomes does Mrs Smith have?   (1)

(ii) What is the chance that her baby will be a girl?   (1)

(iii) Mrs Smith already has two children, Bill and Harry. They are identical twins. Bill weighs 35 kg and Harry weighs 41 kg.

Suggest TWO reasons for this difference.   (2)
(Total 7 marks)

Edexcel GCSE Double Award (Combined) 1524 June 1999, Paper 1F, no. 3

2.   The graph below shows the changes in population size of the snowshoe hare and of its predator, the lynx, between 1890 and 1930.

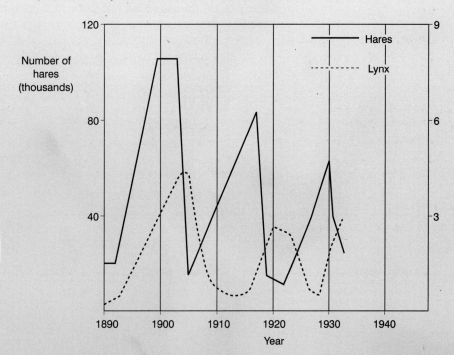

(a)   Why does the population size of the lynx change in the way shown
        (see the dashed line (_ _ _ _ _ _))?   (3)

(b)   Adult snowshoe hares vary in body size. What causes this variation?   (2)
                                                                                    (5 marks)

Edexcel GCSE Double Award (Modular) 1531 June 1998, Paper 1F, no. 5 (abridged
artwork)

3.   The gene for producing insulin can be isolated from human cells. The isolated gene can
        be placed into a bacterial cell.

        The diagram shows a bacterial cell and a human insulin gene.

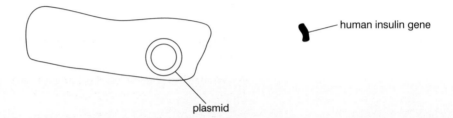

plasmid

(i)   Describe how the human insulin gene is inserted into the bacterial cell.   (3)

(ii) Bacterial cells containing the insulin gene are then cloned. Why are these bacterial
      cells cloned?   (2)

(iii) What are the advantages of using insulin from genetically engineered bacteria to
      treat diabetes?   (2)
                                                                                      (6 marks)

Edexcel GCSE Double Award (Modular) 1531 June 1998, Paper 1F, no. 7 (abridged
artwork)

4   The diagram shows two fruit flies (Drosophila). One has normal wings, the other has short
        wings.

normal wings

short wings

A short-winged fruit fly was crossed with a normal-winged fruit fly. The offspring they produced are shown.

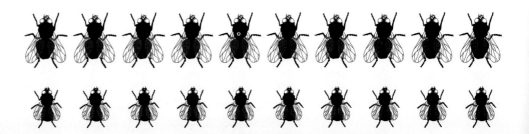

Wing length is inherited. The allele for normal wings (N) is dominant to the allele for short wings (n).

Draw a genetic diagram to show how a fruit fly with normal wings and a fruit fly with short wings can be crossed to produce the offspring shown above.

Your answer should show: the genotypes of both parents
all the gametes formed
the genotypes of the offspring
the phenotypes of the offspring

(5 marks)

Edexcel GCSE (Modular) 1531 June 1998, Paper 1F, no. 6 (abridged artwork)

Glossary 2

Adapted	Plants and animals have special characteristics to suit them to living in a particular environment.
Alleles	Alternative forms of the same gene, such as the gene controlling eye colour.
Amnion	The bag of fluid that surrounds and cushions the developing fetus.
Base pairs	Pairs of chemicals that join together the two halves of a strand of DNA, like the rungs on a ladder. A joins to T, and C joins to G.
Binary fission	Reproducing by the parent splitting in two. Bacteria reproduce by binary fission.
Cervix	The ring of muscle closing the lower end of the uterus.
Clone	An offspring that is genetically identical to its single parent.
Daughter cells	The two genetically identical cells resulting from a cell dividing by mitosis.
Diploid	The total number of chromosomes in a body cell.
DNA	Deoxyribonucleic acid. This is the molecule that genes are made from.
Double helix	Two parallel strands twisted together, a bit like a twisted ladder.
Fertilisation	The joining together of an ovum and a sperm to form a zygote.
Fetus	The stage when the embryo is recognisably a baby, from about 8 weeks after fertilisation until birth.
Gene	The small part of a chromosome that controls a particular inherited characteristic. Each chromosome contains hundreds of genes.
Genotype	The genetic make up of an organism.
Haploid	The number of chromosomes contained in a sex cell, a sperm or an ovum.
Heterozygous	An organism that carries two different alleles for a particular characteristic.
Homologous	Chromosomes that are identical to each other. All but one pair of the chromosomes in a cell come in homologous pairs.
Homozygous	An organism that carries two identical alleles for a particular characteristic.
Human Genome Project	A project in which scientists have mapped out the location of all the different human genes on the human chromosome. There are about 35,000 human genes in total.
Implantation	The ball of cells, resulting from the dividing of a zygote, sinks into the wall of the uterus.

Locus	The place on a chromosome where a particular gene is situated.
Meiosis	The type of cell division that takes place in the ovaries and testes.
Mitosis	The type of cell division that takes place in all body tissues except the sex cells.
Mutation	A change in a gene, causing the genetic code to alter. A mutation may be caused by some environmental factor.
Natural selection	The process by which individuals that are best adapted to an environment survive and breed more successfully than their less well adapted neighbours.
Oestrogen	A hormone involved in the menstrual cycle in females.
Oviduct	The tube along which an ovum travels from the ovary to the uterus.
Ovulation	The process of a mature ovum (egg) being released from an ovary.
Ovum	The female sex cell.
Phenotype	A description of the outward appearance of an organism.
Placenta	The large, disc shaped organ, attached to the wall of the uterus, that allows the exchange of substances between the fetal blood and the mother's blood.
Progesterone	One of the hormones controlling the menstrual cycle in women.
Replication	The process when a strand of DNA makes an exact copy of itself, just before a cell divides in two.
Selective breeding	Breeding animals or plants with a desired characteristic with other individuals showing the same desired characteristic.
Semen	The liquid that carries the sperm from the testes to the penis.
Sperm	The male sex cell.
Testosterone	The hormone that controls the production of sperm in males.
Umbilical cord	The cord of blood vessels that connects the fetus to the placenta.
Uterus	The muscular organ in which a fertilised ovum develops into a baby.
Zygote	A single fertilised ovum. It is about the size of a full stop.

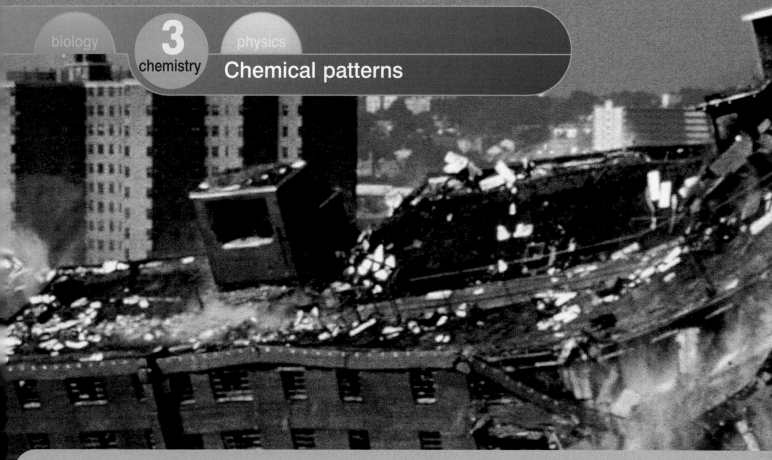

There are many thousands of different chemicals but they are all made from the same building blocks. These building blocks are called elements. Scientists like to find patterns to help them understand things. In this module you will learn how the Russian scientist, Dimitri Mendeléev, found a pattern in the elements. This pattern formed the first periodic table. The periodic table is still important today; it helps us to sort the elements into groups with similar properties.

To understand why the elements fit into groups, you will need to learn about the structure of atoms. It is the electrons in atoms that are so important in chemical reactions. One group of elements is called the halogens. The halogen family contains the elements fluorine, chlorine, bromine and iodine.

These are all toxic substances but they do have their uses. Chlorine was used to kill soldiers in the First World War but it also has an important modern day use as it kills harmful microbes in water, preventing the spread of disease.

Rusting is a slow chemical reaction, whereas explosions are fast chemical reactions. This module looks at how reactions can be speeded up or slowed down? Speeding up reactions is important in industry; if you can make more of a product then you can make more profit! Catalytic converters are now fitted to many cars, but what are they and how do they work? This module will help you to understand chemical catalysts, and also the important catalysts in our bodies, called enzymes.

3

Learning outcomes

After completing the work in this topic you will be able to:

- recall that there are about 100 elements in the periodic table, arranged in order of ascending atomic number

- understand that elements are the building blocks of all materials

- explain where metals and non-metals are found in the periodic table, and the positions of the alkali metals, the halogens and the noble gases

- recall that elements in the same group of the periodic table have similar chemical properties and that there is a gradual change in the properties of the elements from the top to the bottom of each group

Did you know?

Lawrencium (Lw) was first made in 1961 by nuclear scientists. It does not occur naturally.

You should already know that **elements** are chemical substances in their simplest form, and that they are represented by symbols. There are about 100 naturally occurring elements. They combine with other elements to form compounds. Elements are shown in the **periodic table** and can be classified as metals or non-metals.

The periodic table...

The full version of the periodic table contains all the elements (Figure 3.1). You don't need to know anything about the elements in the bottom section, so these are usually left out.

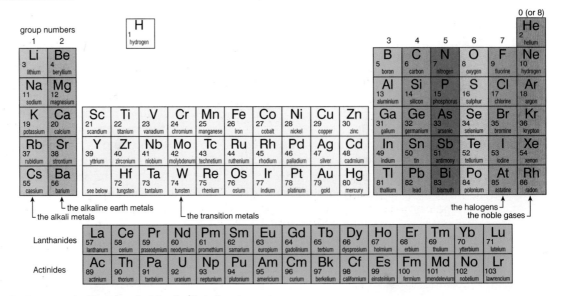

Figure 3.1 The periodic table. Each colour shows a chemical family of similar elements.

In the periodic table, the elements are arranged in order of increasing **atomic number**. A **group** is a vertical column of the periodic table. All the elements in one group have similar properties and are called a chemical family. The **halogens**, including fluorine, chlorine, bromine and iodine, are one chemical family. In each family, there is a gradual variation in properties from the top to the bottom of the group. A **period** is a horizontal row of the periodic table. As you can see in Figure 3.1, the third period contains all the elements from potassium to krypton.

The metals are found to the left of the periodic table and the non-metals are found to the right. The elements on the boundary between the metals and the non-metals have properties of both metals and non-metals. They are called **metalloids**. They include the important **semi-conductors**, silicon and germanium (Figure 3.2).

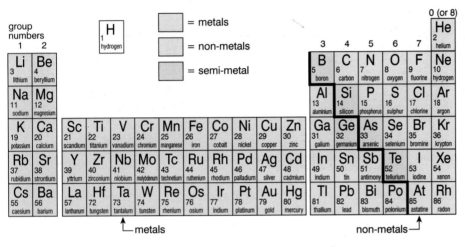

Figure 3.2 The periodic table showing metals to the left and non-metals to the right.

Key Facts

- The elements are the building blocks of all materials.
- The periodic table arranges elements in order of increasing atomic number.
- Elements with similar properties line up in vertical columns called groups.
- There is a gradual change in the properties of the elements from the top to the bottom of each group.
- The horizontal rows are called periods.

Questions

1. Copy and complete:

   Elements are the .... kind of chemical substance. When elements combine .... are formed. The periodic table lists all elements in order of increasing .... The vertical columns in the periodic table are called .... These contain elements with .... properties. As you go down a group, the properties .... change.

2. Use the periodic table to find out:

   a) The symbol for calcium.

   b) The atomic number of carbon.

   c) The name of an element in the second period.

   d) The name of a non-metal.

   e) The name of an element in group one.

   f) The name of an element with similar properties to sodium.

3. The numbers in the diagram show elements in the periodic table.

   Which of these elements are:

   a) metals?

   b) in the second period?

   c) in group 0?

   d) halogens?

   e) alkali metals?

Atomic structure

There are three types of particle inside an atom, called **protons**, **neutrons** and **electrons**. Their basic properties are shown in Table 3.1.

Particle	Charge	Mass
proton	+1	1
neutron	0	1
electron	−1	1/1840

Table 3.1 The particles inside an atom showing relative charge and relative mass.

The three different types of particle (Figure 3.3) have the following properties:
- Protons and neutrons have the same mass.
- Electrons are very light. 1840 electrons have the same mass as 1 proton.
- Protons and neutrons are in the **nucleus** of the atom.
- Electrons **orbit** the nucleus.
- Protons have a positive charge, neutrons have no charge and electrons have a negative charge.

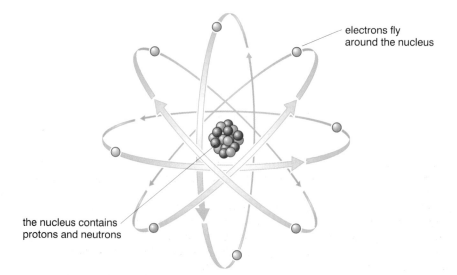

electrons fly around the nucleus

the nucleus contains protons and neutrons

Figure 3.3 Electrons orbit the small dense nucleus of an atom.

Atoms are electrically neutral, which means they do not have an overall positive or negative charge. Therefore, they must contain equal numbers of protons and electrons so that the charges are balanced. The number of protons in an atom is called the atomic number of that element. All atoms of the same element contain the same number of protons. The protons and the neutrons are in the nucleus and the very light electrons orbit around the nucleus. Table 3.2 shows the atomic number of three common elements and the number of protons contained in the nucleus of each atom.

Element	Atomic number	Number of protons
hydrogen	1	1
oxygen	8	8
calcium	20	20

Table 3.2 The atomic number and the number of protons in the nucleus of three common elements.

Electron shells...

Electrons are arranged in **shells** around the nucleus. These are sometimes called orbitals or energy levels. The first shell can only hold two electrons, while the second shell can hold eight electrons. The third shell can also hold eight electrons. The shells nearest to the nucleus are filled first (Figure 3.4).

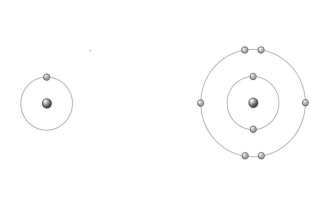

hydrogen has 1 electron   oxygen has 8 electrons   calcium has 20 electrons

Figure 3.4 The electrons in atoms are arranged in shells around the nucleus.

Links to the periodic table...

The first period in the table contains two elements, and the first electron shell holds two electrons. The second period contains eight elements, and the second shell holds eight electrons.

Table 3.3 shows the relationship between the number of electrons and the electron structure of the first 20 elements in the periodic table. When you compare this with Figure 3.1 on page 84, you will see that the number of electrons in the outer shell is the same for each element in the same group of the periodic table. For example, lithium, sodium and potassium all have one outer electron.

The reactions of an element depend on the arrangement of the electrons in its atoms. This is why elements in the same group have similar reactions.

Key Facts

Key Facts

- Atoms contain three types of particles.
- Protons have a positive charge and are in the nucleus.
- Neutrons have no charge and are in the nucleus.
- Electrons have a negative charge and are in shells around the nucleus.
- The electron configuration of an atom shows the arrangement of the electrons in the shells.
- Elements in the same group of the periodic table have the same number of outer electrons.

Element	Number of electrons	Arrangement of electrons
hydrogen	1	1
helium	2	2
lithium	3	2,1
beryllium	4	2,2
boron	5	2,3
carbon	6	2,4
nitrogen	7	2,5
oxygen	8	2,6
fluorine	9	2,7
neon	10	2,8
sodium	11	2,8,1
magnesium	12	2,8,2
aluminium	13	2,8,3
silicon	14	2,8,4
phosphorus	15	2,8,5
sulphur	16	2,8,6
chlorine	17	2,8,7
argon	18	2,8,8
potassium	19	2,8,8,1
calcium	20	2,8,8,2

Table 3.3 The relationship between the number of electrons and the electron configuration of different elements.

Questions

1 Copy and complete:

There are .... types of particles in .... The nucleus contains .... and .... The shells contain .... Every element in a .... of the periodic table has the same number of ....

electrons. This is why the elements in a group have .... reactions.

2 Use the periodic table to help you draw diagrams of the following atoms.

   a) helium   b) carbon
   c) sodium

3 An atom of an element has the electron configuration 2,8,7.

   a) Draw a diagram of this atom.

   b) What is the name of this element?

   c) Which group of the periodic table is the element in?

chemistry

Learning outcome

After completing the work in this topic you will be able to:

- describe the early attempts of scientists to find patterns in the elements

Finding a pattern in facts and information aids understanding. At the beginning of the 19th century, many new elements were discovered, but finding a pattern was difficult. One problem was that some of the substances that were thought to be elements were in fact compounds. Another problem was that some elements had not yet been discovered but the scientists did not know this at the time.

At that time, one important thing known about most of the elements was their **atomic weight**. This is the weight of an atom of the element compared with the weight of an atom of hydrogen. It is now called the **relative atomic mass** (see Module 8).

The German chemist Johann Döbereiner made the first attempt to find a pattern. He studied groups of three elements which were similar chemically, such as chlorine, bromine and iodine. He thought that bromine seemed halfway between chlorine and iodine in its properties. He also noticed that the atomic weight of bromine was approximately halfway between the other two elements.

He looked for other examples and called them 'triads'. Two examples are shown in Table 3.4.

Element	Atomic mass
chlorine	35
bromine	80
iodine	127

Element	Atomic mass
calcium	40
strontium	88
barium	137

Table 3.4 Two examples of Johann Döbereiner's triads.

Döbereiner's ideas were published in 1829. His ideas were not taken very seriously because most of the elements could not be fitted into his scheme. In 1864, the English chemist John Newlands arranged the elements that were known at the time in order of increasing atomic weight. These did not include the noble gases as none of these had been discovered. He noticed that: 'The eighth one starting from a given one is a kind of repetition of the first'. Table 3.5 illustrates this point.

Element	Li	Be	B	C	N	O	F
Atomic weight	7	9	11	12	14	16	19
Element	Na	Mg	Al	Si	P	S	Cl
Atomic weight	23	24	27	28	31	32	35

Table 3.5 The pattern observed by John Newlands.

Key Facts

- Scientists, including Johann Döbereiner and John Newlands, tried to find a pattern in the elements.
- The Russian chemist Dimitri Mendeléev published the periodic table in 1869.

Did you know?

The missing element technetium was not discovered until 1937, long after the idea of the periodic table had been accepted.

For example, John Newlands noticed that sodium resembles lithium, magnesium resembles beryllium and chlorine resembles fluorine. Newlands called this the 'law of octaves'. However, the law of octaves stops working after the first 17 elements, so this idea was again not taken seriously.

It was in 1869 that a Russian chemist, Dimitri Mendeléev, published his periodic table. He succeeded because he realised that Newlands had made two mistakes. One was to assume that all the elements had been discovered and the other was to think that the 'law of octaves' would work throughout the table with seven elements in every row. Mendeléev arranged the elements by property and left spaces. He suggested that the spaces would be filled with as yet undiscovered elements. He even made predictions for these elements. It was nearly 100 years before some of these elements were eventually discovered (Figure 3.5).

One missing element was between silicon and tin in group 4. In 1886, the element germanium was discovered. It had almost identical properties to those that Mendeléev had predicted. This helped considerably to get his ideas accepted.

| | Group | | | | | | | |
	1	2	3	4	5	6	7	8
Period 1	H							
Period 2	Li	Be	B	C	N	O	F	
Period 3	Na	Mg	Al	Si	P	S	Cl	
Period 4	K Cu	Ca Zn	? ?	Ti ?	V As	Cr Se	Mn Br	Fe Co Ni
Period 5	Rb Ag	Sr Cd	Y In	Zr Sn	Nb Sb	Mo Te	? I	Ru Rh Pd

Figure 3.5 Mendeleev's periodic table.

Questions

1 Copy and complete: Mendeléev produced the first .... table. He arranged the elements by placing those with .... properties in the same group. This left some spaces and Mendeléev .... that new elements would be .... He published his ideas in ....

2 A complete group of elements is missing from Mendeléev's table.
   a) What is this group?
   b) Why is it missing?

3 Give the symbols and names of the four missing elements from Mendeléev's periodic table.

4 How did Mendeléev know about the work of Newlands?

5 Why did other people eventually accept Mendeléev's ideas?

6 Use the Internet or a CD-ROM to find out more about the scientists mentioned in this section.

... more at www.modularscience.co.uk

Learning outcomes

After completing the work in this topic you will be able to:

- represent chemical reactions by word equations
- write simple balanced equations
- use the state symbols (s), (l), (g) and (aq)

You should remember that elements are represented by **symbols**. In two letter symbols, the second letter is always small. For example, Co is the symbol for cobalt. However, CO is the formula for carbon monoxide and it represents one atom of carbon and one atom of oxygen.

Compounds are represented by **formulae**. The formula for sodium chloride is NaCl, which represents one atom of sodium combined with one atom of chlorine. The formula for ammonia is NH_3, which indicates one atom of nitrogen combined with three atoms of hydrogen.

Chemical reactions can be represented by **word equations**. For example:

magnesium + oxygen $\rightarrow$ magnesium oxide

Equations and formulae...

A symbol equation shows exactly how the atoms in a chemical reaction have been rearranged. For example:

$$Mg(s) \quad + \quad CuSO_4(aq) \quad \rightarrow \quad MgSO_4(aq) \quad + \quad Cu(s)$$

This shows that solid magnesium has reacted with copper sulphate solution to form magnesium sulphate solution and solid copper (Figure 3.6). You should remember that this is a displacement reaction.

The symbols (s) and (aq) are called **state symbols**. The state symbols are (s) solid, (aq) in solution (aqueous), (l) liquid, (g) gas. They are not always included in symbol equations.

Figure 3.6 Magnesium displaces copper from copper sulphate solution.

Writing formulae...

Why is the formula of ammonia NH_3 and not NH? This is because one atom of nitrogen combines with three atoms of hydrogen. To write formulae you have to know the combining power of atoms or groups of atoms.

In general, the combining power of atoms can be calculated from the following rules:

- Groups 1 to 4 of the periodic table have the same combining power as their group number. For example, aluminium is in group 3 and it has a combining power of 3.
- For group 5 the combining power is 3.
- For group 6 the combining power is 2.
- For group 7 the combining power is 1.

For example, chlorine is in group 7 and has a combining power of 1. Aluminium is in group 3 and has a combining power of 3. This means that one atom of aluminium combines with three atoms of chlorine and the formula of aluminium chloride is $AlCl_3$.

These rules are a useful guide but they don't always work. For example, sulphur in hydrogen sulphide H_2S has a combining power of 2 but sulphur in sulphur dioxide SO_2 has a combining power of 4.

Did you know?

Formulae are not all simple. Insulin has the formula $C_{254}H_{377}N_{65}O_{75}S_6$

Key Facts

- Chemical equations can be represented by word equations.
- The symbols (s), (aq), (l) and (g) are called state symbols.
- To balance an equation, the number of atoms of each element on both sides of the equation must be the same.

Symbol equations...

Example 1
Write a symbol equation for the reaction of iron with sulphur.

word equation:	iron	+	sulphur	$\rightarrow$	iron sulphide
write in the formulae:	Fe	+	S	$\rightarrow$	FeS
balance the equation:	there are already equal amounts of each atom on both sides				

Example 2
Write a symbol equation for the reaction of magnesium with oxygen.

word equation:	magnesium	+	oxygen	$\rightarrow$	magnesium oxide
write in the formulae:	Mg	+	O_2	$\rightarrow$	MgO
balance the equation:	2Mg	+	O_2	$\rightarrow$	2MgO
	2 magnesium atoms + 2 oxygen atoms				2 magnesium atoms + 2 oxygen atoms

To balance an equation, the number of atoms of each element on both sides of the equation must be the same. Atoms are not created or destroyed in a chemical reaction, they are just rearranged, so equations must always balance.
When you are writing an equation, you must not change the formulae. You can only change the number of atoms by putting numbers in front of the formulae.

Questions

1 Write the formulae for:
   a) sodium chloride
   b) calcium oxide
   c) magnesium chloride
   d) calcium chloride
   e) aluminium chloride
   f) sodium nitrate
   g) calcium sulphate
   h) ammonium sulphate
   i) magnesium nitrate
   j) aluminium sulphate

2 How many atoms of each element are present in:
   a) $Mg(NO_3)_2$
   b) $(NH_4)_2SO_4$
   c) $Ca_3(PO_4)_2$

3 Balance these equations:
   a) $H_2 + O_2 \rightarrow H_2O$
   b) $Na + H_2O \rightarrow NaOH + H_2$
   c) $H_2 + Cl_2 \rightarrow HCl$
   d) $Fe + O_2 \rightarrow Fe_2O_3$
   e) $Mg + HCl \rightarrow MgCl_2$
   f) $Ca(OH)_2 + HNO_3 \rightarrow Ca(NO_3)_2 + H_2O$
   g) $N_2 + H_2 \rightarrow NH_3$
   h) $C_2H_6 + O_2 \rightarrow CO_2 + H_2O$
   i) $HCl + CaCO_3 \rightarrow CaCl_2 + H_2O + CO_2$
   j) $KMnO_4 + HCl \rightarrow KCl + MnCl_2 + H_2O + Cl_2$

4 Write balanced symbol equations for:

   a) The reaction of copper with oxygen to form copper oxide.
   b) The displacement of iron from iron(III) chloride solution by magnesium.
   c) The reaction of zinc with sulphuric acid to form zinc sulphate and hydrogen.
   d) The reaction of sodium hydroxide solution with sulphuric acid to form sodium sulphate and water.
   e) The reaction of calcium carbonate with nitric acid to form calcium nitrate, water and carbon dioxide.

... more at www.modularscience.co.uk

The halogens

After completing the work in this topic you will be able to:

• describe the variation in colour, the trends in boiling point and the physical
  states at room temperature of the halogens: fluorine, chlorine, bromine and
  iodine

Group 7 of the periodic table is made up of the halogens, which is a group of non-
metals. One of the group, astatine, is a rare radioactive element. Its properties are not
accurately known. Table 3.6 shows some of the properties of the halogens.

Name	Symbol	Atomic number	Electron configuration	Appearance at room temperature	Melting point (°C)	Boiling point (°C)
fluorine	F	9	2,7	pale yellow gas	−220	−188
chlorine	Cl	17	2,8,7	green-yellow gas	−101	−35
bromine	Br	35	2,8,18,7	red-brown liquid	−7	59
iodine	I	53	2,8,18,18,7	dark grey solid	114	187
astatine	At	85	2,8,18,32,18,7	not known		

Table 3.6 The halogens and their properties.

Properties of halogens...

As a group, the halogens have the following properties:
• They are all coloured – the colour gets darker as you go down the group.
• They have very low melting points and boiling points, which increase as you go down
  the group.
• They change from gases to liquids to solids at room temperature as you go down
  the group.
• They all exist as **diatomic** molecules, for example Cl_2

Other properties...

Chlorine turns moist universal indicator red and then bleaches it. All the halogens act
as bleaches but the effect is less further down the group (Figure 3.7).

Figure 3.7 The indicator paper turns white when it is bleached by
chlorine.

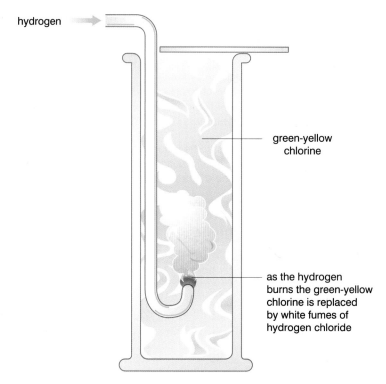

Figure 3.8 Hydrogen burns in chlorine to form hydrogen chloride.

The halogens react with hydrogen to form hydrogen halides. The reaction of hydrogen with fluorine is explosive.

$$H_2 \quad + \quad F_2 \quad \rightarrow \quad 2HF$$
hydrogen   fluorine   hydrogen fluoride

If a jet of burning hydrogen is lowered into a gas jar of chlorine it continues to burn, forming white fumes of hydrogen chloride (Figure 3.8).

$$H_2 \quad + \quad Cl_2 \quad \rightarrow \quad 2HCl$$
hydrogen   chlorine   hydrogen chloride

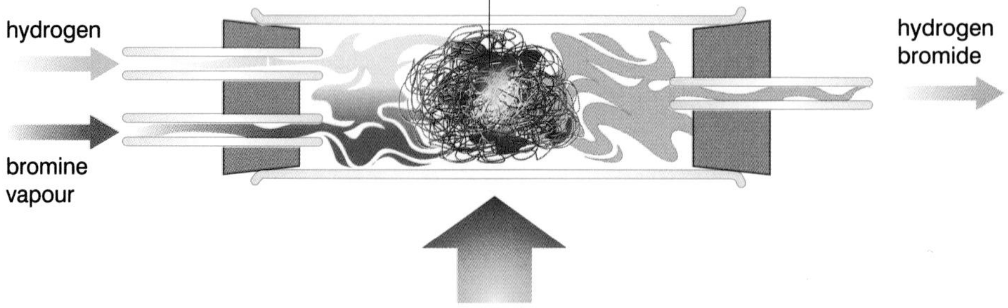

Figure 3.9 Hydrogen and bromine combine to form hydrogen bromide.

Did you know?

Fluorine is the most reactive of all the non-metallic elements; it even attacks glass.

Hydrogen and bromine vapour burn with a weak flame when lit but will combine when passed over a hot catalyst (Figure 3.9).

$$H_2 \quad + \quad Br_2 \quad \rightarrow \quad 2HBr$$
hydrogen   bromine   hydrogen bromide

It is difficult to get hydrogen to react with iodine. The reaction of the halogens with hydrogen shows the normal trend for this group.

F
Cl
Br
I

reactivity increases

Key Facts

- The halogens form Group 7 of the periodic table.
- Halogens are elements with similar chemical properties.
- There is a gradual change in properties from the top to the bottom of the group.

Questions

1 Copy and complete:
   Group 7 of the periodic table contains the .... This family of elements contains fluorine, ..., ... and .... The most reactive element in the group is .... At room temperature .... is a green gas and .... is a grey solid.

2 Use the information in Table 3.6 to make predictions about astatine.
   Predict:
   a) its colour
   b) its melting point
   c) its boiling point
   d) its physical state at room temperature

3 Explain why the melting points and boiling points of the halogens increase as you move down the group.

4 The reactivity decreases as you move down the halogen group. Justify this statement by referring to the reactions of the halogens with hydrogen.

... more at www.modularscience.co.uk

Figure 3.10 Chlorine gas.

Chlorine and Dutch metal...

Dutch metal is an alloy of copper and zinc which is supplied in thin sheets. If a piece of it is lowered into a gas jar of chlorine, it bursts into flames (Figure 3.10).

$$Cu \ (s) \quad + \quad Cl_2 \ (g) \quad \rightarrow \quad CuCl_2 \ (s)$$
copper   chlorine   copper chloride

$$Zn \ (s) \quad + \quad Cl_2 \ (g) \quad \rightarrow \quad ZnCl_2 \ (s)$$
zinc   chlorine   zinc chloride

Chlorine and sodium...

If a small piece of burning sodium is placed in a gas jar of chlorine it continues to burn, forming white fumes of sodium chloride (Figure 3.11).

$$2Na \ (s) \quad + \quad Cl_2 \ (g) \quad \rightarrow \quad 2NaCl \ (s)$$
sodium   chlorine   sodium chloride

Chlorine and iron...

If dry chlorine is passed over heated iron, iron(III) chloride is formed (Figure 3.12).

$$2Fe \ (s) \quad + \quad 3Cl_2 \ (g) \quad \rightarrow \quad 2FeCl_3 \ (s)$$
iron   chlorine   iron(III) chloride

Figure 3.11 Sodium burning in chlorine.

Did you know?

Sodium chloride is common salt, which is used to flavour our food. It can be formed from the reaction of a very reactive metal with a poisonous gas.

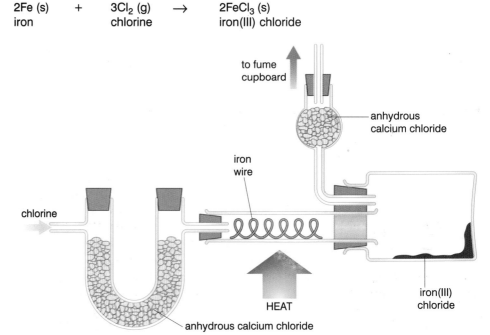

Figure 3.12 Iron and chlorine combine to form iron(III) chloride.

Other halogens with metals...

The same group trends are shown in the reactions of the halogens with metals.

F
Cl   reactivity
Br   decreases
I

The reaction of halogens with hot iron are shown in Table 3.7 and Figure 3.13.

Halogen	Reaction with hot iron
chlorine	reacts rapidly to form iron(III) chloride $2Fe + 3Cl_2 \rightarrow 2FeCl_3$
bromine	reacts slowly to form iron(III) bromide $2Fe + 3Br_2 \rightarrow 2FeBr_3$
iodine	reacts very slowly to form iron(III) iodide $2Fe + 3I_2 \rightarrow 2FeI_3$

Table 3.7 The reaction of halogens with hot iron.

Key Facts

- Metals react with halogens to form halides.
- Fluorine forms fluorides in very vigorous reactions.
- Chlorine forms chlorides in vigorous reactions.
- Bromine forms bromides in slow reactions.
- Iodine forms iodides in very slow reactions.

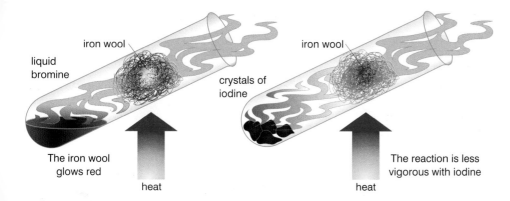

iron wool
liquid bromine
crystals of iodine
iron wool
The iron wool glows red
heat
The reaction is less vigorous with iodine
heat

Figure 3.13 Iron reacts more vigorously with bromine than with iodine.

Questions

1 Copy and complete:

The most reactive halogen is .... Reactivity .... as you move down the group. All the halogens react with metals to form .... When sodium reacts with chlorine .... is formed. When iron reacts with ...., iron(III) bromide is formed.

2 Write balanced equations for the following reactions:

a) sodium with chlorine

b) iron with bromine

c) zinc with bromine

3 Explain how the reaction of the halogens with iron shows a typical group trend.

One general rule for halogens is that a more reactive halogen will displace a less reactive one from solutions of its compounds. So, if chlorine is passed into potassium bromide solution, a reddish brown colour is produced as bromine is **displaced** (Figure 3.14).

Did you know?

Bromine is obtained by bubbling chlorine through seawater, which contains bromide ions. The bromine is displaced.

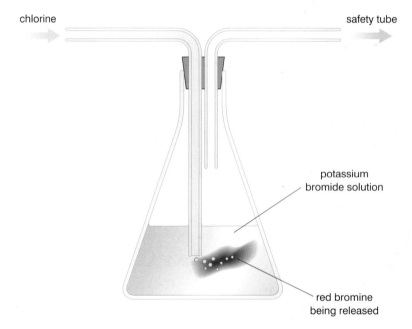

chlorine   safety tube

potassium
bromide solution

red bromine
being released

Figure 3.14 Chlorine displaces bromine when it is bubbled into potassium bromide solution.

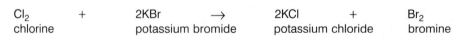

Cl_2	+	$2KBr$	$\rightarrow$	$2KCl$	+	Br_2
chlorine		potassium bromide		potassium chloride		bromine

In the same way, if bromine solution (bromine water) is dripped into potassium iodide solution, dark brown iodine is released (Figure 3.15).

Br_2	+	$2KI$	$\rightarrow$	$2KBr$	+	I_2
bromine		potassium iodide		potassium bromide		iodine

Reactivity...

The high reactivity of the halogens is due to their electronic structure. They all have seven electrons in their outer shell and require an extra electron to fill it. They therefore react by gaining one electron to form negative **ions** (Figure 3.16). As you go down the group, the atoms become larger. The positive nucleus is less able to attract electrons and the reactivity decreases.

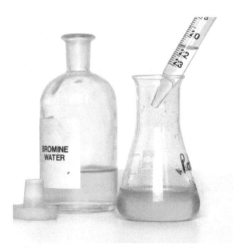

Figure 3.15 Bromine displaces iodine when bromine water is dripped into potassium iodide solution.

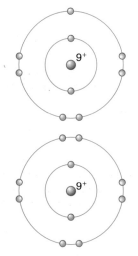

A fluorine atom has 7 electrons in its outer shell

A fluorine atom has 9 electrons (2,7)

A fluoride ion has 8 electrons in its outer shell

A fluoride ion has 10 electrons (2,8)

Figure 3.16 A fluorine atom and a fluoride ion. The fluoride ion has gained an electron in the outer shell.

Uses of halogens

Uses of fluorine...

One of the better-known uses of fluorine is in the form of fluorides in toothpaste and water supplies. Fluorides are added to drinking water and toothpaste to strengthen tooth enamel and reduce tooth decay. The addition of sodium fluoride to drinking water has caused much debate since it was first permitted in 1985. Two newspaper reports from 1999 show the different points of view.

Water firms seek legal protection under plans for mass fluoridation

Anti-fluoride campaigners say that the use of the chemical in drinking water amounts to mass medication and is potentially harmful. They point to research linking high doses of fluoride with bone disease.

Water companies are concerned that they will be responsible for any legal claims if fluoride is added to water supplies.

Dentists back fluoridation campaign

The British Dental Association has published a new report which gives more evidence that fluoridation benefits older people as well as children.

Dentists say that all the new evidence reinforces the positive aspects of fluoride in water.

Compounds of fluorine...

Compounds of fluorine have many important uses. Teflon (polytetrafluoroethylene) is an important 'non-stick' coating (Figure 3.17).

In the early 1960s, chlorofluorocarbons (CFCs) found many uses as solvents, aerosol propellants and in refrigerators. We now know that releasing these compounds into the atmosphere destroys ozone. The use of CFCs is now banned in most industrialised countries.

Figure 3.17 Teflon, which is a fluorine compound, stops the eggs sticking to the pan.

Chemical patterns **99**

Uses of chlorine...

Figure 3.18 shows some of the many uses for chlorine.

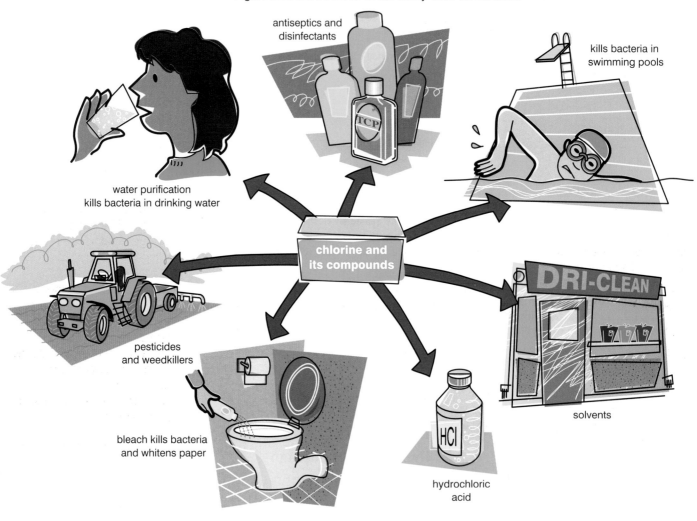

Figure 3.18 Some of the uses of chlorine.

Uses of bromine...

Bromine is used in making fire-retardant materials, pesticides and medicines. Silver bromide is sensitive to light and is used in photography.

Uses of iodine...

Iodine is used as an antiseptic. A solution of iodine in ethanol is used to treat cuts (Figure 3.19). Compounds containing iodine are added to animal feeds and silver iodide is also sensitive to light and is used in photography.

Did you know?

If silver iodide is fired into clouds it can cause rain. This is known as seeding. The USA used cloud seeding in the Vietnam war to produce flooding.

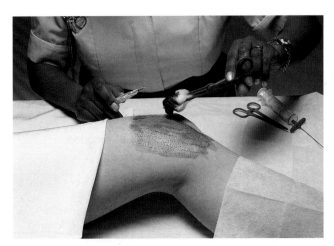

Figure 3.19 Iodine kills bacteria.

Production of halogens...

Chlorine is by far the most important of the halogens. Table 3.8 shows the annual world production of fluorine, chlorine, bromine and iodine.

Halogen	Annual world production
fluorine	15 000 tonnes
chlorine	39 million tonnes
bromine	550 000 tonnes
iodine	13 000 tonnes

Table 3.8 The annual world production of four halogens.

Key Facts

- The most reactive halogen is fluorine. The reactivity of halogens decreases down the group as the size of the atom increases.
- A more reactive halogen will displace a less reactive one from solutions of its compounds.
- The uses of chlorine include water purification and bleaching.
- A common use of iodine is as an antiseptic.

Questions

1 Copy and complete:

   The least reactive of the halogens fluorine, chlorine, bromine and iodine is .... This halogen also has the .... atoms. Chlorine will displace .... from sodium iodide solution. Chlorine will not displace .... from sodium fluoride solution because chlorine is .... reactive than fluorine. Chlorine is used in swimming pools to kill .... Iodine is used as an antiseptic to kill ....

2 Write balanced equations for the reactions of:

   a) Chlorine with sodium bromide solution.

   b) Bromine with potassium iodide solution.

3 Explain why iodine does not react with sodium chloride solution.

4 Design a poster to explain why dentists believe that sodium fluoride should be added to drinking water.

5 Is chlorine a friend or foe?

   Prepare a short talk to explain why chlorine can be regarded as both a friend and a foe.

Learning outcomes

After completing the work in this topic you will be able to:

- recall how to measure the speed at which chemical reactions take place

Figure 3.20 The formation of rust is a slow chemical reaction.

Figure 3.21 This is a fast chemical reaction.

Some chemical reactions happen slowly, others occur much faster. Figures 3.20 and 3.21 illustrate this point. We say that fast reactions have a high **rate of reaction**.

Measuring reaction rates

We can measure rates of reaction by measuring how quickly a **product** is formed or how quickly a **reactant** is used up. Usually it is easier to measure the product being formed.

Volume of gas formed...

Experiment 1
When marble chips (calcium carbonate) react with dilute hydrochloric acid, carbon dioxide is formed (Figure 3.22).

$$CaCO_3(s) + 2HCl(aq) \rightarrow CaCl_2(aq) + H_2O(l) + CO_2(g)$$

The total volume of carbon dioxide formed every 30 seconds in the experiment can be measured and the results can be recorded in a table (Table 3.9).

Time (s)	Volume of carbon dioxide (cm^3)
0	0
30	
60	

Table 3.9 Volume of carbon dioxide produced in Experiment 1.

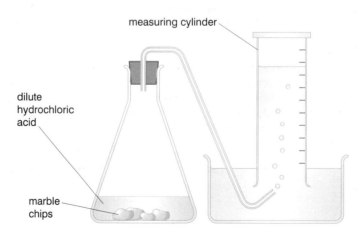

Figure 3.22 An experiment to measure the rate of reaction between marble chips and hydrochloric acid by measuring the volume of gas given off.

Experiment 2
When magnesium reacts with dilute hydrochloric acid, hydrogen is formed (Figure 3.23).

$$Mg(s) + 2HCl(aq) \rightarrow MgCl_2(aq) + H_2(g)$$

The total volume of hydrogen formed every 30 seconds in the experiment can be measured and the results can be recorded in a table (Table 3.10).

Time (s)	Volume of hydrogen (cm^3)
0	0
30	
60	

Table 3.10 Volume of hydrogen produced in Experiment 2.

Key Facts

- Some chemical reactions are fast, others are slow.
- Rates of reaction can be measured by finding out how quickly a product is formed or how quickly a reactant is used up.
- Examples of measuring reaction rates include measurement of the volume of a gas formed and measurement of the loss in mass when a gas is given off.

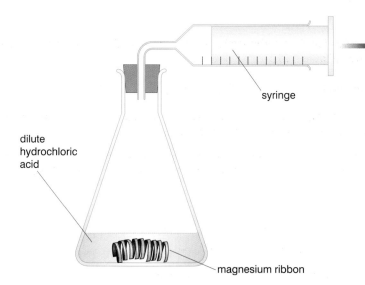

syringe

dilute hydrochloric acid

magnesium ribbon

Figure 3.23 An experiment to measure the rate of reaction between magnesium and hydrochloric acid by measuring the volume of gas given off.

Mass of gas formed...

In any reaction, the total mass of reactants is equal to the total mass of products. If a gas is given off during a reaction, some products are lost to the surroundings, so the total mass of the reaction flask plus the contents will decrease. To show this, the flask is placed on a balance (figure 324). The total mass every 30 seconds can be measured in order to find the rate of reaction (Table 3.11)

Time (s)	Mass (g)	Loss of mass (g)
0		0
30		
60		

Table 3.11 Mass of gas formed

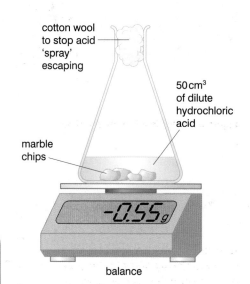

cotton wool to stop acid 'spray' escaping

50 cm^3 of dilute hydrochloric acid

marble chips

-0.55 g

balance

Figure 3.24 An experiment to measure the rate of reaction between marble chips and hydrochloric acid by measuring the mass of gas given off.

Graphs for reaction rates...

In Figure 3.25, the slope (or gradient) of the graph gives you the rate of the reaction. The steeper the slope, the faster the reaction. Usually, reactions start fast and then slow down as the reactants are used up. The reaction stops when all of one of the reactants is used up.

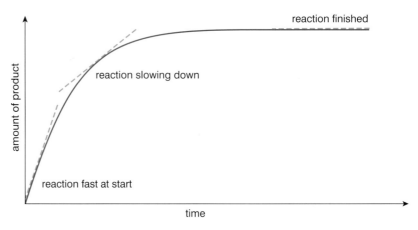

Figure 3.25 Graph to show the rate of a reaction as the reactants are used up.

Questions

1 Copy out each description of a reaction. Then match the reaction to its description:

A slow reaction that makes alcohol.

A useful reaction that makes unwanted products.

A fast, unwanted reaction.

A slow reaction that is not usually wanted.

A slow reaction that destroys cars.

    rusting
    fermenting sugar
    burning fuels
    a house fire
    milk turning sour

2 Marble chips were added to dilute hydrochloric acid. Figure 3.26 shows how the volume of

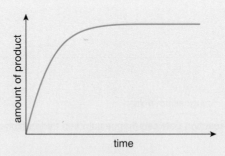

Figure 3.26 Graph for question 2.

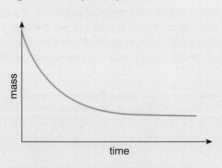

Figure 3.27 Graph for question 3.

gas given off changed with time.

a) When was the rate of reaction fastest?

b) Describe and explain what happened to the rate of reaction with time.

3 A conical flask containing marble chips and dilute hydrochloric acid was placed on a top-pan balance. The graph in Figure 3.27 shows how the mass of the flask and contents changed with time.

a) Why did the mass fall?

b) Why did the mass never fall to zero?

c) Explain the shape of the graph.

... more at www.modularscience.co.uk

Learning outcome

After completing the work in this topic you will be able to:

- understand that the rate of a chemical reaction increases if the temperature is increased

Marble chips and dilute hydrochloric acid...

Figure 3.28 shows an experiment to find out the effect of temperature on the rate of reaction between marble chips and dilute hydrochloric acid. Marble chips are made of calcium carbonate. The equation for this reaction is:

$$CaCO_3(s) \quad + \quad 2HCl(aq) \quad \rightarrow \quad CaCl_2(aq) \quad + \quad H_2O(l) \quad + \quad CO_2(g)$$

| calcium carbonate | hydrochloric acid | | calcium carbonate | water | carbon dioxide |

cotton wool to stop acid 'spray' escaping

50 cm³ of dilute hydrochloric acid

marble chips

-0.75 g

balance

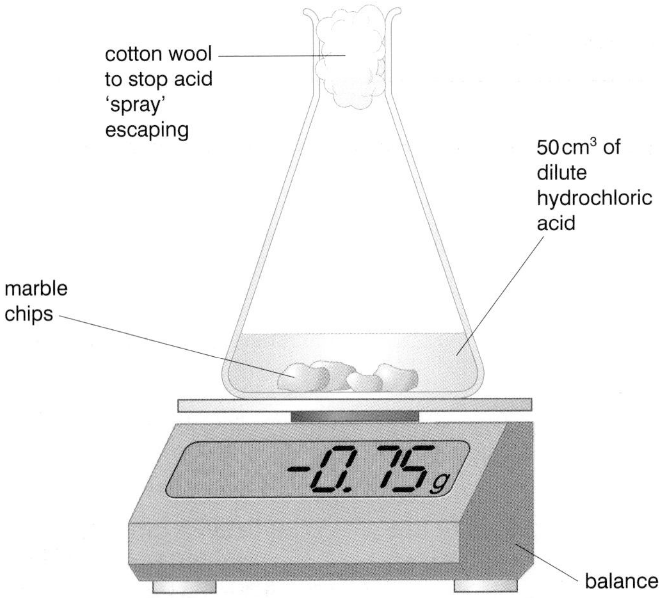

Figure 3.28 Marble chips reacting with hydrochloric acid. This experiment is conducted at different temperatures.

The graph in Figure 3.29 shows the results of the experiment at different temperatures. The line for 40°C is steeper than the others at the start, showing that the rate of reaction at the start of the experiment is faster at the higher temperature. The final loss in mass is the same. The reaction stops when one of the reactants has been used up.

Sodium thiosulphate and dilute hydrochloric acid...

As hydrochloric acid is added to sodium thiosulphate solution, sulphur is formed. The equation for this reaction is:

$$2HCl(aq) \quad + \quad Na_2S_2O_3(aq) \quad \rightarrow \quad S(s) \quad + \quad 2NaCl(aq) \quad + \quad SO_2(g) \quad + \quad H_2O(l)$$

| hydrochloric acid | sodium thiosulphate | | sulphur | sodium chloride | sodium dioxide | water |

Key Facts

- Increasing the temperature increases the rate of chemical reactions.

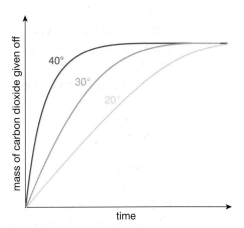

Figure 3.29 Graph to show the rate of reaction between marble chips and hydrochloric acid at different temperatures.

Figure 3.30 The reaction between hydrochloric acid and sodium thiosulphate solution. The cross can be seen through the clear solution at the beginning of the experiment but not through the cloudy solution as the reaction takes place.

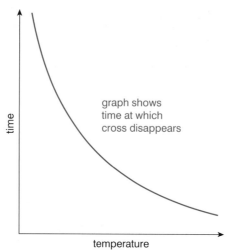

graph shows time at which cross disappears

Figure 3.31 The reaction is faster at higher temperatures.

Figure 3.30 shows one way of measuring the rate of this reaction. As the reaction takes place, the solution becomes cloudy and will slowly obscure a cross drawn on a piece of paper. The experiment is conducted at different temperatures, and by measuring the time it takes for the cross to disappear, the rate of the reaction can be found. This is shown in Figure 3.31.

Questions

1 Copy and complete:

If the temperature of a chemical reaction is increased, this will increase the .... of the reaction, making the reaction happen .... Hydrochloric acid reacts with sodium thiosulphate to produce solid ....

2 Explain the following observations:

a) Milk turns sour faster in summer.

b) Statues in warm countries are eroded faster by acid rain than those in cold countries.

3 Magnesium ribbon was placed in excess dilute hydrochloric acid. The time for the magnesium to disappear at different temperatures was measured.

The results are shown in the table.

Temperature (°C)	10	20	30	40	50	60
Time (s)	25	19	14	10	7	5

a) Draw a graph of the results. Plot temperature on the x axis.

b) From your graph, work out the time for the reaction at 25°C.

c) Why is it important to use the same concentration of acid throughout the experiment?

d) Write a balanced equation for the reaction.

4 Dilute hydrochloric acid was added to sodium thiosulphate solution. The solution turned cloudy. The time taken for the cloudiness to obscure a cross on a piece of paper was measured. The experiment was repeated at several different temperatures.

The results are shown in the table.

Temperature (°C)	18	29	40	48	58
Time (s)	35	23	18	8	4

a) Draw a graph of these results. Plot temperature on the x axis.

b) Which result appears to be incorrect?

c) Explain with the aid of a balanced equation why the solutions turn cloudy when mixed.

Solutions can be concentrated or dilute (Figure 3.32).

Magnesium and hydrochloric acid...

When magnesium is mixed with dilute hydrochloric acid, hydrogen gas is produced (Figure 3.33). This is collected in the gas syringe. Different **concentrations** of acid can be used with the same mass of magnesium and graphs of the volume of gas produced against time can be plotted. With excess acid, a graph like the one in Figure 3.34 is obtained. The steeper gradient shows that the rate of reaction at the start is faster for the more concentrated solution. Both lines level off at the same point when all the magnesium has reacted.

Figure 3.32 The concentrated orange squash is diluted before drinking it.

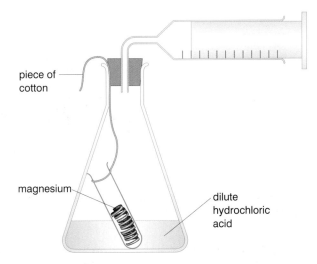

Figure 3.33 Measuring the effect of concentration on reaction rate.

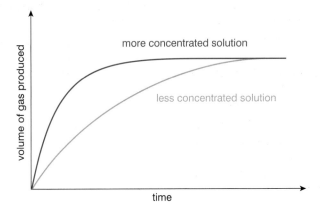

Figure 3.34 An experiment to find the relationship between concentration and reaction rate.

Marble chips and dilute hydrochloric acid...

Different concentrations of hydrochloric acid can be obtained by diluting the acid with water. This is shown in Table 3.12.

Acid (cm^3)	Water (cm^3)	Acid concentration (%)
50	0	100
40	10	80
30	20	60
20	30	40
10	40	20

Table 3.12 Dilution of hydrochloric acid.

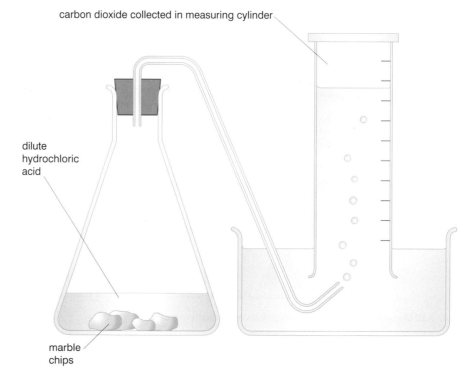

Figure 3.35 An experiment to find the relationship between concentration and reaction rate.

The experiment to find the relationship between concentration and the rate of reaction is shown in Figure 3.35. In this reaction, the marble chips are usually in excess so that the reaction stops when the acid has been used up. The equation for the reaction is:

$$CaCO_3(s) + 2HCl(aq) \rightarrow CaCl_2(aq) + H_2O(l) + CO_2(g)$$

Gas reactions...

If the pressure of a gas is increased, the gas particles are pushed closer together so the gas becomes more concentrated. In reactions between gases, increasing the pressure increases the rate of reaction.

Questions

1 Copy and complete:

Chemical reactions happen faster if the concentration of the reactants is .... A less concentrated solution is a more .... solution. To increase the concentration of a gas you increase the ....

2 The graph in Figure 3.36 shows the results of an experiment in which dilute hydrochloric acid was added to excess marble chips in a conical flask.

a) When was the rate of reaction fastest?

b) What has happened to the rate of reaction at point X compared with the start of the experiment?

c) Explain why the rate of reaction is different at point X compared with the rate of reaction at the start of the experiment.

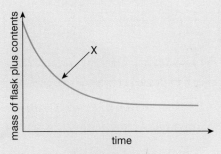

Figure 3.36 Graph for question 2.

3 Two experiments were carried out on the reaction between hydrochloric acid and excess calcium carbonate. The results of the first experiment are shown in the table.

Time (s)	0	15	30	45	60	75	90
Volume of gas (cm³)	0	36	56	67	74	76	76

The second experiment was carried out using the same volume of a more dilute acid.

a) What gas is given off?

b) Write a balanced equation to show how a gas is produced in this reaction.

c) Draw a graph of these results for the first experiment.

d) Explain the shape of your graph.

e) On the same graph, sketch the curve you would expect for the second experiment. Label it curve 2.

modularscience.co.uk

... more at www.

Learning outcome

After completing the work in this topic you will be able to:

* recall that the rate of a chemical reaction increases if the surface area of a solid reactant is increased

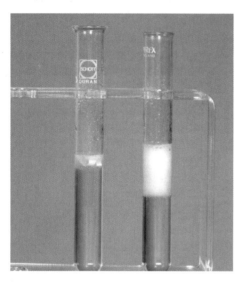

Figure 3.37 When a solid reactant is made into small pieces it reacts faster than it would in large pieces. The froth forms because the reaction is faster with the powder.

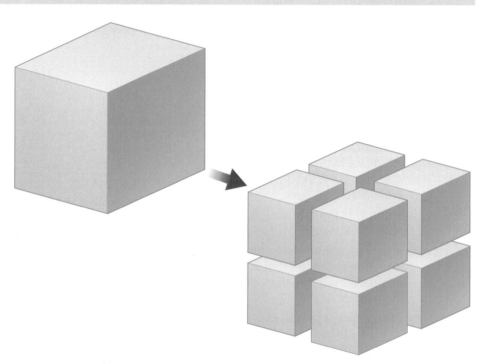

Figure 3.38 Making the particles smaller increases the surface area.

Figure 3.39 Lumps of coal burn slowly in a domestic fire but in a power station the coal is ground to a fine dust to increase the rate of reaction.

If a solid reactant is made into smaller pieces it will react faster than if it is in large pieces (Figure 3.37). Reactions between solids and liquids happen on the surface of the solid. Making the particles smaller increases the **surface area**. When the solid cube in Figure 3.38 is cut up into smaller cubes, the surface area is increased. More atoms of the solid are at the surface ready to react.

Increasing surface area in order to increase the rate of reaction has important everyday applications. We cut food up when cooking it to speed up the rate of reaction. We also chew our food to increase the surface area and speed up digestion, which involves chemical reactions. Increasing surface area to speed up reactions also has many important industrial applications (Figure 3.39).

Did you know?

In 1982, a flour mill at Metz in France was wrecked by an explosion. Flour has very small particles and so reacts quickly with air if ignited.

Marble chips and hydrochloric acid...

The effect of changing particle size can be investigated using the reaction between marble chips and dilute hydrochloric acid. The same mass of different sized chips is combined with the same volume of acid at the same concentration. A graph of the mass of carbon dioxide produced against time for each chip size can be plotted (Figure 3.40). With suitable equipment, graphs can be produced directly on a computer.

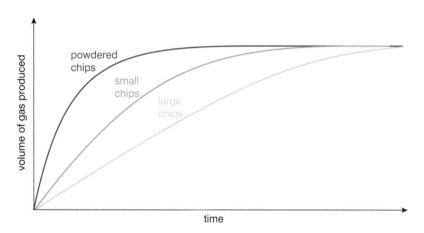

Figure 3.40 The gas is produced more quickly with smaller chips.

Key Facts

• Making particles smaller increases the rate of reaction because it increases the surface area of the solid reactant.

Questions

1 Copy and complete:

A solid reacts with a liquid where its .... touches the liquid. Grinding up a solid .... its surface .... Smaller pieces react ....

2 Explain the following observations:

a) Coal dust can explode in coal mines.

b) Vegetables cook quicker if cut into smaller pieces.

c) Fires are easier to light with small sticks than with large logs.

d) Joints of beef can be kept for longer in a freezer than minced beef.

e) Hot iron wool burns in oxygen but a hot iron nail does not.

3 In an experiment, a piece of magnesium ribbon reacted with hydrochloric acid. The graph in Figure 3.41 shows how the volume of gas produced changed with time.

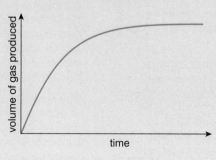

Figure 3.41 Graph for question 3.

a) Write a balanced equation to show how a gas is produced in this reaction.

b) Copy the graph into your book and add a second line to suggest the results that would be obtained with magnesium powder.

c) Explain why the results for magnesium powder are different from those for magnesium ribbon.

Man-made catastrophes

When something goes wrong in the chemical industry, the consequences can be severe. The combination of high temperatures, pressures and poisonous chemicals can often prove lethal.

The worst accident in the chemical industry's history happened in the Indian city of Bhopal in December 1984. Poisonous gas leaking from a pesticide factory in the city killed at least 3,500 people, though some estimates put the death toll much higher. A recent Greenpeace report found that the land surrounding the now-abandoned factory is still heavily contaminated with toxic chemicals, some seventeen years later.

The disaster happened when water entered a storage tank holding 40 tons of a chemical called methyl isocyanate which is used in fertiliser production. This started a chemical reaction which quickly grew out of control and caused an explosion. Clouds of the poisonous methyl isocyanate then escaped and drifted into the sleeping city, along with gases like hydrogen cyanide formed during the reaction.

The factory was owned by the American chemical company Union Carbide. Some people say that the accident was Union Carbide's fault, saying that the water entered the storage tanks through a leaking valve. The company blames an act of deliberate sabotage by a disgruntled employee. Whatever the cause, several medical surveys of the region have shown that tens of thousands of people are still living with the effects, suffering from a range of disorders including eyesight problems, persistent coughs, depression and nerve damage.

The worst chemical accident in Great Britain occurred at Flixborough in northeast England in 1974. On June 1, an explosion destroyed a chemical plant owned by the company Nypro, killing 28 people. Nypro was making chemicals used to manufacture nylon. The plant mixed air with cyclohexane, a flammable hydrocarbon gas with similar physical properties to petrol, to make cyclohexanone and cyclohexanol. The gases were made in a series of reactors, one of which developed a leak. The faulty reactor was taken away for repair and a temporary pipe was put in its place. The workmen who had been asked to design and install the pipe were not experts however, the plant's work engineer had left and his replacement had not yet arrived.

The temporary pipe meant that the plant was up and running again in a few days but it was not strong enough to hold the high temperature, pressurised and flammable gases flowing through it from one reactor to the next. It eventually gave way, releasing forty tons of cyclohexane in about a minute before it reached some kind of ignition source and the vapour exploded.

Accidents don't only happen on dry land. On July 6 1988, an explosion and fire on the oil rig Piper Alpha killed all but 61 of the rig's 228 employees. The rig had been pumping oil since 1976 and, in its prime, brought in some 10 per cent of all profits from the North Sea oilfields. The disaster began when a pump used to provide the oil rig with power broke down. It was quickly replaced with another pump, but this one was being serviced, and exploded when it was turned on. The explosion was not that serious but the area was not protected by blast walls, so the fire quickly spread. Even then, the fire could perhaps have been brought under control, but two other oil rigs that were connected by oil pipelines kept pumping oil towards Piper Alpha, feeding the flames. An investigation blamed the disaster entirely on human error, including bad communication, bad management and bad safety procedures.

Even nature can cause chemical spills and disasters. Two of the most famous cases happened in the African country of Cameroon. In 1984 and two years later in 1986, clouds of carbon dioxide were released from the depths of two lakes. Although not poisonous in itself, carbon dioxide kills people because it smothers them and stops them breathing. (Its oxygen starvation properties are what make the gas an ideal fire extinguisher.) Due to the fact that carbon dioxide is heavier than air, it slipped down the African valleys, hugging the ground.

The second incident killed over 1,700 people. Nobody is quite sure why the lakes, which have lots of natural carbonated water in their depths, 'erupted'. In fact the Cameroon government kept the 1984 incident secret at first, because it thought terrorists might have been involved.

The collision theory

biology

3.12
chemistry

physics

Learning outcome

After completing the work in this topic you will be able to:

- understand that reactions can occur when particles collide and that the rate of a reaction is increased by increased frequency of the collisions and greater energy of the collisions

For a chemical reaction to happen, the reactants must first collide with each other (Figure 3.42). However, just colliding is not enough. For a reaction to take place, the reactants must collide with enough energy (Figure 3.43).

Effect of temperature...

At higher temperatures, the faster moving particles have more **kinetic energy**. This means that they are moving quicker and will collide more often. They also have more energy when they collide, meaning that the higher temperature increases the number of effective collisions in which the particles collide with enough energy for a reaction to occur. Raising the temperature by 10°C doubles the rate of many reactions.

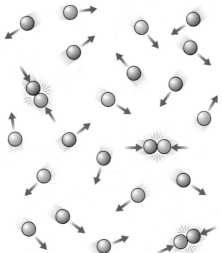

Figure 3.42 In a chemical reaction, the reactants collide with each other.

low speed collision

high speed collision

Figure 3.43 At slow speeds, the collision causes very little damage, but at high speeds the energy is greater and the result is very different.

Effect of concentration...

More concentrated solutions contain more particles in the same space, making them more likely to collide (Figure 3.44). The increase in the number of collisions with sufficient energy increases the rate of reaction.

In reactions involving gases, increasing the pressure moves the particles closer together, making collisions more likely (Figure 3.45). If the particles collide with enough energy to react, then more collisions will increase the rate of reaction.

Figure 3.44 When people are crowded together they are more likely to bump into each other.

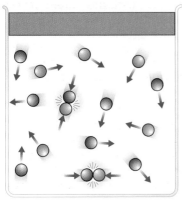

low pressure

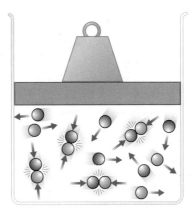

high pressure

Figure 3.45 When the particles are closer together, the number of collisions increases.

Chemical patterns 113

Key Facts

- For a reaction to take place, particles must collide.
- The rate of reaction is increased if the number of collisions increases or if the particles collide with greater energy.
- Increasing the temperature increases both the number of collisions and the energy of the particles.
- Greater concentration and greater surface area increase the number of collisions.

Effect of surface area...

If more surface area is available, the number of particles of the solid reactant available for collision will increase. If more collisions occur, it is likely that there will be more collisions with sufficient energy to successfully lead to a reaction (Figure 3.46).

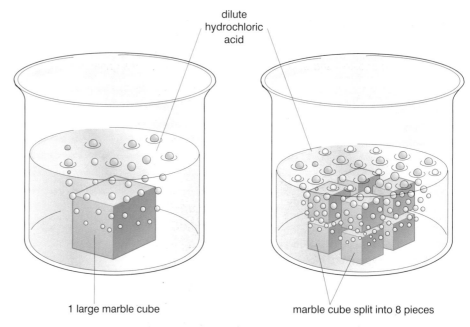

dilute hydrochloric acid

1 large marble cube

marble cube split into 8 pieces

Figure 3.46 When the marble cube is split up, more of its surface can react with the acid.

Questions

1   Copy and complete:
    For substances to react, their particles must .... For the collision to cause a reaction, the particles must have enough .... At higher temperatures, particles move .... This causes .... collisions with enough .... for a reaction to take place.

2   Explain with the aid of diagrams why:
    a) Gas particles react faster if the pressure is increased.

    b) Increasing the concentration of acid makes a piece of magnesium ribbon react faster.

    c) Small marble chips react faster than large marble chips.

3   If a piece of coal is heated it burns.
    a) Which of the following would increase the rate of burning?
       i)   Heating the coal less strongly.
       ii) Heating the coal more strongly.

    iii) Crushing the coal to a fine powder.
    iv) Doing the experiment up a high mountain.
    v)   Blowing hot air on to the coal.

    b) In each of the cases in which you think the coal would burn faster, explain why it burns faster?

Catalysts

After completing the work in this topic you will be able to:

- recall that the rate of a chemical reaction increases when a catalyst is used

A substance which changes the rate of a chemical reaction without being used up itself is called a **catalyst**. You have probably heard of catalytic converters, which are fitted to car exhausts (Figure 3.47). These use a catalyst to help convert harmful exhaust gases, such as carbon monoxide and oxides of nitrogen, into less harmful gases.

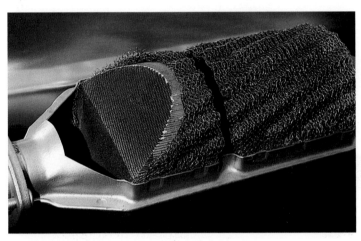

Figure 3.47 In this catalytic converter, there are many fine tubes to give a large surface area.

Did you know?

Chlorine atoms from CFCs catalyse the destruction of atmospheric ozone.

Breaking down hydrogen peroxide...

Hydrogen peroxide solution breaks down slowly into water and oxygen.

$$2H_2O_2(aq) \rightarrow 2H_2O(l) + O_2(g)$$
hydrogen   water   oxygen
peroxide

This is a good way of making oxygen if the reaction can be speeded up. The best way to do this is to add a catalyst of manganese(IV) oxide (Figure 3.48). Most catalysts are used to speed up chemical reactions but sometimes they are used to slow them down. This type of catalyst is called a negative catalyst or inhibitor. An inhibitor is added to antifreeze solutions to slow down corrosion in a car cooling system.

Investigating catalysts...

Zinc reacts with dilute sulphuric acid to produce hydrogen gas.

$$Zn(s) + H_2SO_4(aq) \rightarrow ZnSO_4(aq) + H_2(g)$$
Zinc   sulphuric acid   zinc sulphate   hydrogen

If a little copper sulphate is added, the reaction speeds up. The copper sulphate acts as a catalyst. This reaction could be investigated by trying the effect of other copper salts, and the effect of other transition metal ions.

- Catalysts change the rate of chemical reactions but are not used up in the reaction.

Figure 3.48 a) Hydrogen peroxide solution. b) Adding manganese(IV) oxide makes the hydrogen peroxide split up faster. c) The manganese(IV) oxide is still there and can be used again.

Questions

1 Copy and complete:

A .... is a substance which changes the .... of a chemical reaction, but is .... chemically at the end of the reaction. Most catalysts are used to .... the rate of a chemical reaction but some called .... are used to .... down chemical reactions.

2 Many catalysts are made from very expensive materials. Explain why this is not a major problem when using catalysts in industrial processes.

3 Chlorine atoms from CFCs catalyse the breakdown of atmospheric ozone. Explain why a small number of chlorine atoms can destroy large amounts of ozone.

4 Use the Internet or a CD-ROM to find out more about the breakdown of atmospheric ozone.

5 Hydrogen peroxide decomposes to form water and oxygen. The reaction is catalysed by some transition metal oxides.

a) What is a catalyst?

b) Write a balanced equation for the decomposition of hydrogen peroxide.

c) If you had oxides of copper, manganese and nickel, how would you find out which was the best catalyst?

Enzymes

Hydrogen peroxide breaks down slowly to form water and oxygen. This reaction can be speeded up by using a catalyst. The usual catalyst used in the laboratory is manganese(IV) oxide. Pieces of liver, celery and potato will also speed up this reaction because these materials contain a biological catalyst called catalase. Catalase is an **enzyme**. Enzymes are biological catalysts.

Enzymes in our bodies...

The enzyme catalase is present in our bodies to break down harmful peroxides, which are poisons. Enzymes are **specific** in their action, which means each enzyme catalyses a particular reaction. Since there are a large number of chemical reactions going on in our bodies, we need a large number of different enzymes to catalyse these reactions.

Enzyme action

When enzymes work...

Enzymes can only work within certain temperature limits. They work best at an **optimum temperature**. Below this temperature, the rate of the reaction slows down. At high temperatures, enzymes are **denatured**. This means that they can no longer work because their shape has been changed. In most mammals, the enzymes work best between 35°C and 40°C (Figure 3.49). Fish and other cold-blooded animals have enzymes with lower optimum temperatures.

Enzymes also have an **optimum pH**. Many enzymes work best in neutral conditions but the enzyme pepsin works in acidic conditions in the stomach (Figure 3.50).

Did you know?

Enzymes act very quickly. One catalase molecule can break down 6 million molecules of hydrogen peroxide in one minute.

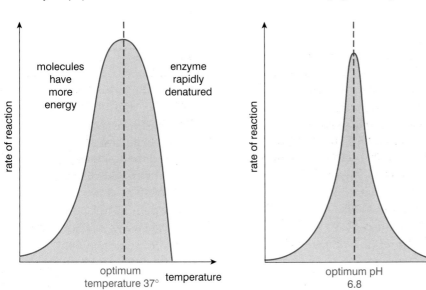

Figure 3.49 This enzyme works best at 37°C. Figure 3.50 This enzyme works best at pH 6.8.

Key Facts

- Enzymes are biological catalysts.
- Enzymes are proteins.
- Enzymes have a special shape. This causes each enzyme to be specific to a reaction.
- Enzymes work best at an optimum temperature and pH. If the temperature or pH is changed too much, the enzyme's shape changes and it is denatured.

How enzymes work...

An enzyme is a special protein molecule. Each enzyme has its own special shape so that it can work with one material called its **substrate** (Figure 3.51).

Every enzyme molecule is a different shape. Bonds within the molecule hold it in this shape. High temperatures or changes in pH can break these bonds and allow the shape to change. This is known as denaturing.

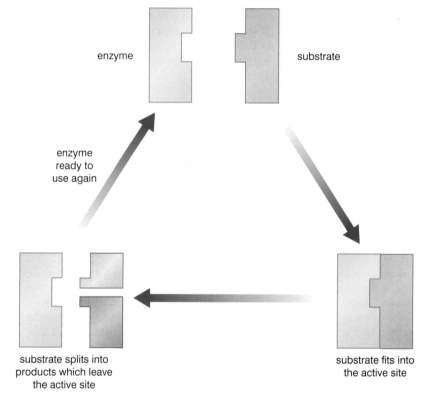

Figure 3.51 The lock-and-key model for enzyme action.

Questions

1 Copy and complete:

Enzymes are .... molecules which act as .... catalysts. The temperature at which enzymes work best is called the .... temperature. Above this temperature, enzymes are .... Enzymes also work best at an optimum ....

Enzymes only work with one .... We say that they are .... to a reaction.

2 Explain why enzymes in mammals work best between 35°C and 40°C.

3 Explain why the optimum temperature for enzymes in fish is lower than 35°C.

4 The breakdown of hydrogen peroxide is catalysed by both blood and manganese(IV) oxide. Which catalyst would work best at:

a) 37°C   b) 50°C?

In each case explain the reasons for your choice.

group numbers																	0 (or 8)
1	2											3	4	5	6	7	He 2 helium

H
1 hydrogen

Li 3 lithium	Be 4 beryllium																
Na 11 sodium	Mg 12 magnesium											B 5 boron	C 6 carbon	N 7 nitrogen	O 8 oxygen	F 9 fluorine	Ne 10 hydrogen
K 19 potassium	Ca 20 calcium	Sc 21 scandium	Ti 22 titanium	V 23 vanadium	Cr 24 chromium	Mn 25 manganese	Fe 26 iron	Co 27 cobalt	Ni 28 nickel	Cu 29 copper	Zn 30 zinc	Al 13 aluminium	Si 14 silicon	P 15 phosphorus	S 16 sulphur	Cl 17 chlorine	Ar 18 argon
Rb 37 rubidium	Sr 38 strontium	Y 39 yttrium	Zr 40 zirconium	Nb 41 niobium	Mo 42 molybdenum	Tc 43 technetium	Ru 44 ruthenium	Rh 45 rhodium	Pd 46 palladium	Ag 47 silver	Cd 48 cadmium	Ga 31 galium	Ge 32 germanium	As 33 arsenic	Se 34 selenium	Br 35 bromine	Kr 36 krypton
Cs 55 caesium	Ba 56 barium	La 57 lanthanum	Hf 72 tungsten	Ta 73 tantalum	W 74 tunsten	Re 75 rhenium	Os 76 osium	Ir 77 indium	Pt 78 platinum	Au 79 gold	Hg 80 mercury	In 49 indium	Sn 50 tin	Sb 51 antimony	Te 52 tellurium	I 53 iodine	Xe 54 xenon
												Tl 81 thallium	Pb 82 lead	Bi 83 bismuth	Po 84 polonium	At 85 astatine	Rh 86 radon

1. Sodium and chlorine both form ions. Ions can have either a positive or a negative charge. Electrons have a negative charge.

(a) Copy and complete the table. The periodic table above may help you.

	Symbol		Number of electrons	
	atom	ion	atom	ion
sodium	Na	Na$^+$	11	10
chlorine	Cl	Cl$^-$	17	18

(3)

(b) Use the periodic table provided to help you describe how the electrons are arranged in a sodium atom.

(3)
(Total 6 marks)

Edexcel GCSE Double Award (Modular) 1531 June 2000, Paper 2H, no. 11

2. A student investigated how long it took for marble chips to react with acid. She set up three test tubes. She used two different sizes of marble chips, as shown in the diagram. In each test tube she used the same mass of marble chips and the same volume of acid. The reaction caused fizzing. She timed how long it took for the fizzing to stop in each test tube.

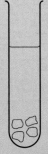
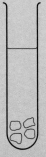

acid
large marble chips
at 25°C

acid
large marble chips
at 50°C

acid
small marble chips
at 50°C

She recorded times of 60 s, 120 s and 180 s for the fizzing to stop in the three test tubes. What is the correct time for each test tube.

(Total 3 marks)

Edexcel GCSE Double Award (Modular) 1531 June 1999, Paper 1F, no. 9)

3. (a)   Use the periodic table to give:

(i)   the symbol for an atom of sulphur: (1)

(ii) an element in the same group as sodium;   (1)

(iii) an element in group 2;   (1)

(iv) an element in group 6;   (1)

(v)   the atomic number of neon;   (1)

(vi) an element in period 2.   (1)

(b)   Elements can be classified as metals or non-metals.
        Give the names of TWO non-metals.   (2)

(c)   List the TWO properties of most metals.

They are shiny.

They are soft.

They break easily.

They conduct electricity.   (2)

(d)   You have an unknown solid element. Describe a test to find out if it is a metal.   (3)

(Total 13 marks)

Edexcel GCSE Double Award (Combined) 1524 June 1999, Paper 2F, no. 1

4. (a)   Copy and complete the sentences using words from the box.

atom   compound   formula   metal   mixture   property

An element contains only one type of ....

When elements combine, they form a ....

Iron combines with sulphur to form iron sulphide. This is not magnetic because it has a different physical .... to iron.

Iron sulphide is represented as FeS. This is its ....   (4)

(b)

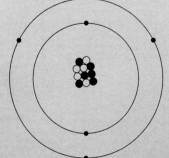

The diagram shows an atom of boron.

(i)   How many electrons are in this atom?   (1)

(ii) How many neutrons are in this atom?   (1)

(Total 6 marks)

Edexcel GCSE Double Award (Modular) 1524 June 1999, Paper 2F no. 8

5. The table contains information about the halogens.

Name	Symbol	Appearance at room temperature
fluorine	F	pale yellow gas
chlorine	Cl	green gas
bromine	Br	red-brown liquid
iodine	I	grey solid

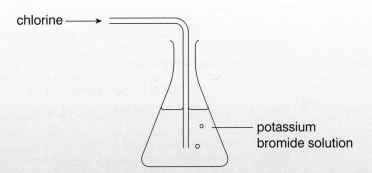

chlorine

potassium
bromide solution

(a) When chlorine is bubbled into potassium bromide solution, the solution turns red-brown. Explain this observation and give the reason why the reaction takes place.

(3)

(b) When moist Universal indicator paper is placed in chlorine, the paper turns red then white. Explain why the paper first turns red and then turns white. (2)

(c) A mixture of chlorine and hydrogen reacts violently to form hydrogen chloride when exposed to sunlight. Write a balanced equation for this reaction. (2)

(Total 7 marks)

Edexcel GCSE Double Award (Modular) 1531 June 1999, Paper 1H, no. 9

Glossary 3

Atomic number	The number that shows how many protons an element contains. Elements in the periodic table are arranged in order of atomic number.
Atomic weight	The weight of an atom of an element compared with the weight of a hydrogen atom.
Catalyst	A substance that changes the rate of a chemical reaction without actually being used up during the reaction.
Compounds	These are made of elements, chemically bound together.
Concentration	Concentrated solutions contain a smaller volume of solvent.
Denatured	When an enzyme has its shape changed, such as by high temperatures, so that it can no longer work, it is said to be denatured.
Diatomic	Molecules that always exist as atoms bound together in pairs.
Displaced	When an element is replaced by another more reactive element.
Electron	A particle orbiting around the nucleus of an atom, with an electric charge of −1 and a mass of 1/1840 the mass of a proton.
Elements	Chemical substances in their simplest form. There are about 100 different chemical elements.
Enzyme	A biological catalyst, that speeds up the rate of biological reactions.
Formula	The letters and sometimes numbers used to represent a chemical. The formula for the compound sodium chloride (salt) is NaCl.
Group	A group is a collection of elements with similar properties. They are shown as a vertical column of the periodic table.
Halogens	The name of one group of elements in the periodic table. The halogens include fluorine, chlorine, bromine and iodine.
Ions	An atom that has become electrically positively or negatively charged by losing or gaining electrons.
Kinetic energy	The energy that atoms or molecules have because they are moving about. The faster they move, the more kinetic energy they have.
Metalloids	Elements which have characteristics of both metals and non-metals.
Neutron	A particle in the nucleus of an atom, with an electric charge of 0 and a mass of 1.
Nucleus	The centre part of an atom, made up of protons and neutrons tightly bound together.

Optimum pH	The level of acidity or alkalinity in which an enzyme works best. Most enzymes work best in a neutral pH.
Optimum temperature	The temperature at which an enzyme works best to speed up a reaction.
Orbit	To go round another body. An electron orbits the nucleus of an atom in a similar way to the way the planets orbit the Sun.
Period	A horizontal row of the periodic table.
Periodic table	A table that classifies chemical elements into groups according to their characteristics.
Product	The new compound or element that forms as a result of a chemical reaction.
Proton	A particle making up the nucleus of an atom, with an electric charge of 1+1 and a mass of 1.
Rate of reaction	How quickly chemicals form or change in a chemical reaction.
Reactant	The compound or element that is being 'used up' in a chemical reaction to make a new compound or element.
Relative atomic mass	This is the relative mass of an atom of an element, compared with an atom of hydrogen. It is also called atomic weight.
Semi-conductors	Metalloid elements that have a varying electrical conductivity, partway between that of metals and insulators, and increasing as temperature increases.
Shell	The electrons can only orbit the nucleus at particular distances. Each distance that can hold a collection of orbiting electrons is called a shell.
Specific	Only affecting one thing. A catalyst is specific to a particular reaction. It will not affect the rate of other reactions.
State symbol	The letters, s, aq, l and g used to show whether a chemical is solid, aqueous (in solution), liquid or gas.
Substrate	The material which has the correct shape to enable an enzyme to work best.
Surface area	The amount of area around the outside of particles of a material, where chemical reactions can take place.
Symbols	A single letter or pair of letters used to represent each element.
Word equation	A means of showing the reactants and products in a chemical reaction.

Chemical reactions are involved in making many of the things you use every day. In this module you will learn about some of the important chemical reactions that provide you with the things you need. Crude oil is the source of different types of fuel and many important chemicals, including chemicals used to make dyes, drugs and plastics. Crude oil is sorted into useful products in oil refineries.

Prospecting for crude oil is an important business. You will find out in this module how crude oil was formed. Oil is the starting material for many polymers including important plastics and synthetic fibres. You will learn about the early work on plastics, the development of nylon and its use in the Second World War, the problems associated with the disposal of plastics, and the attempts to overcome these problems by recycling and making biodegradable plastics.

Another group of very important reactions are those controlled by substances called enzymes. Enzymes are used to make alcoholic drinks, bread, cheese and yoghurt, so they are very important. The module finishes with explanations about a few other useful reactions, such as those used to make lime, fertilisers, glass and cement. When you have finished, you will have a better understanding of how widely used chemistry is in our everyday lives.

4

Crude oil

Did you know?

Some scientists have questioned the generally accepted idea that crude oil is a fossil fuel. They believe that it was trapped deep inside the Earth when the Earth was formed. They think the deposits slowly seep upwards towards the Earth's surface.

Figure 4.1 Finding oil under the sea.

Crude oil is a **fossil fuel**. It was formed millions of years ago when large areas of the Earth were covered by sea. Tiny sea creatures called plankton lived in the oceans. When they died, their remains settled on the seabed together with sand and silt. Their bodies did not decay completely because the bacteria feeding on them had little or no oxygen. Further layers of sand and silt were turned into sedimentary rock, which covered the remains of the plankton. High pressure and high temperatures turned the remains of the plankton into crude oil. Natural gas often occurs with crude oil.

The oil is obtained by drilling down through the rock to create an oil well. Originally, oil was found by drilling on land but as supplies reduced and prices increased, oil companies started to look for oil under the sea (Figure 4.1). The UK has used oil from under the North Sea since 1972. Oil exploration is now being carried out in deep water off the northwest coast of Scotland.

What is crude oil?...

Crude oil is a mixture of substances, most of which are **hydrocarbons**. A hydrocarbon is a compound containing only hydrogen and carbon. Most of the hydrocarbons in crude oil are **alkanes** (Figures 4.2 and 4.3). The general formula of an alkane is C_nH_{2n+2} where n can be any number (Table 4.1).

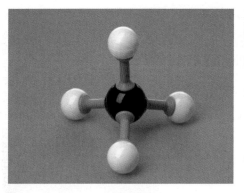

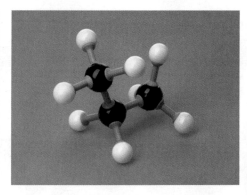

Figure 4.2 Models of methane, ethane and propane.

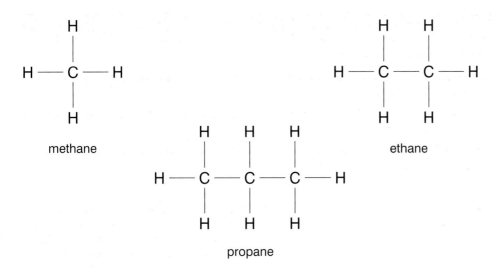

methane

ethane

propane

Figure 4.3 Methane, ethane and propane.

Alkane	Formula
methane	CH_4
ethane	C_2H_6
propane	C_3H_8
butane	C_4H_{10}
pentane	C_5H_{12}
hexane	C_6H_{14}
heptane	C_7H_{16}
octane	C_8H_{18}

Table 4.1 Alkanes.

Questions

Copy and complete:

1 Crude oil was formed .... of years ago at the bottom of .... Dead creatures called .... which lived in the .... fell to the bottom and were covered in layers of .... and .... The remains of their bodies slowly changed into .... because of the effects of .... and .... together with the lack of ....

2 Design a poster to show how crude oil was formed.

3 Decane is an alkane with ten carbon atoms.
a) Work out its formula.
b) Draw its structure.

4 *Alkanes* are *hydrocarbons* found in *crude oil*. Explain what is meant by each of the words written in italics.

5 Use the Internet to obtain up-to-date information about oil exploration in Britain.

Separating crude oil

4.02 chemistry

Learning outcome

After completing the work in this topic you will be able to:

- describe how the mixture of substances in crude oil can be separated by fractional distillation to yield fractions with different properties due to the different size of their molecules

Crude oil is a strong-smelling thick black liquid (Figure 4.4). In this form it is not much use but it contains many valuable substances. The molecules in crude oil are many different sizes. Because of this, they all have different boiling points. This difference in boiling points is used to separate crude oil into **fractions** (Figure 4.5).

When the crude oil is gently heated, the lower boiling point molecules change to vapours and are condensed to form the first fraction. When the temperature reaches 70°C, a second fraction is collected. This process does not separate the crude oil into single substances. Each fraction contains several different substances with similar-sized molecules (Table 4.2).

Figure 4.4 Crude oil.

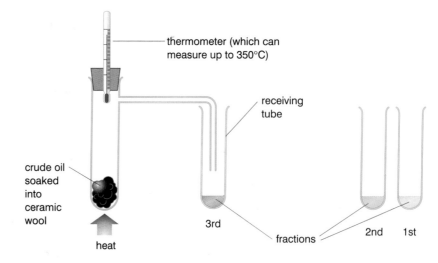

Figure 4.5 The separation of crude oil in the laboratory.

Fraction	Colour	Thickness	How does it burn?	Number of carbon atoms in molecule
1 boils below 70°C	pale yellow	runny	easily, with clean yellow flame	4–6
2 boils between 70°C and 120°C	yellow	fairly runny	quite easily, with some smoke	6–8
3 boils between 120°C and 170°C	dark yellow	thicker	harder to burn, with some smoke	8–10
4 boils between 170°C and 240°C	brown	thick (viscous)	hard to burn, with smoky flame	10–16

Table 4.2 The fractions separated from crude oil.

Fractional distillation...

At an oil refinery, crude oil is separated into fractions. In the laboratory, each fraction is boiled and separated in turn. In industry, the whole of the crude oil is vaporised and the fractions are collected as they condense and turn back to liquids. This is carried out in a fractionating tower, which is about 100 m tall (Figure 4.6).
At the bottom of the tower, large molecules with high boiling points condense to liquid. Smaller molecules with lower boiling points remain as vapours and rise up the tower. Different fractions condense at different levels.

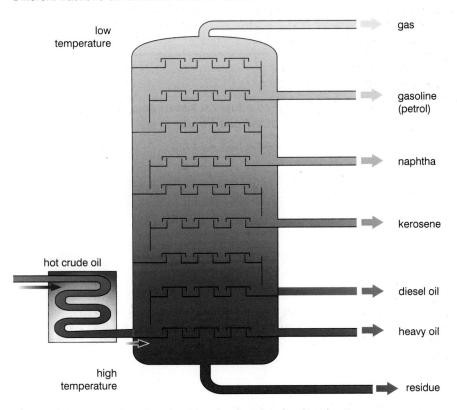

Figure 4.6 The separation of crude oil into fractions in a fractionating tower.

Questions

1 Copy and complete:
Crude oil is .... into fractions using fractional .... The crude oil is heated to .... it. The .... falls to the bottom of the tower, but everything else .... up the tower. About halfway up the tower .... vapour .... and turns to a liquid.

2 Describe the differences between the separation of crude oil in the laboratory and the separation in industry.

3 Explain why gasoline collects near the top of a fractionating column while diesel collects near the bottom. Your answer should make reference to the size of the molecules.

4 Prepare a five-minute talk to explain the process of fractional distillation.

... more at www.modularscience.co.uk

Petroleum
fractions

biology

4.03
chemistry

physics

The different fractions produced in a **fractionating tower** at an oil refinery (Figure 4.7) can be put to many uses. Table 4.3 shows some of these.

Fraction	Boiling range (°C)	Number of carbon atoms	Uses
refinery gas	below 25	1–4	used as a fuel on site or sold as bottled gas for use in camping stoves
gasoline (petrol)	25–70	5–9	used as a fuel for cars
naphtha	70–180	8–10	source of chemicals for making plastics, drugs, medicines and fabrics
kerosene (paraffin)	180–240	10–16	major use as fuel for aircraft
diesel	240–340	15–20	fuel for diesel engines, trains and central heating
residue	over 340	over 20	further separation of this gives lubricating oil, fuel oil for power stations and for ships, and bitumen for roads and waterproofing

Table 4.3 Some of the uses of the fractions separated from crude oil.

Figure 4.7 The tall tower is a fractionating tower.

Crude oil composition...

The composition of crude oil varies depending on the oil field it comes from. Table 4.4 shows the composition of crude oil from five different countries.

There is a higher demand for the lower boiling point fractions so the oil from Venezuela is less useful.

Country of origin	Refinery gas, naphtha and gasoline	Kerosene and diesel	Residue
North Sea	23	35	42
Nigeria	25	37	38
Middle East	20	32	48
North Africa	30	40	30
Venezuela	1	19	80

Table 4.4 The composition of crude oil from different countries (expressed as percentage by volume) .

Where would we be without oil?

Many of the products we use every day are manufactured from the chemicals found in crude oil. Figure 4.8 shows some of them. As a source of organic chemicals, crude oil is used to make textiles, such as acrylic and nylon; pesticides and insecticides; antifreeze, brake fluid and lubricating oil for machinery; and even lipstick, explosives, paints and drugs.

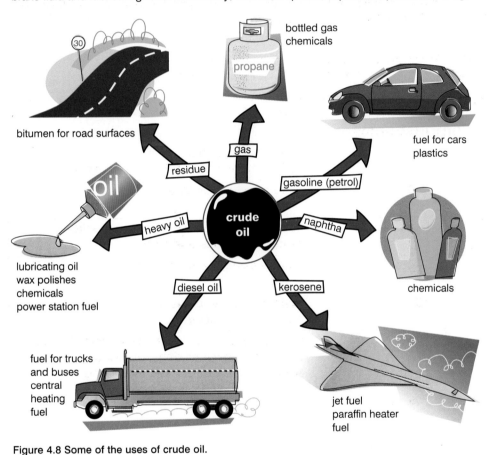

bitumen for road surfaces

residue

gas

gasoline (petrol)

heavy oil

crude oil

naphtha

diesel oil

kerosene

bottled gas
chemicals
propane

fuel for cars
plastics

chemicals

lubricating oil
wax polishes
chemicals
power station fuel

fuel for trucks
and buses
central
heating
fuel

jet fuel
paraffin heater
fuel

Figure 4.8 Some of the uses of crude oil.

Did you know?

The sap of the gopher tree contains about 30% hydrocarbons. Petrol could be made from this.

Key Facts

- Crude oil is the main source of fuel and organic chemicals in Britain.
- As a fuel, oil is used for transport and heating.
- As a source of organic chemicals, crude oil is used to make many things, including fabrics, pesticides, antifreeze, lubricating oil, explosives, paints and drugs.
- Crude oil is a very important chemical, which we are rapidly using up.

Questions

1 Copy and complete:
Gasoline is used as a .... for cars. It is more commonly known as .... The fuel for aircraft is known as .... or .... A third fuel, which is used for road transport and trains, is ....

2 Design a poster to show the uses of crude oil in the chemical industry. Do not include its uses as a fuel.

3 Explain why some people think that using crude oil as a fuel is a waste.

4 Petrol for use in cars is a blend of different hydrocarbons with different boiling points. The blend is changed several times each year. Suggest why it is important to change the blend.

Fuels

When fuels burn, energy is released as **thermal energy**. The fuel natural gas is mainly composed of the alkane called methane.

Combustion

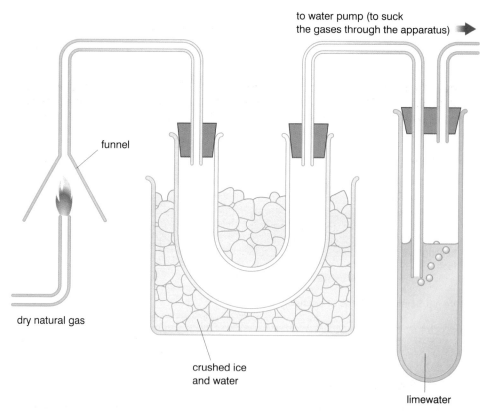

Figure 4.9 Experiment to find out the products of combustion.

Figure 4.9 shows an experiment to find out what happens when natural gas burns. This is known as **complete combustion** and takes place in a plentiful supply of oxygen. In the experiment, the limewater turns cloudy showing the presence of carbon dioxide. A colourless liquid forms in the u-tube surrounded by crushed ice and water. This liquid turns cobalt chloride paper from blue to pink showing that the liquid is water. So, the equation for the reaction is:

$$CH_4 \quad + \quad 2O_2 \quad \rightarrow \quad CO_2 \quad + \quad 2H_2O$$

methane   oxygen   carbon dioxide   water

In this reaction, oxygen is added to the methane. The methane is **oxidised** to water and carbon dioxide. **Oxidation** is the addition of oxygen to a substance. All the fuels we obtain from crude oil produce carbon dioxide and water when we burn them in plenty of oxygen. If there is a lack of oxygen, then carbon (as soot) or carbon monoxide may be formed. The equations for this type of combustion are:

$$CH_4 + O_2 \rightarrow C + 2H_2O$$
methane   oxygen   carbon   water

$$2CH_4 + 3O_2 \rightarrow 2CO + 4H_2O$$
methane   oxygen   carbon monoxide   water

This is known as **incomplete combustion**. It happens when there is not enough oxygen available for complete combustion. You can see that less oxygen is used in incomplete combustion if the equation is written like this:

$$CH_4 + 1\tfrac{1}{2}O_2 \rightarrow CO + 2H_2O$$
methane   oxygen   carbon monoxide   water

Other fuels...

Many of the products from crude oil are used as fuels. Figure 4.10 shows the main uses of crude oil in Britain. You can see that more than 85% of the products are burnt as fuels. The fuels with small molecules are easy to burn. With larger molecules, the fuels are more difficult to ignite (Table 4.5).

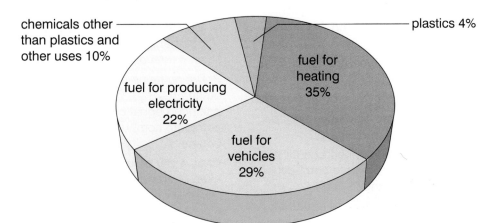

Figure 4.10 The uses of crude oil in Britain.

Fuel	Use	How it is burnt
petroleum gas	bottled gas	easily lit in camping stoves
petrol	cars	vaporised before ignition
kerosene	jet aircraft engines	sprayed into a blast of compressed air
diesel	diesel engines	special fuel injection system
fuel oil	power stations and ships	sprayed into combustion chamber as fine mist

Table 4.5 The uses of different types of fuel.

Key Facts

- Burning hydrocarbon fuels in a plentiful supply of air produces carbon dioxide and water.
- Thermal energy is released when fuels burn.
- Much of the crude oil we produce is used as fuel.

Did you know?

Biodiesel can be made from rapeseed oil. This means it is a renewable fuel, but even if all of the fields in Britain were planted with rape it would only produce between 7% and 10% of the diesel we need.

Figure 4.11 Bottled gas to use as a fuel.

Bottled gas...

Bottled gas contains either liquid propane or liquid butane. In Figure 4.11, the blue cylinders contain butane and the red cylinders contain propane. Table 4.6 shows that different alkanes vaporise at different temperatures.

Bottled gas can be a problem when the weather gets cold. If the temperature drops to 0°C, the butane in the blue cylinders does not vaporise so there is no gas to use. Winter caravanners need to use propane from a red cylinder since this will vaporise at temperatures as low as −40°C.

Alkane	Boiling point (°C)
methane	−161
ethane	−88
propane	−42
butane	−1

Table 4.6 Temperature at which alkanes vaporise.

Questions

1 Copy and complete:
Natural gas is mainly .... When natural gas burns in .... of oxygen .... and .... are produced. If there is not enough oxygen then .... combustion takes place, which may form ....

2 Explain the differences between complete and incomplete combustion.

3 When methane is burnt in air, carbon dioxide and water are formed.

a) How can you test for carbon dioxide?

b) How can you test for water?

c) What two elements must be present in methane?

d) Write a balanced equation for the complete combustion of methane?

e) Write a balanced equation for the complete combustion of ethane?

f) Explain why the combustion of ethane is an example of an oxidation reaction.

4 Petrol contains the alkane octane (C_8H_{18}). Write a balanced equation for the complete combustion of octane.

5 Draw a bar chart to show the uses of crude oil in Britain. Use information from the last page.

... more at www.modularscience.co.uk

Carbon monoxide

biology **4.05** chemistry physics

Learning outcomes

After completing the work in this topic you will be able to:

- understand that incomplete combustion can occur in faulty gas appliances and other heating appliances, producing carbon and carbon monoxide – a toxic gas

Figure 4.12 shows an experiment to show that when hydrocarbon fuels burn in plenty of air they produce carbon dioxide and water, but if they burn without enough oxygen the hydrocarbons do not burn completely. Then they produce soot and carbon monoxide. The equation for this is:

$2CH_4$	+	$3O_2$	$\rightarrow$	$2CO$	+	$4H_2O$
methane		oxygen		carbon monoxide		water

Carbon monoxide is a toxic gas. It combines with haemoglobin in the blood, preventing the haemoglobin from carrying oxygen to the cells of the body. It is colourless, so you can't see it. It is odourless, so you can't smell it. This is why it is sometimes called the silent killer. Headlines like the one in Figure 4.13 are far too common. But why do people die from carbon monoxide poisoning?

Many people heat their homes with gas fires or gas central heating boilers. If these appliances are faulty or have insufficient air, carbon monoxide will be produced by incomplete combustion. Lack of oxygen can be caused when people seal doors and windows, or cover up ventilation grills to prevent draughts.

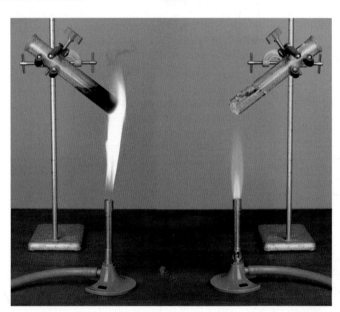

Figure 4.12 When the air hole is open, there is plenty of oxygen and no soot is produced. When the air hole is closed, there is less oxygen and soot is produced.

THE SILENT KILLER STRIKES AGAIN

Man dies in suspected carbon monoxide poisoning

Figure 4.13 This type of headline is far too common.

Did you know?

Poisonous carbon monoxide is also present in cigarette smoke and vehicle exhaust fumes.

Mother's gift prevents death from fumes

Figure 4.14 Carbon monoxide detectors can save lives.

Key Facts

- Carbon monoxide is produced from the incomplete combustion of hydrocarbon fuels.
- Carbon monoxide is toxic.
- Carbon monoxide is colourless and odourless so you do not know it is there.
- Carbon monoxide detectors can help to prevent deaths from carbon monoxide poisoning.

To prevent carbon monoxide poisoning:
- Have gas appliances serviced regularly.
- Do not block ventilation grills.
- Fit a carbon monoxide detector.

Carbon monoxide detectors (Figure 4.15) can be used to show whether appliances are producing carbon monoxide. The newspaper report in Figure 4.14 tells how a mother was worried after reading about carbon monoxide poisoning. She bought a detector for her son's student flat. When the detector started flashing, an expert was called in. He found that carbon monoxide was leaking from a cooker every time it was used.

Figure 4.15 One of these could save your life.

Questions

1   Copy and complete:
    Carbon monoxide is a
    .... gas produced by
    the incomplete .... of
    .... fuels. Carbon
    monoxide cannot be ....
    or .... Carbon
    monoxide forms if ....
    are faulty or if there is
    insufficient ....

2   Design a poster warning
    people about the dangers of
    carbon monoxide poisoning.

3   Explain why the following are
    dangerous:

a) Sealing doors and windows.

b) Having a car engine running
   in a garage with the doors
   closed.

c) Not having gas appliances
   serviced regularly.

Alkanes and alkenes

biology **4.06** chemistry physics

Learning outcomes

After completing the work in this topic you will be able to:

- recall the formulae of the alkenes – ethene and propene – and the structures of their molecules

- describe how bromine water is used to distinguish between alkenes and alkanes

You have already met the family of hydrocarbons called alkanes (Figure 4.16). These have the general formula C_nH_{2n+2}

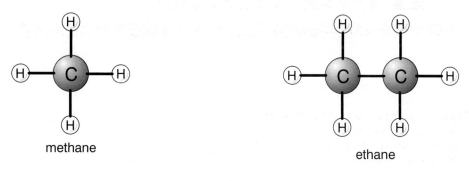

methane

ethane

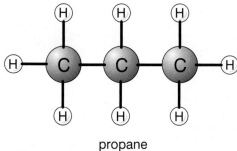

propane

Figure 4.16 Methane, ethane and propane.

There are other families of hydrocarbons. One of these is the **alkene** family.

Name	Number of carbon atoms	Formula	Boiling point (°C)
ethene	2	C_2H_4	−104
propene	3	C_3H_6	−48
butene	4	C_4H_8	−6

Table 4.7 The alkenes.

Alkenes have the general formula C_nH_{2n}. An alkene has fewer hydrogen atoms than the corresponding alkane.

ethane   ethene
C_2H_6 C_2H_4

Chemistry in action 135

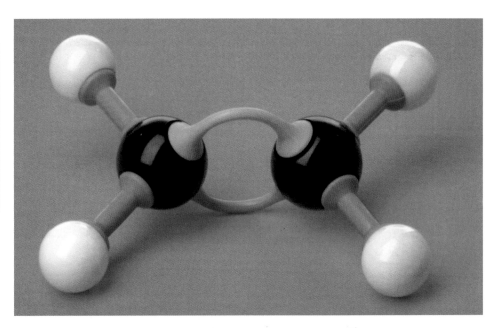

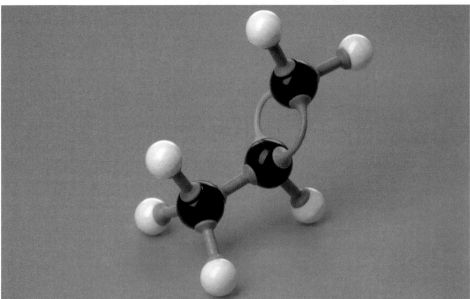

Figure 4.17 Models of ethene and propene.

The alkene family all contain a **carbon–carbon double bond** and are said to be **unsaturated** (Figures 4.17 and 4.18).

The alkane family do not contain a carbon–carbon double bond and are said to be **saturated**.

Reaction with bromine...

Bromine joins with alkenes in an **addition reaction**.

$$C_2H_4 \quad + \quad Br_2 \quad \rightarrow \quad C_2H_4Br_2$$

ethene   bromine   1,2-dibromoethane

Bromine is a red-brown colour. When the bromine reacts with an alkene, the colour disappears (Figure 4.19). The decolourising of bromine water is a standard test for unsaturation. It is used to distinguish between alkanes which are saturated, and alkenes which are unsaturated and contain a carbon–carbon double bond.

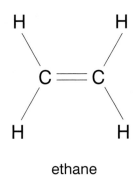

ethane

Figure 4.19 Bubbling ethene into bromine water removes the colour of the bromine.

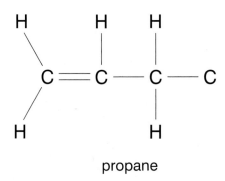

propane

Figure 4.18 Ethene and propene.

Key Facts

- The alkenes are a family of hydrocarbons which all contain a carbon–carbon double bond.
- The alkenes are unsaturated; they react with bromine water and decolourise it.

Questions

1 Copy and complete:
Alkenes are .... molecules with a carbon–carbon .... bond. The alkenes are .... and will remove the .... colour from bromine water.

2 Design a leaflet to warn people about the dangers of too much saturated fat in their diet.

3 a) Use the information on the previous page to estimate the boiling point of pentene C_5H_{10}

b) Draw the structure of pentene.

c) Find out the boiling points of the alkanes – ethane, propane and butane. How do these compare with the boiling points of the corresponding alkenes?

4 Explain why ethene decolourises bromine water.

5 Write a balanced equation for the complete combustion of ethene.

6 The first member of the alkane family of hydrocarbons is methane. Explain why an alkene called methene does not exist.

... more at www.modularscience.co.uk

Power without the pollution

Science Today

Fuel cells do not burn fuel in the same way as power stations and car engines. Instead, they work like a battery, drawing electricity from a chemical reaction between the fuel and the oxygen. This makes them very efficient. Burning fuel is dirty and throws heat out in all directions, wasting most of it.

Like batteries, fuel cells have positive and negative terminals. The negative terminal (the cathode) of a fuel cell strips oxygen from the air. This changes the electrical charge of the oxygen atom and makes it an 'ion'. The positive terminal (the anode) attracts these oxygen ions and combines them with fuel. This reaction frees electrons from the fuel and allows electricity to flow.

The biggest problem with fuel cells is their cost. Cars, lap-top computers and even mobile telephones have already been developed and are powered by fuel cells, but they are much more expensive than those using conventional engines and batteries. This is because these fuel cells run on hydrogen, which is difficult to make and dangerous to store.

Cost is no object to NASA of course and the volatile mixture of hydrogen and oxygen used as rocket fuel actually make fuel cells the best energy source for spacecraft. The fuel cells used on the Apollo missions to the moon for example, generate power twice as efficiently as the best car engines.

But these fuel cells need pure hydrogen to work. Scientists make this by combining steam and methane (natural gas) at very high temperatures. This process, called reforming, is expensive. It is much cheaper just to burn the methane to produce electricity in a power station – as most people do.

Fuel cells that run on more everyday fuels made from oil and coal are already in existence, but they are plagued with problems. These problems are mainly caused by the electrolyte, the third crucial component in any battery or fuel cell. The electrolyte is needed to transfer electrons between the electrodes, completing the circuit and therefore allowing electricity to flow.

Not all materials work as electrolytes. Electrolytes used in some fuel cells are often corrosive liquids, which can eat away at their own electrodes. Others are solid but need to be kept at high temperatures. These, however, produce lots of soot, which build up on the electrodes like a dirty chimney and break the electrical circuit.

But fuel cells are gradually being invented that could directly tap the hydrogen locked up inside fossil fuels such as methane and petrol, without the costly reforming middle step or electrolyte problems. For example, scientists in America at the University of Pennsylvania have now discovered how to run a fuel cell, not on hydrogen, but on methane and other hydrocarbon fuels such as butane. This could eventually make them cheap enough to compete with petrol, methane and coal.

The electrodes in this new cell do not gather soot, and the cell produces electricity as long as fuel is fed to it. The technique is not perfect – it can only produce about one-tenth of the power of hydrogen-fuelled fuel cells – but the scientists think they can improve this enough to make their fuel cell almost as good, but much cheaper.

Cracking

Learning outcome

After completing the work in this topic you will be able to:

- explain how some oil fractions are cracked to yield useful hydrocarbon molecules, some of which are unsaturated since they contain carbon–carbon double bonds

The lower boiling point fractions obtained from fractional distillation are in greater demand than the higher boiling point ones.

Fraction	Percentage produced	Percentage demand
refinery gas	2	4
petrol	7	22
naphtha	10	5
kerosene	13	8
diesel	20	23
residue	48	38

Table 4.8 The demand for the different fractions in crude oil.

As can be seen from Table 4.8, the demand for petrol far exceeds the supply. This has led scientists to find a way of breaking some of the larger molecules into smaller ones. The big molecules are passed over a hot catalyst in a process known as **cracking**. The plant in which this process is carried out is called a **catalytic cracker**. Temperatures of about 800°C are used, but by changing the temperature and pressure, different products can be obtained (Figure 4.20).

Did you know?

Some countries have no oil. In South Africa, petrol is made from coal and in Brazil ethanol made from sugar cane is used as fuel.

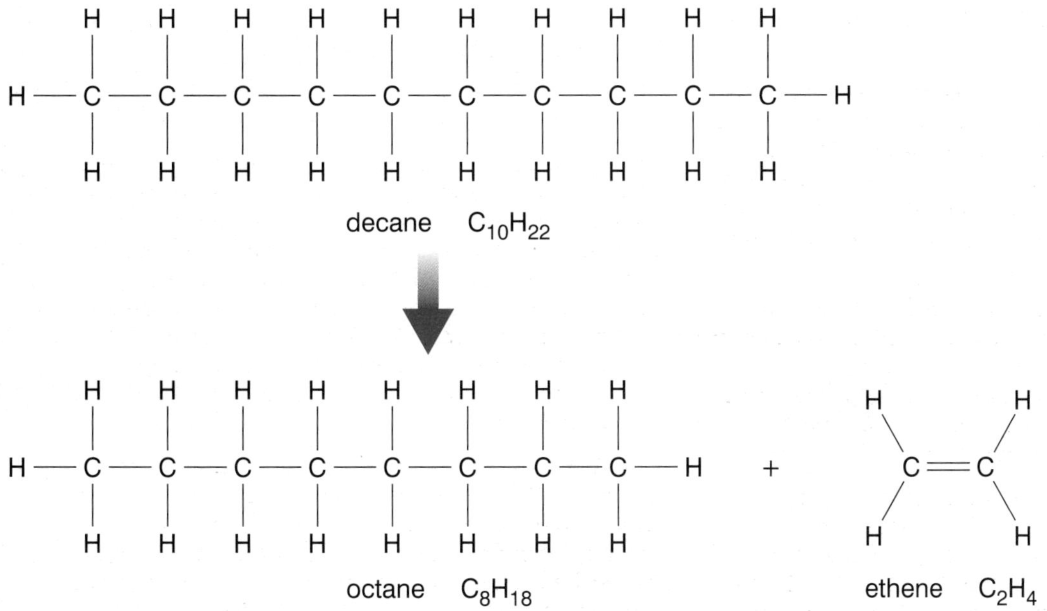

decane $C_{10}H_{22}$

octane C_8H_{18} + ethene C_2H_4

Figure 4.20 The cracking of decane to produce octane and ethene.

4.07 Cracking

Cracking is important because it produces more petrol and finds a use for some of the fractions of crude oil for which there is less demand. Cracking also produces **alkenes** containing double bonds. The alkene ethene is the starting point for many chemicals, including poly(ethene) (Figure 4.21). In fact, ethene is so important that large quantities of it are now produced by cracking the ethane obtained from natural gas.

$$C_2H_6 \rightarrow C_2H_4 + H_2$$
ethane   ethene   hydrogen

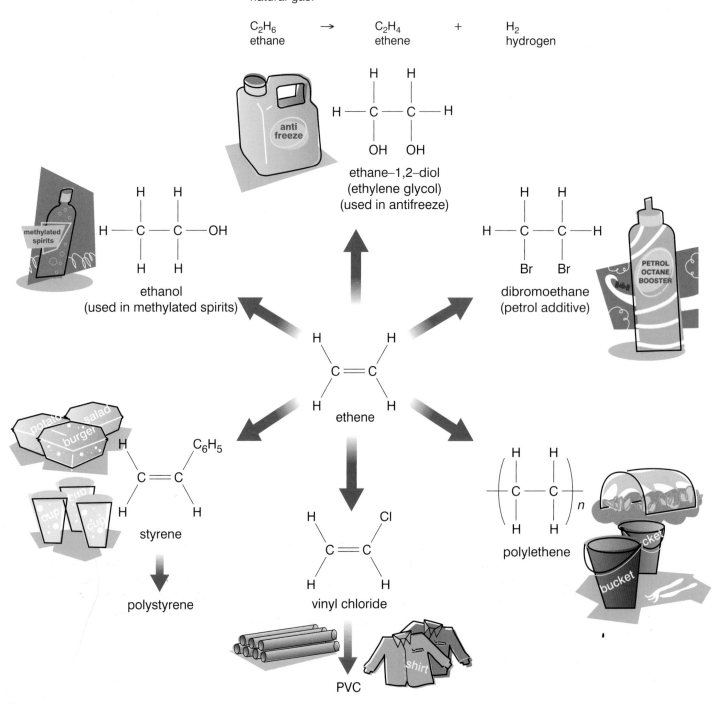

Figure 4.21 Some of the products made from ethene.

Cracking in the laboratory...

Figure 4.22 shows the method used for cracking liquid paraffin in the laboratory. The liquid paraffin is broken into smaller molecules. The ethene gas can be tested with bromine water to show that it is unsaturated.

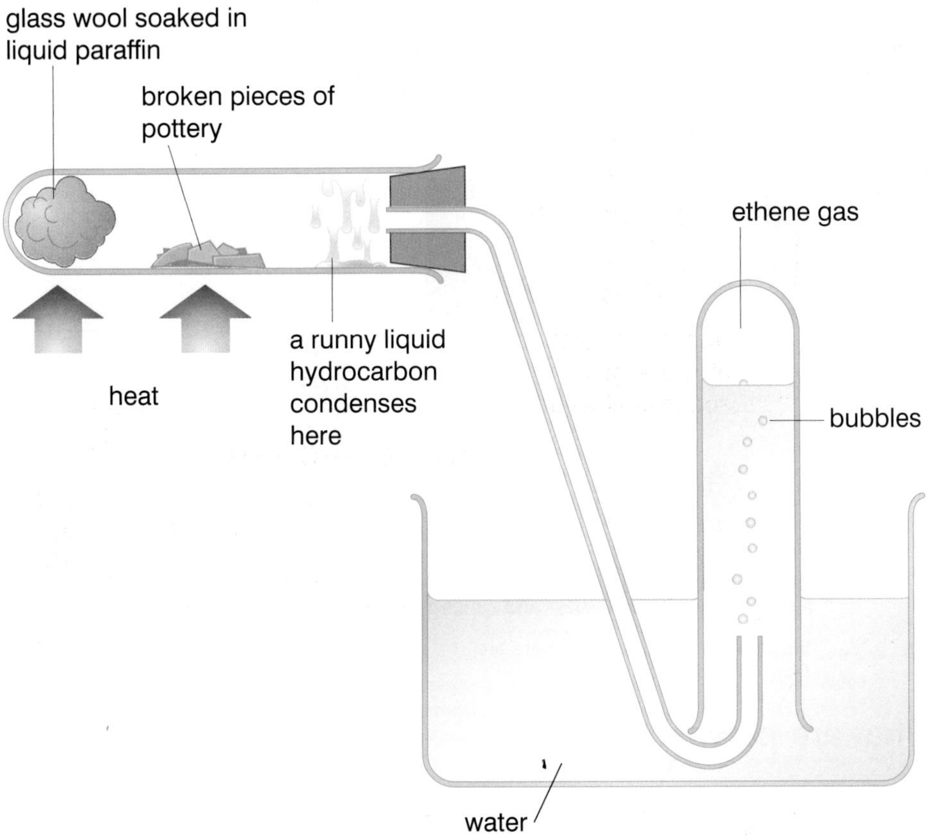
glass wool soaked in liquid paraffin
broken pieces of pottery
heat
a runny liquid hydrocarbon condenses here
ethene gas
bubbles
water

Figure 4.22 The apparatus for cracking liquid paraffin in the laboratory.

Key Facts

- Cracking is used to break large hydrocarbon molecules into smaller ones.
- Some of these molecules are alkenes containing carbon–carbon double bonds.

Questions

1 Copy and complete:
Large .... molecules are broken into .... ones by .... This involves the use of a .... Some of the .... molecules contain a carbon–carbon .... These molecules are ....

2 Explain what is meant by each of these:
a) cracking
b) alkene
c) carbon–carbon double bond
d) unsaturated

3 Eicosane has the formula $C_{20}H_{42}$. Draw the structures of three possible pairs of smaller molecules obtained when eicosane is cracked.

Polymers

Learning outcome

After completing the work in this topic you will be able to:

- explain how addition polymers are formed from unsaturated monomers

All living things are built from **natural polymers**. Starch, cellulose and proteins are natural polymers. Rubber, silk, cotton and wool are also natural polymers. **Synthetic polymers** are now very important in our lives but they were only first used on a large scale in the late 1940s and early 1950s (Figures 4.23, 4.24 and 4.25).

Figure 4.23 Synthetic polymers are used in packaging.

Figure 4.24 Synthetic polymers are used for clothes.

Figure 4.25 Synthetic polymers are used in many sports.

What are polymers?

Polymers are made from lots of small molecules joined together. Starch and cellulose are both polymers of glucose, but the glucose molecules are joined in different ways, giving starch and cellulose different properties. The small molecules are called **monomers**; glucose is the monomer for both starch and cellulose. During **polymerisation**, monomers join together to form polymers (Figure 4.26).

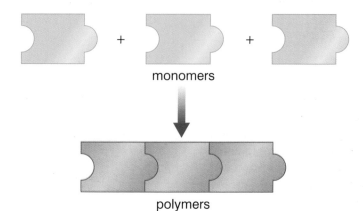

monomers

polymers

Figure 4.26 Polymerisation.

Did you know?

The polymer fibre Nomex can be used to make fireproof clothing for special applications (Figure 4.28).

Alkenes and polymerisation...

All alkenes are reactive because of their carbon–carbon double bond. This allows an alkene molecule to react with another alkene molecule to form an **addition polymer**. Ethene reacts in this way to form poly(ethene) usually known as polythene (Figure 4.27).

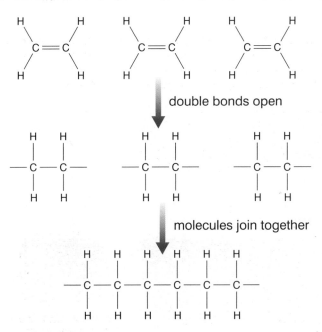

Figure 4.27 Polymerisation of ethene.

Figure 4.28 Special fibres can save lives.

Polymer properties...

By varying the conditions used during its manufacture, it is possible to make many different types of polythene. Different temperatures, pressures and catalysts can affect the length of the polymer chain and the number of branches to the chain. There are two basic types of polythene: low-density poly(ethene) and high-density poly(ethene). These are used for different purposes. Other alkenes can be polymerised, and polymers can even be made from a mixture of alkenes.

Some polymers are made from molecules that are not alkenes, but in all types of polymerisation, small molecules join together to form larger molecules.

Key Facts

- Small monomer molecules join together to form larger molecules called polymers.
- When ethene joins with other ethene molecules, it forms the addition polymer poly(ethene) or polythene.

Questions

1 Copy and complete:
Polymers can be .... or synthetic. An example of a synthetic polymer is ....
Poly(ethene) is made by joining together .... molecules in a process called ....

2 Explain what is meant by each of these words:
a) monomer
b) polymer
c) poly(ethene)
d) synthetic

3 Prepare a five-minute talk to explain how addition polymers are formed from unsaturated monomers.

... more at www.modularscience.co.uk

Chemistry in action 143

Plastics are materials that can be moulded when they are soft, and then set into solid shapes. The first plastics were made from natural polymers. This was achieved by dissolving the natural polymer in a suitable solvent. When the solvent evaporated, the original material had changed. The new material was known as a semi-synthetic polymer. In the 1850s, Alexander Parkes changed cellulose into the first plastic, which he called **Parkesine**. Parkes was awarded a prize for his display at the Great Exhibition in London in 1862 (Figure 4.29). Unfortunately, one problem with Parkesine was its flammability, and Parkes's company went bankrupt in less than two years.

An American, John Hyatt, modified Parkes's methods. He developed **celluloid**, the first commercially successful plastic. This was developed to make artificial ivory for billiard balls, although it is probably best known for its use as movie film. However, like Parkesine, it is also highly flammable. It may even burst into flames while a film is being projected if the lamp gets too hot.

Figure 4.29 Objects made from Parkesine.

Cellulose acetate...

In the early 1900s, another plastic based on cellulose was developed. This was made by dissolving cellulose in ethanoic (acetic) acid and was called **cellulose acetate**. During the First World War, it was used as 'dope' to tighten the fabric on aircraft wings. After the war, demand for dope dropped and cellulose acetate was widely used for screwdriver handles, pens, toys and steering wheels. It was also used to make photographic film. Cellulose acetate was made into fibres by dissolving it in propanone (acetone) and forcing the solution through hundreds of tiny holes. The propanone evaporated, leaving a solid fibre known as artificial silk or **rayon**.

Did you know?

Casein was discovered by accident in 1890. The German chemist Spittler had a mouse in his laboratory. While chasing the mouse, his cat knocked over a bottle of methanal (formaldehyde). Some of this fell onto some cheese in a mousetrap. The cheese became the hard material casein.

Bakelite and **casein** are two other semi-synthetic polymers that were developed in the early 1900s (Figure 4.30).

Figure 4.30 This radio is made from bakelite.

Polythene...

In 1933, two ICI research chemists, Eric Fawcett and Reginald Gibson, were attempting to react ethene with benzaldehyde at a pressure of 1900 atmospheres. They were hoping to make new substances for the dye industry. They left the mixture to react but their equipment leaked. They found that they had produced a small amount of a white waxy solid, the first **poly(ethene)**. They had difficulty in repeating the experiment until they realised that the reaction would only work if a small amount of oxygen was present.

Large molecules...

As recently as the 1920s, the idea of large molecules was not accepted. The chemical theory at the time regarded naturally occurring materials, such as starch and cellulose, and also the newly invented plastics, as being composed of bundles of small molecules held together by some unknown force.

The German chemist Hermann Standinger challenged this idea. He began his work on large molecules in 1922 and first used the term 'macromolecules'. His idea of large molecules met with fierce opposition. One colleague, Professor Weiland, advised him: "Drop the idea of big molecules. There are no molecules with a molecular weight higher than 5000. If you purify your compounds, they will crystallise."

Figure 4.31 Hermann Standinger is making a speech. Standinger's wife was a scientist and she helped him with his work. Some of the best ideas may have been hers.

The bulk of Standinger's work was carried out between 1926 and 1951, when he retired at the age of 70. He led a team of research workers who produced 644 publications (Figure 4.31). Standinger is regarded as one of the fathers of polymer chemistry. He was awarded the Nobel Prize in 1953.

Nylon...

In 1931, Wallace Carothers, an American chemist working for the Du Pont Company, published an article on polymerisation showing his understanding of the process. A few years later he produced **nylon**, the first fully synthetic polymer. In 1939, nylon was produced on a large scale for use in ladies' stockings. The factory-made material, rayon, had proved unsuitable because it did not cling properly and wrinkled at the knees. Carothers was a brilliant chemist but was very critical of his own work. He felt he had not achieved much and thought that he had run out of ideas. In 1937 he committed suicide at the age of 41 by taking cyanide.

During the Second World War, supplies of natural silk from the Far East were cut off. Silk was used for parachutes but nylon proved even better. It was also used for inflatable life rafts. The understanding of polymer chemistry that arose from the work of Standinger and Carothers led to the rapid development of a polymer industry.

Questions

1 Copy and complete:

The first plastic was called .... This material was .... which caused problems. Artificial silk or rayon is made from .... Wallace Carothers produced ...., the first synthetic polymer.

2 Explain the following:

a) In1915, there was high demand for cellulose acetate.

b) Celluloid cinema film can be dangerous to use.

c) Some accidents can be very useful.

d) Nylon was important in the Second World War.

e) Publishing research work helps scientific progress.

3 Discuss the differences between the ideas that were generally accepted for the structure of polymers in 1922 and the ideas of Standinger.

4 Explain why the polymer industry has developed rapidly since the early 1950s.

5 Produce a short talk on the history of polymers.

6 Use the Internet or a CD-ROM to find out more about Wallace Carothers.

... more at www.modularscience.co.uk

Learning outcome

After completing the work in this topic you will be able to:

- recall some of the uses of poly(ethene), poly(propene), poly(styrene) and poly(chloroethene)

Synthetic polymers have a wide range of uses (Figure 4.32). For many purposes, they have replaced wood, stone, glass, leather, natural fabrics and metals because they have the advantage of being light, strong and hardwearing. Synthetic plastics are made from synthetic polymers with other materials added to improve or modify their properties.

Figure 4.32 Products made from plastics.

Poly(ethene) (polythene) is easily moulded and is used to make flexible containers, including plastic bags (Figure 4.33). Over 52 million tonnes of polythene are produced each year.

Figure 4.33 Products made from poly(ethene).

Poly(propene) (polypropene) is made into film for packaging. It is also used to make car bumpers and battery (Figure 4.34). It can be made into fibres to make carpets and thermal underwear, as well as ropes and fishing nets. Over 23 million tonnes of polypropene are produced each year.

Figure 4.34 One use for poly(propene).

Poly(styrene) (polystyrene) is used for toys, furniture, household items, cups and cartons. In its expanded form it is used for insulated containers and packaging (Figure 4.35). Over 8 million tonnes of polystyrene are produced each year.

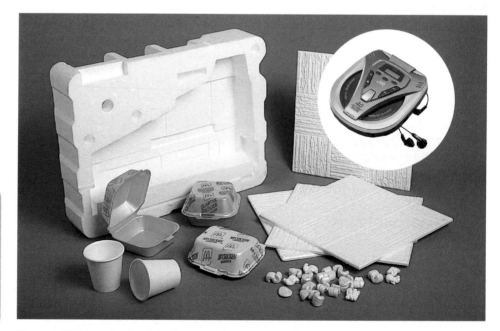

Figure 4.35 The packaging, CD Player and fast-food containers are made from polystyrene.

Did you know?

The crude oil that is used to produce the petrol for a 400-mile car journey could be used instead to make 10 shirts or 250 pairs of tights.

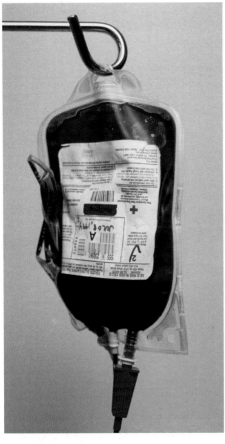

Poly(chloroethene) is more commonly known as poly(vinyl chloride) or PVC (polyvinyl chloride). This material has a wide range of uses, which include rainwater gutters and pipes, windows, electrical cables, and the plastic folders you keep your work in. It also has many medical uses (Figure 4.36). 27 million tonnes of PVC are produced each year.

Figure 4.36 PVC has many medical uses, including blood bags and flexible tubing.

Key Facts

- Polymers are important materials with many uses.
- The properties of synthetic polymers have allowed them to replace many natural materials.

Questions

1 Copy and complete:

The polymer that is used the most is .... Bowls and buckets are made from .... Car bumpers are made from .... Polychloro(ethene) is more commonly known as .... or .... Insulated food containers are made from ....

2 Copy out this list of uses for polymers. After each use, add the name of the polymer that is normally used.
a) fishing nets
b) plastic carrier bags
c) windows
d) rainwater pipes
e) insulated fast-food containers

3 What material was used to make the following articles before the use of polymers? What are the advantages of using polymers rather than the original material?
a) gutters and drainpipes
b) fizzy drink bottles
c) buckets
d) carrier bags
e) toy soldiers
f) car bumpers

4 Some people think it is a waste to burn oil. Explain why they think this.

Plastic waste

Learning outcome

After completing the work in this topic you will be able to:

• describe the problems associated with the disposal of some plastics

Did you know?

The tyres on a jumbo jet can be retreaded six times before being scrapped.

Figure 4.37 Pollution by plastics.

Vast quantities of the plastic materials manufactured today are used for packaging and then thrown away. Something has to be done with this waste (Figure 4.37). One advantage of plastics is that they are resistant to bacteria and chemicals, but this also makes them hard to get rid of. Plastics do not rot away because they cannot be broken down by bacteria and fungi; they are **non-biodegradable**.

Landfill sites...

One of the main methods for the disposal of waste is to find a suitable hole in the ground to put the rubbish in. However, suitable landfill sites are becoming difficult to find. Rubbish tips are unsightly and some people think that plastic waste is too valuable to dump and should be recycled.

Burning the waste...

Plastic waste can be burnt to produce heat. This can be used for heating buildings or to generate electricity. The main problem is that poisonous fumes can be formed. For example, carbon monoxide is formed if there is insufficient oxygen, and hydrogen chloride is formed when PVC is burned.

Figure 4.38 Bales of plastic for recycling.

Recycling...

Recycling plastic waste may appear to be the best answer for the disposal of plastics, but it is not easy in practice. The main problem with recycling is that plastic waste is difficult to sort into individual types of plastic. Research into recycling continues and each year progress is made. Dunlop has a factory in Liverpool that makes new PVC Wellington boots from recycled PVC.

Tyres are made from polymers and are also difficult to dispose of. Some tyres are retreaded, which means putting a new tread on the old tyre. Eventually, however, the tyres have to be disposed of. New ways of getting rid of tyres must be found since a European ban on dumping in landfill sites will come into effect in 2003. Recent research has been looking at including shredded rubber into road surfaces. This would make the surface more flexible and would reduce noise and maintenance (Figure 4.38). Recycled plastics can also be used in the clothing industry (Figure 4.39).

Figure 4.39 Clothes can be made from recycled plastics.

Pyrolysis...

Pyrolysis involves the heating of waste plastics in the absence of air, at temperatures between 400°C and 800°C. The polymers break up to form a mixture of small molecules. Some of these, such as ethene, can then be used to make new polymers.

Biodegradable plastics...

Unlike normal plastics, biodegradable plastics will decompose. Some break down in sunlight, others are broken down by bacteria, and one even dissolves in water. One of these plastics made by ICI is called Biopol. It is used for packaging cosmetics in Germany. Italy also uses biodegradable plastics and, since 1989, the use of non-biodegradable plastics for food wrappings has been illegal in Italy.

Key Facts

- Over 75 million tonnes of plastics are produced in the world every year. Much of this ends up as waste. Most plastic waste is non-biodegradable.
- Suitable landfill sites are difficult to find. Burning plastic waste releases energy for heating but also produces toxic fumes.
- Plastics are difficult to recycle because plastic waste is made up of many different polymers.
- Research is being carried out into the recycling of plastics, breaking plastics down by pyrolysis and into the manufacture of biodegradable plastics.

Questions

1 Copy and complete:
Plastic waste often causes .... of the environment. Materials that do not rot away are called .... A hole in the ground in which rubbish is buried is called a .... Burning plastics can produce .... fumes.

2 Explain the meaning of the following:
a) pollution
b) landfill site
c) recycling
d) pyrolysis
e) biodegradable

3 Some people think that plastics are too valuable to bury in landfill sites. Explain why?

4 Use a computer to produce a poster that tries to persuade people to recycle plastics.

Fermentation

If the apparatus shown in Figure 4.40 is set up, bubbles appear in the limewater and the limewater turns cloudy, showing that the bubbles are carbon dioxide. There is also a smell of alcohol. This is because fermentation has changed the sugar into carbon dioxide and ethanol.

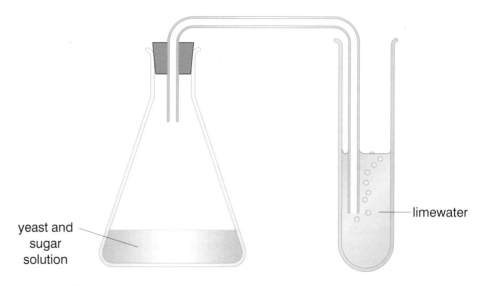

limewater

Figure 4.40 Experiment to find the products of yeast fermentation.

yeast and sugar solution

$$C_6H_{12}O_6 \rightarrow 2C_2H_5OH + 2CO_2$$
glucose ethanol carbon dioxide

People have used fermentation for thousands of years to make alcoholic drinks. The process was probably discovered by the Babylonians in 6000 BC. The ethanol produced during fermentation makes the drink alcoholic and the carbon dioxide adds fizz. Table 4.9 shows the source of sugar for a range of alcoholic drinks.

Drink	Source of sugar
beer	barley
cider	apples
wine	grapes
sherry	grapes
whisky	barley
gin	wheat
vodka	potatoes

Table 4.9 Source of sugar for various alcoholic drinks.

Did you know?

Enzymes were discovered by accident in 1897. Edward Buchner extracted juice from yeast to see if it would cure diseases. Before he could test it, the juice went bad. He tried to preserve the juice using sugar. When fermentation took place, Buchner realised that only part of the yeast was needed for fermentation. Before this, people had thought that sugar could only be fermented by living yeast.

Beer, cider and wine are made by fermentation. Sherry is a fortified wine with extra alcohol added. Whisky, gin and vodka are spirits. In these, the alcohol is first produced by fermentation; it is then concentrated by **distillation** in equipment called a still (Figure 4.41). Biological catalysts found in the yeast, called enzymes, control the reactions. These enzymes work best at a temperature of 37°C, which is called their optimum temperature.

Figure 4.41 Making whisky.

Figure 4.42 Carbon dioxide makes bread rise.

Bread-making...

Fermentation is also used to make bread. In this case, it is the carbon dioxide that is important. Dough is made from flour, water and yeast, and is kept in a warm place. Fermentation takes place and the carbon dioxide produced makes the dough rise. The ancient Egyptians discovered this process in about 4000 BC (Figure 4.42).

Questions

1 Copy and complete:
Fermentation changes sugar into .... and ....
Yeast contains ....
These are biological ....
Catalysts work best at an .... temperature.
Alcoholic drinks contain .... Bread rises because bubbles of .... form in the dough.

2 a) The first stage of whisky production involves the fermentation of malted barley in large vats. These are kept warm. Why?

b) Describe how the alcohol content of whisky is increased after the first stage.

c) Why are alcoholic drinks expensive?

3 A recipe for homemade bread contains the following instructions:

1 Mix yeast with a little sugar in warm water.

2 Mix flour with a little yeast.

3 When the yeast froths, add it to the flour.

4 Mix and knead the dough.

5 Leave the dough in a warm place for one hour.

6 Bake in a hot oven.

a) Why must the water be warm in step 1?

b) Why is the dough left in a warm place in step 5?

c) What does baking in a hot oven do to the enzymes in the yeast?

The dairy industry is concerned with making things from milk. For thousands of years, people have made cheese and yoghurt from milk.

Making cheese...

Milk is pasteurised to kill harmful bacteria. This involves heating the milk to 70°C for 30 minutes. To make cheese, the milk is then cooled to 30°C and special useful bacteria are added. These produce an enzyme that makes the milk turn sour. A sugar in the milk, called lactose, is changed into lactic acid. Rennet is then added; this contains the enzyme rennin, which makes the milk curdle. The lumpy solids produced are curds and the watery liquid is whey (Figure 4.43).

Did you know?

Rennet is usually obtained from the stomachs of calves. It is present in the stomachs of young mammals to solidify the milk from their mothers. Rennet made from fungi is now used to make 'vegetarian' cheese.

Figure 4.43 Making cheese.

Cottage cheese is basically curds. To make other cheeses, bacteria or fungi (moulds) are added. These ripen the cheese and give each variety of cheese its characteristic smell and flavour (Figure 4.44).

Figure 4.44 Bacteria give off carbon dioxide, which makes the holes in some cheeses. Fungi (moulds) cause the blue veins in other cheeses.

Making yoghurt...

Yoghurt is very popular in Britain (Figure 4.45). It is thought that it was first made in the Middle East. As in cheese-making, the milk is pasteurised, and after cooling to 30°C, the bacteria are added. Enzymes change the lactose to lactic acid. Fruit and flavourings are then added to some yoghurts.

Figure 4.45 Different types of yoghurt.

Washing powders...

Washing powders are used to remove dirt from clothes (Figure 4.46). Some of the dirt is soluble in water but some stains cannot simply be washed out. These stains can be digested using enzymes, but because enzymes are specific in their action, a complex mixture is required. This includes protease to remove protein, lipase to remove fats, amylase to remove starch and cellulases to remove loose 'bobbles'.

Figure 4.46 All these washing powders will get clothes clean but some use enzymes to help.

Key Facts

- Cheese and yoghurt are products of the dairy industry. Enzymes made by microbes are used in the production of cheese and yoghurt.
- Enzymes are added to some washing powders to digest stains.

Questions

1   Copy and complete:
    Cheese and yoghurt are both made from .... Enzymes change lactose into .... In cheese-making, rennet which contains the enzyme .... is used. Yoghurt often has .... and .... added to change its flavour.

2   Look at these examples of nutrition information taken from cheese and yoghurt labels. Use this information to explain why eating yoghurt is healthier than eating cheese.

Mature cheddar Nutrition information per 100 g	
Energy	1700 kJ
Protein	25.0 g
Carbohydrate	0.1 g
Fat	34.4 g

Yoghurt Nutrition information per 100 g	
Energy	468 kJ
Protein	4.2 g
Carbohydrate	19.1 g
Fat	1.9 g

3   Explain what is meant by vegetarian cheese. Suggest why some vegetarians would be happy to eat this cheese but others would consider it unsuitable for a vegetarian diet.

4   Produce a poster to explain why it is not healthy to eat large amounts of cheese.

5   Explain why the enzymes in some washing powders are said to digest stains.

6   Use the Internet to find out more about enzymes in washing powders.

... more at www.modularscience.co.uk

Neutralisation

Neutralisation...

The reaction of a base with an acid to produce a neutral substance is called **neutralisation**. Neutralisation is used to make salts. For example:
- nitric acid gives nitrates
- sulphuric acid gives sulphates
- hydrochloric acid gives chlorides

Ammonium nitrate, ammonium phosphate and potassium chloride are all important salts used in fertilisers.

base		acid		salt
$NH_3(g)$	+	$HNO_3(aq)$	$\rightarrow$	$NH_4NO_3(aq)$
ammonia		nitric acid		ammonium nitrate

Limestone...

Limestone is an important raw material. It is used in blast furnaces when iron is extracted from its ore. It is also the starting point for some important chemicals. Limestone is a form of calcium carbonate. When it is heated, it breaks down. Decomposition caused by heating is called **thermal decomposition**. The equation for this reaction is:

$$CaCO_3(s) \xrightarrow{\text{heat}} CaO(s) + CO_2(g)$$

$CaCO_3(s)$	$\xrightarrow{\text{heat}}$	$CaO(s)$	+	$CO_2(g)$
calcium carbonate		calcium oxide		carbon dioxide

This reaction was carried out in many of the old lime kilns you see in the countryside (Figure 4.47). It is now carried out in modern lime kilns. The calcium oxide produced is known as quicklime. Calcium oxide is a base and has many important uses, including neutralising acidic gases. In agriculture, it is used to break down clay soils and to neutralise acidity in soil.

Figure 4.47 An old lime kiln.

Did you know?

Limewater, which is used to test for carbon dioxide, is made by dissolving a little calcium hydroxide in cold water.

... more at www.modularscience.co.uk

Key Facts

- Thermal decomposition and neutralisation are two types of chemical reaction.
- In thermal decomposition, a compound is broken down by the action of heat. An example of this in industry is the manufacture of calcium oxide (quicklime).
- Neutralisation involves reacting an acid with a base to produce a salt. This process is important in the manufacture of some fertilisers.

When water is slowly added to lumps of quicklime, it is absorbed until the lump breaks open, forming a white powder:

$$CaO(s) \quad + \quad H_2O(l) \quad \rightarrow \quad Ca(OH)_2(s)$$

calcium oxide $\qquad$ water $\qquad\qquad$ hydrated lime

The white powder is slaked or hydrated lime. Because it is a base, it is used by farmers and gardeners to neutralise acidic soils (Figure 4.48). Hydrated lime is also an important industrial chemical.

Figure 4.48 Farmers neutralise acid soil using lime.

Questions

1 Copy and complete:

When a compound is broken down by heating, the process is called .... Limestone breaks down when .... to form quicklime and .... The chemical name for limestone is .... The chemical name for quicklime is .... Neutralisation occurs when a .... reacts with an ....

2 Describe how a sample of limewater can be made from limestone. Include relevant symbol equations.

3 Suggest how the following salts can be formed. In each case, write a symbol equation:

a) sodium chloride from sodium hydroxide

b) copper sulphate from copper(II) oxide

c) ammonium sulphate from ammonia

d) calcium nitrate from calcium carbonate

e) zinc chloride from zinc

Learning outcomes

After completing the work in this topic you will be able to:

- recall that calcium carbonate is used in the production of glass, cement and iron
- recall further examples of different types of chemical reactions

Glass production...

Limestone (calcium carbonate) is one of the raw materials used to make glass. The most common glass is soda-lime-silica glass. This glass is made by mixing and heating sand (silicon dioxide), limestone (calcium carbonate) and sodium carbonate.

Glass recycling...

Many glass containers are used in Britain. Some of these are thrown away, forming litter. All litter spoils the appearance of our towns and countryside, but glass is also dangerous to people and animals. Glass on beaches is responsible for many of the cuts that require treatment at first-aid posts. Small mammals, such as mice, voles and shrews, crawl into bottles because they are attracted by the smell of milk or a sugary drink. Once inside, they may drown or be unable to crawl back out.

Figure 4.49 A bottle bank to collect glass for recycling.

Even if empty containers are disposed of safely in dustbins and rubbish dumps, it is still a waste. Making glass uses raw materials and also large amounts of energy to heat the furnace. If waste glass is collected in bottle banks, it can easily be melted to form new glass objects (Figure 4.49). This uses less energy than making new glass.

Making cement...

Cement is another important material that is made from limestone. Its manufacture involves heating limestone with clay in a rotary kiln (Figure 4.50).

Figure 4.50 Cement is another useful product made from limestone.

Did you know?

Glass is made when molten liquid cools too quickly for the atoms in it to form crystals. Obsidian is a natural glass formed when molten rock from a volcano reaches the Earth's surface.

Copper carbonate...

Copper carbonate undergoes thermal decomposition on heating (Figure 4.51).

$$CuCO_3(s) \rightarrow CuO(s) + CO_2(g)$$

| copper carbonate | | copper oxide | | carbon dioxide |

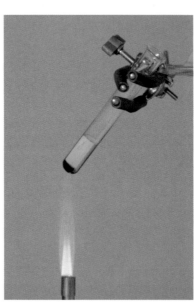

Figure 4.51 Copper carbonate turns black when it is heated, as copper(II) oxide forms. This is an example of thermal decomposition which is easily shown in the school laboratory.

Questions

1 Copy and complete:
   Limestone is an important .... It is used in the .... when iron is .... from its ore. To make glass, limestone is heated with .... and .... Cement is made in a .... by heating limestone with ....

2 Reusable bottles need to be stronger than non-returnable bottles and cost more to manufacture. Each time they are reused, they need to be washed, filled and returned to the shops.

	Reusable	Non-returnable
Energy to make bottle (MJ)	7.0	4.6
Energy to wash, fill and transport bottle (MJ)	2.5	2.1

   a) Use the information in the table to compare the amount of energy used if three non-returnable bottles are used compared with using a new reusable bottle and then refilling it twice.

   b) Give two reasons why the energy needed to wash, fill and transport a reusable bottle is greater than the energy needed for a non-returnable bottle.

3 Design a leaflet to encourage people to recycle glass.

4 Explain why heating copper carbonate is an example of thermal decomposition.

5 In groups, research and prepare a short talk to explain to your class the problems caused by the use of large quantities of limestone as a raw material.

... more at www.modularscience.co.uk

1.   Copy and complete the sentences using words from the box.

     cracking   crude oil   poly(ethene)   polymerisation   poly(styrene)

     The material used to produce useful hydrocarbon molecules is ....

     Large molecules are broken down into small molecules by a process called ....

     Carrier bags are often made from ....

                                                             (Total 3 marks)

     Edexcel GCSE Double Award (Combined) 1524 June 1999, Paper 5H no. 6

2.   Propene (C_3H_6) can be obtained by cracking alkanes.

     (a)   Draw the structure of a molecule of propene showing **all** the bonds.   (1)

     (b)   One molecule of the alkane decane ($C_{10}H_{22}$) was cracked to give two molecules of propene and one molecule of another alkane.

            Write the balanced equation for this reaction.   (2)

     (c)   Propene is used to make poly(propene).

            (i)   What feature of a propene molecule enables it to form poly(propene)?   (1)

            (ii)   Draw the structure of the repeating unit in poly(propene).   (2)

            (iii) Poly(ethene) is used to make many types of bottle. Suggest why the more expensive poly(propene) is used to make bottles for fizzy drinks.   (1)

                                                             (Total 7 marks)

     Edexcel GCSE Double Award (Combined) 1524 June 1999, Paper 5F, no. 8

3.   The table gives the names and formulae of three monomers used to make plastics.

Name of monomer	ethene	propene	chloroethene
Formula of monomer	H, H / C=C / H, H	CH₃, H / C=C / H, H	Cl, H / C=C / H, H

     (a)   (i)   Which of these monomers are hydrocarbons?

            (ii)   Explain your answer.   (1)

     (b)   Ethene can be changed into the polymer poly(ethene). Part of the structure of this polymer is shown below. Show the structure of poly(propene), which can be formed from propene.

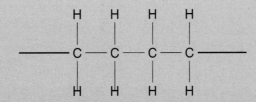

                                                                   (1)

                                                                   (Total 2 marks)

     Edexcel GCSE Double Award (Modular) 1531 June 1999, Paper 1H, no.10

Glossary 4

Addition polymer   A polymer that is made by the joining together of alkene molecules with a double carbon-carbon bond.

Addition reaction   A reaction where a new compound is formed by adding an extra atom onto the 'spare' bond of an existing compound.

Alkane   A hydrocarbon where the number of hydrogen atoms is 2 more than twice the number of carbon atoms. So if an alkane had 4 carbon atoms it would have $(4 \times 2) + 2 = 10$ hydrogen atoms.

Alkene   A hydrocarbon where the number of hydrogen atoms is twice the number of carbon atoms. So if the number of carbon atoms were 4 there would be 8 hydrogen atoms.

Bakelite   A semi-synthetic polymer developed in the early 1900s.

Carbon–carbon double bond   A carbon–carbon double bond consists of two carbon atoms held together by two bonds instead of the usual single bond.

Casein   A semi-synthetic polymer developed in the early 1900s.

Catalytic cracker   The plant in which large molecules are broken up by cracking.

Celluloid   The first commercially successful plastic.

Cellulose acetate   A plastic made by dissolving celluloid in ethanoic (acetic) acid.

Complete combustion   Complete combustion of a hydrocarbon leaves only carbon dioxide and water. Complete combustion can only take place if there is plenty of oxygen.

Cracking   Breaking large molecules into smaller ones by passing the substance over a hot catalyst.

Distillation   The process used to concentrate the alcohol in fermented drinks, converting them into spirits.

Fermentation   The process of breaking a sugar down into carbon dioxide and an alcohol using enzymes in yeast.

Fossil fuel   A fossil fuel is a fuel formed from dead plants and animals that lived millions of years ago.

Fraction   A mixture of substances in crude oil, all with very similar molecule size and very similar boiling points. Crude oil contains several fractions.

Fractionating tower   A tower for separating the fractions in crude oil by boiling and condensing them.

Hydrocarbon   A compound made only from hydrogen and carbon atoms.

Incomplete combustion   Combustion of a hydrocarbon that leaves carbon (soot) or carbon monoxide. Incomplete combustion takes place when the supply of oxygen is limited.

Monomer   A small molecule that joins together in long chains to make a polymer.

Natural polymer   A naturally occurring long chain molecule made from many smaller molecules joined together.

Neutralisation   The reaction of an acid with a base to produce a neutral substance.

Non-biodegradable   Substances that cannot be broken down by bacteria or fungi, so they do not rot.

Nylon   The first fully synthetic polymer developed in 1931 by Wallace Carothers. It was used by the fashion industry as a cheap substitute for silk.

Oxidation   The process of adding oxygen to a substance to form new substances.

Parkesine   The first type of plastic, made by Alexander Parkes in the 1850s.

Poly(ethene)   A very important plastic developed by accident when two ICI research chemists were trying to make new substances for the dye industry.

Polymerisation   The process of joining together lots of monomers to make a polymer.

Rayon   Artificial silk made by forcing a solution of cellulose acetate fibres through tiny holes.

Saturated   A compound which does not have 'spare' bonds and reacts by substituting a different atom for one of its original atoms.

Synthetic polymer   An artificially created long chain molecule made from many smaller molecules joined together.

Thermal decomposition   Breaking a compound down by heating it.

Thermal energy   Heat energy that is released when fuels are burned.

Unsaturated   A compound that has 'spare' bonds and reacts by adding extra atoms onto those spare bonds.

In this module you will learn about energy. Modern life relies on energy, from cooking food and heating buildings to batteries for mobile phones and electricity for computers and televisions.

Electricity is the perfect source of energy. It is clean, quiet and instantaneous. But electricity has to be generated, either by a battery or in power stations, and this always causes pollution somewhere. Electricity also has to be transmitted to where it is used and this requires miles of cables carrying highly dangerous voltages. Perhaps science should find a better way of providing us with electricity? Maybe there are other ways of giving us the energy we take for granted in modern life? Or should we change our lifestyle so that we no longer require so much energy in our homes?

This module looks at the way electricity is generated now and looks at possibilities for the future from renewable sources of energy. Is sustainable energy technology ever going to deliver what it promises? The module also looks at how electricity is transmitted and asks if we really need all those overhead cables. It looks at how we, as users, are always in danger from electricity and the steps that are taken to protect us from injury and death, inside our homes and outside.

Electricity is an expensive luxury and it is set to become more expensive as the 'polluter pays' system comes into play. The module also looks at how we pay for our electricity and how we can reduce our bills while improving our quality of life.

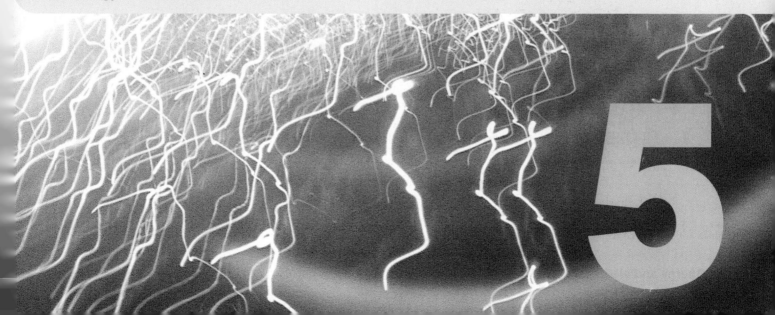

Who's who?...

André Marie Ampère, Count Alessandro Volta, Georg Simon Ohm, James Prescott Joule and James Watt have something in common (Figure 5.1). Their names have become part of the international language of science as units for measuring electrical quantities:

* amp (A) for current
* volt (V) for voltage
* ohm (Ω) for resistance
* joule (J) for energy
* watt (W) for power

Figure 5.1 Ampère, Ohm, Volta, Watt and Joule are well-known scientists. Without their work we wouldn't have the hundreds of electrical devices we rely on in our homes and at work.

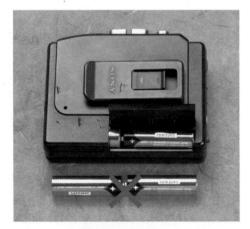

Figure 5.2 A personal stereo only works if the batteries are inserted correctly.

Electric current and voltage

There is a big difference between current, measured in amps, and voltage, measured in volts. This section explains that difference.

Batteries...

The batteries in a personal stereo must be put in the right way round. The batteries are needed to send an electric current around the circuit to make the device work. The electric current from a battery or cell is called **direct current** because it flows only one way round a circuit. If you accidentally put in your batteries facing in opposite directions, they will try to send their currents in opposite directions (Figure 5.2). The current can go nowhere and the stereo will not work!

Direct current...

It is easy to imagine electric current as particles moving through a wire, a bit like water flowing along a pipe. These particles are called 'electrons', which is where we get the word electricity (Figure 5.3).

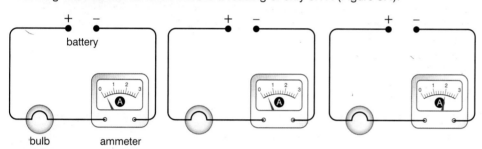

Figure 5.3 Particles called electrons flow through the wire when a battery is connected. This is called an electric current.

wire   electrons

Speeding up...

The faster the electrons move, the higher the current. An **ammeter** measures the current in amps. It simply detects the charge on the electrons as they flow through it. You have to connect an ammeter in series so that it can sense the charge flowing through it. If an ammeter reads 0.2 A, it indicates that the charge is flowing twice as fast as when there is a reading of only 0.1 A (Figure 5.4).

battery

bulb   ammeter

Figure 5.4 A higher current shows that the electrons are moving more quickly through the wires as they pass around the circuit.

Voltage

Voltage is more complex. The voltage marked on a battery lets you know how much energy each charged particle is carrying. The particles will use this energy as they go around the circuit. The more energy (voltage) an electron is given, the faster it will flow around a particular circuit. So increasing the voltage is a way to get a higher current (Figure 5.5).

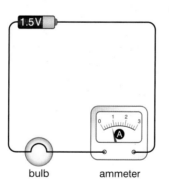

bulb   ammeter

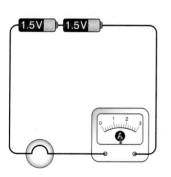

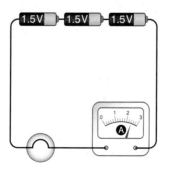

Figure 5.5 A higher voltage means the electrons have more energy so they move more quickly. We can see this as higher currents on the ammeters.

Key Facts

- Direct current from batteries passes in one direction round a circuit.
- An ammeter is connected in series in a circuit to measure the current (in amps).
- A voltmeter is connected across a device to measure the voltage (in volts).

Did you know?

A voltmeter is one of the most useful pieces of kit for electrical engineers (Figure 5.7). They can work out which part of a circuit is not working by simply touching the voltmeter probes onto each end of the device to see if any energy is being used in it. A zero reading means the device is not working.

Figure 5.7 The voltmeter is an important piece of an electrical engineer's tool kit.

Energetically does it...

A **voltmeter** works out how much energy is used as the current flows through a particular device (resistor). It measures the energy on the way in and on the way out then works out the difference. Voltage is sometimes called 'potential difference' for this reason.

A voltmeter has to be connected in parallel with a resistor (piggy-back) so that it can measure the energy of the current before and after, and then work out how much each charged particle has used (Figure 5.6).

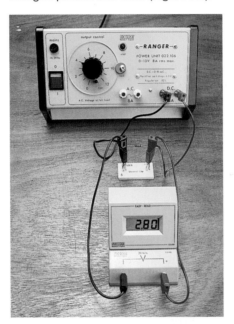
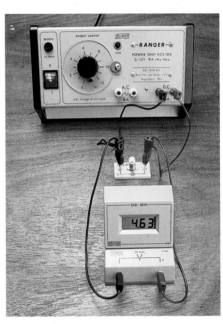

Figure 5.6 The voltmeter measures how much energy the electrons use as they pass through a device.

Questions

1. Copy and complete:

   Cells and batteries supply direct .... The word 'direct' means that the .... passes .... around the circuit. The .... measures the current in a circuit. If the charged particles are flowing more quickly, the .... will show a .... current. The .... measures the energy used in a circuit. This is called the voltage and is measured in .... In identical circuits, a higher voltage will give a .... current because it makes the electrons move ....

2. Make a short instruction leaflet for a device, such as a personal stereo, which explains how to insert the batteries and why it is important to insert them the right way round.

3. Why does an electrical engineer need a voltmeter? Why is it easier to use than an ammeter for testing a circuit?

Resistance

Learning outcomes

After completing the work in this topic you will be able to:

- explain how changing the resistance in a circuit changes the current and how this can be achieved using a variable resistor

- describe how the resistance of a light dependent resistor changes with light intensity and the resistance of a thermistor changes with a change of temperature

Resisting the flow...

One way to slow down the current is to put a resistor in the way. A resistor does exactly what it says – it resists the current going through it and so slows the current down all round the circuit. A large resistor has more of an effect and so the current in the circuit will be lower.

A simple dimmer switch can be made using a **variable resistor**. As you turn the knob, you change the **resistance** and therefore you change the current. A higher current – because of a lower resistance – gives a brighter light (Figure 5.8).

Figure 5.8 Increasing the resistance reduces the current so the light becomes dimmer.

Dependent on light...

Light dependent resistors (LDRs) do exactly what they say. They are like variable resistors except that their resistance changes in light and dark conditions. In light conditions, an LDR has low resistance so a current easily flows through it. In the dark, it has a high resistance so only a small current can flow through it (Figure 5.9).

Figure 5.9 The resistance of the LDR changes in the light and dark. Shining light on it makes its resistance go down, so current flows easily through the circuit. This can be used to operate a circuit, perhaps to close the blinds automatically or switch on a secuirity light.

Did you know?

At very low temperatures, some materials have no electrical resistance at all. They are called superconductors. An electric current in a superconductor can keep going around a circuit forever without needing a battery to keep it going. This is because there is no electrical resistance to slow it down. There is a ring of superconductor in America where the current has been going round and round for over 40 years!

Energy and electricity

Key Facts

- Changing the resistance in a circuit changes the current.
- In a light dependent resistor (LDR), the resistance goes up if it is not illuminated.
- In a thermistor, the resistance goes up if it is not heated.

Heating up...

Thermistors change their resistance as they get hot. A warm thermistor has a low resistance so a higher current flows through it. When the thermistor is cold, its resistance is high so only a tiny current can flow. Thermistors can switch on the heating when things get cold (Figure 5.10).

Figure 5.10 The resistance of the thermistor changes in the hot and cold. Making it warm will make its resistance go down so current flows more easily through the circuit. This can be used to operate a circuit, perhaps to open windows automatically.

Questions

1 Copy and complete:

Increasing the voltage of a power supply can increase the current in a circuit. Another way to increase the current is to .... the resistance in the circuit. A variable resistor can change the resistance in a circuit. When the resistance of the variable resistor is high, the............... in the circuit will be low. Shining a light on a light dependent resistor (...............) will make its resistance go .... This means the current will flow............... through the circuit. Making a thermistor .... will make its resistance go up. This means the .... will flow less easily through the circuit.

2 Some people describe a resistor in a circuit slowing down the flow of charge like climbing over a stile slows down a group of walkers. Think of some other ways to describe a resistor's action in a circuit.

3 Copy and fill in the table, which summarises how the resistance of an LDR and a thermistor can be changed.

4 Make a half page advertisement for a dimmer switch to go in a magazine. Explain how the resistance of the dimmer switch can be used to control the light level in a room.

Current level required in circuit	Resistance level required in circuit	Changes required to light dependent resistor	Changes required to thermistor
high current			
low current			

Ohm's law

Learning outcome

After completing the work in this topic you will be able to:

- understand how to use the equation:

  voltage (V) = current (A) × resistance (Ω)

  V = I × R

Herr Ohm...

Georg Ohm was a popular and talented teacher in Germany in the early 19th century (Figure 5.11), although his scientific work did get him into trouble with the school governors, who thought his work unworthy of a good teacher! It is ironic that Ohm's law is now part of the physics taught to students in every country in the world.

Electricity seemed a complex subject at the time but Ohm's work led him to uncover the basic law of electricity – that electrical current in a conductor depends upon both:
- the voltage applied and
- the resistance of the resistor

A higher voltage gives the charged particles more energy so they flow faster, making a higher current. A higher resistance slows the charged particles down more, making a lower current.

Georg then worked out the equation we now call Ohm's Law:

voltage (V) = current (A) × resistance (Ω)
V = I × R

The unit of resistance is named after him in recognition of his work. Every resistor has a value such as 20 ohms or 2000 ohms (Figure 5.12). The symbol we use for ohms is the Greek letter omega – Ω e.g. 20 Ω.

Figure 5.11 Georg Ohm was asked to leave his job as a school teacher when the school governors disapproved of his discoveries in electricity.

Figure 5.12 All fixed resistors in electrical circuits are colour coded with their resistance in ohms. This is to make sure the right value resistor is used to make the circuit work properly.

Did you know?

Electrical insulators, such as wood and some plastics, have such high resistance that they stop the current altogether!
Scientists are now developing semi-insulating plastics which allow a very slow flow of charge instead of insulating completely.

Key Facts

• Ohm's Law ($V = I \times R$) tells us that a higher resistance in a circuit will reduce the current (making it harder to flow) while a higher voltage will increase the current (by giving it more energy).

Working it out…

Ohm's Law is used all the time by electrical engineers to work out the value of a resistor in a circuit. For example, in a household lamp, the voltage is 240 V and the current is 2 A. What is the resistance?

voltage (V) = current (I) $\times$ resistance (Ω)

If you rearrange the equation you get:

resistance (Ω) = voltage (V) / current (A)
R = 240 V / 2 A
R = 120 Ω

Questions

1   Copy and complete:
Ohm's law describes how the
.... and .... in a
circuit are related. The
electrical current in a circuit
depends on the .... and
the .... Doubling the
voltage in a circuit with a fixed
resistor will result in the current
.... Doubling the
resistance in a circuit with a
fixed voltage will result in the
current ....The unit of
resistance is the .... Its
symbol is ....

2   Copy the table and use the
equation V = I x R to work out
the missing values.

Voltage (V)	Current (A)	Resistance (Ω)
12		60
240		4800
6	0.2	
	10	2500
1.5		30

3   Make up a question – like the
one in the text – which asks a
GCSE student to use Ohm's
law to calculate the answer.
Write out the question in full
and supply the correct answer.

4   Use secondary sources to find
out about Georg Ohm,
Alessandro Volta or Marie-
Christian Ampere. Did they

know about each other's work?
Why is it important for
scientists to know about what
others are doing?

5   If an engineer needed to
reduce the current in a circuit
to one third of its value, what
should s/he add to the circuit
if there's already a 1000Ω
resistor in it?

... more at www.modularscience.co.uk

Fixing a value…

The simplest resistors to experiment on are 'fixed value resistors' – sometimes called Ohmic resistors because they follow Ohm's law perfectly. It is easy to do an experiment to show that if you double the voltage across a fixed resistor, the current through it also doubles.

If you vary the current and voltage of a resistor, you can plot these pairs of measurements on a graph. This gives a graph with a diagonal straight line, so long as the resistor has not heated up. If you work out the gradient of the line, it gives the value of the resistor in ohms (Figure 5.13).

b) The voltage from the power supply is slowly increased. This makes the voltage across the resistor increase and current in the circuit increase.

Figure 5.13 a) The circuit is set up with the ammeter in series and the voltmeter in parallel with the fixed resistor being tested.

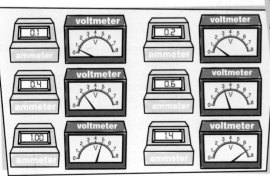

c) Pairs of readings are taken from the ammeter and voltmeter.

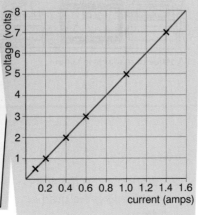

d) The voltage is plotted on the vertical axis and the current is plotted on the horizontal axis. If the gradient is worked out it tells us the resistance of the resistor in ohms.

Breaking Ohm's law…

Filament lamps do not behave like fixed value resistors. Instead of getting a nice straight line, the results are surprising. As you get to higher voltages, the current rises more slowly than you might expect. This is because the filament is getting hot and this makes the resistance of the lamp increase instead of being fixed (Figure 5.14).

Figure 5.14 a) The circuit is set up with the ammeter in series and the voltmeter in parallel with the filament lamp being tested.

b) The voltage from the power supply is slowly increased. This makes the voltage across the lamp increase and current in the circuit increase, but not in the same way as for a fixed resistor. As the lamp gets brighter the current doesn't go up as much as you might expect.

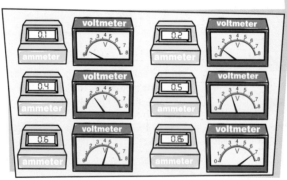

c) A series of readings is taken.

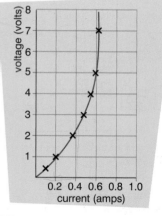

d) The voltage is plotted on the vertical axis and the current is plotted on the horizontal axis. This time you get a curve because the resistance of the lamp is going up as the lamp gets hotter.

Questions

1   Plot your own graph from the reading on the ammeters and voltmeters on page 171 and 172.

2   Work out the resistance by calculating the gradient of each device.

… more at www.modularscience.co.uk

One way only...

A diode is another device that behaves strangely when the voltage is turned up. After a slow start, the current increases much more than expected, so long as the diode is the right way round. But a diode is like a valve, like you have in your heart. It will not let the current flow the wrong way. If you connect it backwards, it simply registers no current flowing through it (Figure 5.15).

Figure 5.15 a) The circuit is set up with the ammeter in series and the voltmeter in parallel with the diode being tested.

b) The voltage from the power supply is slowly increased. This makes the voltage across the diode increase and current in the circuit increase, but not as slowly as you might expect. If you turn the power supply round then increasing the voltage will send almost no current through the diode.

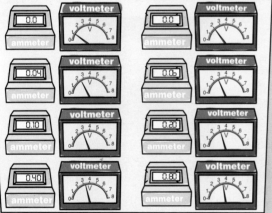

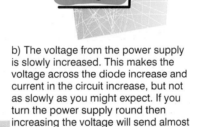

c) A series of readings is taken.

d) The voltage is plotted on the vertical axis and the current is plotted on the horizontal axis. This time you get a curve which shows the current increases slowly at first but then goes up very steeply. This is because the resistance goes down as you put a bigger voltage across the diode.

Questions

1 Write an instruction sheet for a student who has been absent and needs to learn how to test the resistance of a device (a fixed resistor, a filament lamp and a diode). Make sure the student knows what readings to take, how to plot the graph and what it should look like.

2 Make a time-line of inventions that use electricity.

Learning outcomes

After completing the work in this topic you will be able to:

- recall that the mains supply is alternating current and that alternating current changes direction

- understand that the mains supply can provide dangerous currents which can cause injury or death

- describe how to identify the live, neutral and earth conductors in a correctly wired plug and recall the colour of the insulation used on each conductor

- explain the functions of live, neutral and earth wires, and recall that energy flows into a building or appliance through the live wire, that the neutral wire is needed to make a complete circuit, and that the earth wire together with the fuse prevent electrocution

Did you know?

Thomas Edison, the inventor of the light bulb, did all he could to make sure we did not use alternating current in our homes. He even said that the use of a.c. to execute criminals in New York was proof that it was too dangerous to use in the home. Really he wanted to make everyone buy his d.c. generator instead!

A.C.

Mains electricity is **alternating current** (a.c.). It is different from the direct current we obtain from batteries. Instead of the charge flowing round the circuit in one direction, an alternating current changes direction. The mains supply in many countries, including the UK, goes back and forth 50 times per second (called 50 Hertz or 50 Hz). Some other countries use 60 Hz mains electricity.

Left-handers at risk?...

Your body is a good conductor of electricity because it is filled with salty water. When you touch a live wire, the electric current flows through your body. A high enough current will make your muscles contract. This is electrocution. If your heart muscle contracts hard, it may stop beating altogether. Statistics show that left-handed people typically touch live wires with their left hand and so their heart is more affected by the current, and they are more at risk of dying from electrocution (but only slightly!) Many people who are electrocuted suffer serious burns as the electric current escapes from their body into the earth. Some even have large holes blown through the bottom of their feet by the current (Figure 5.16).

Figure 5.16 Mains supply can produce dangerous currents, which can electrocute and even kill. Many victims suffer horrendous burns as the electric current comes out of their body and goes to earth.

Wired for action...

The wires from any device in your home to a plug are blue, brown and, if there is a third wire, green and yellow striped (Figures 5.17 and 5.18). These colours were chosen because they are the least likely to be mixed up by people who are colour-blind. A red-green colour-blind electrician may be in danger because he (colour-blind people are almost always male) could easily mix up the red and green wires that are still used for wiring houses (Figures 5.19 and 5.20).

Figure 5.17 A correctly wired plug.

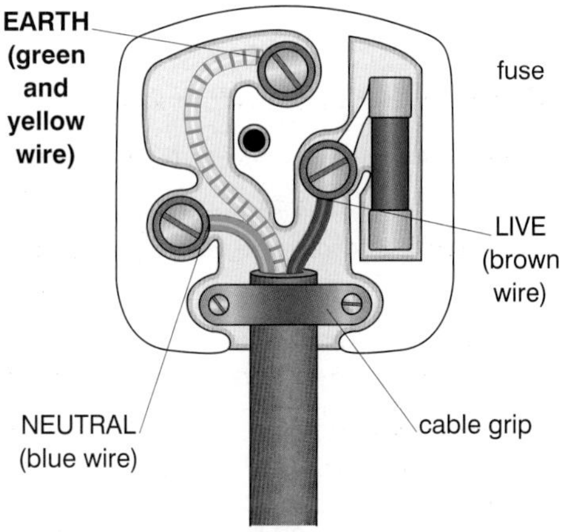

EARTH
(green
and
yellow
wire)

fuse

LIVE
(brown
wire)

NEUTRAL
(blue wire)

cable grip

Figure 5.18 The brown wire is the live wire. Energy flows into the appliance through this wire. The blue wire is the neutral wire. It completes the circuit. If there is a green and yellow wire, it is the earth wire. It is there for safety and helps to prevent electrocution.

Key Facts

- Alternating current from the mains changes direction 50 times per second.
- Mains voltages in the UK are 230 V. This can give a dangerously high current, which can cause serious injury if used carelessly.
- The live (brown) wire carries energy to an appliance.
- The neutral (blue) wire completes the circuit.
- The earth wire (green and yellow stripe), if present, works with the fuse to prevent electrocution.

Safety legislation...

The law now requires that all new electrical appliances must be fitted with a plug. Only a few years ago, this was not required so everyone had to put a plug on every new device they bought. Many people were not very good at getting the wires the right way round and often caused accidents in their homes.

Figure 5.19 A correctly wired household socket.

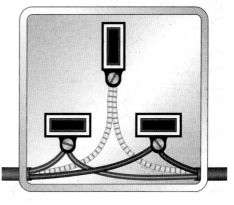

Figure 5.20 The wires in a house are different colours from those used in appliances.

Questions

1   Copy and complete:
    Mains electricity is a.c. This stands for .... It means that the current changes .... Batteries provide d.c., which stands for............... In our homes we use 50 Hz a.c. 50 Hz stands for 50 .... and means that the current .... per second. Appliances have two or three wires connected to their plug. The live wire is coloured .... the earth wire is coloured .... and the .... wire is coloured blue. The function of the live wire is to .... The neutral wire simply .... The purpose of the earth wire is to ....

2   Draw diagrams of incorrectly wired plugs to show what you should not do. Write warnings to explain what is wrong.

Did you know?

The earth pin on a plug has another safety function. It is longer than the live and neutral pins so that it goes into the socket first and pushes aside the sliding covers over the live and neutral connections inside the socket. These covers prevent a small child from pushing anything into the live or neutral holes and being electrocuted.

Safety first…

Some cables have an **earth wire**. One end is connected to 'earth'. The other end is connected to the casing of the appliance. The earth wire is a safety feature to prevent electrocution. If the **live** wire accidentally touches the casing and makes it live and you touch it, you will be electrocuted. Instead the current flows immediately to earth through the earth wire, and blows the **fuse** at the same time. It is much better that the current flows through the earth wire instead of through you! (Figure 5.21).

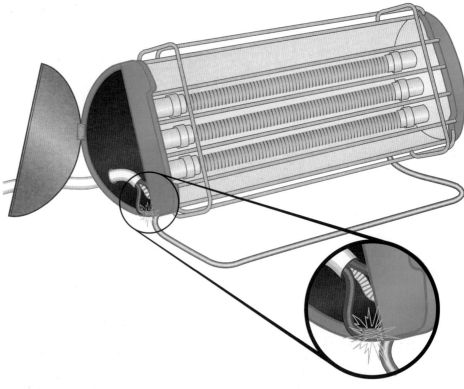

Figure 5.21

My hairdryer has no earth…

A hair dryer has a plastic case. Plastic is a good electrical insulator. Even if the live wire touches the casing, a current will not flow through it so you cannot get electrocuted (Figure 5.22). Other appliances, such as vacuum cleaners and drills, are also **double insulated**.

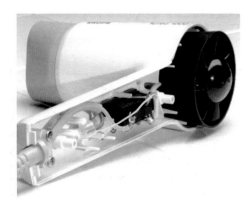

Figure 5.22 Double insulated appliances such as this hairdryer do not require earth connections as the plastic casing acts as an electrical insulator and prevents the operator from receiving an electric shock.

RCCBs…

In the instructions for most electrical tools, such as lawnmowers or drills, you will be advised to use an RCCB (residual current circuit breaker). These clever devices detect any difference between the current in the live and the neutral wires. In a perfect device, the current in the two wires must be the same. If any current escapes down the earth wire, the current in the live wire will be different from the current in the neutral wire. The RCCB detects that there is a difference and immediately 'trips' and switches everything off before the operator is hurt (Figure 5.23). The other advantage of an RCCB is that it can be reset and is immediately ready for use – although it would be sensible to check out what caused it to 'trip' in the first place!

Figure 5.23 Residual current circuit breakers are now recommended for anyone using an appliance such as a lawn mower or power tools. The RCCB acts quickly to cut off the supply if any current leaks to earth. This protects the user from electrocution.

Key Facts

• The earth wire and fuse act together to prevent electrocution.
• Some appliances have no earth wire as they are 'double insulated'. Their casing is made of an insulating material so the user cannot receive a shock from it.
• A residual current circuit breaker protects the appliance user by detecting a difference between the current in the live wire and the neutral wire, and breaking the circuit. It can easily be reset.

Questions

1 Copy and complete:

   If there is a problem with an appliance, the earth wire helps prevent the user from being …………… The earth wire is connected to the appliance's …………… If current leaks onto the appliance's …………… it will flow immediately to …………… and blow the fuse at the same time. Double insulated appliances such as …………… and …………… do not need an earth wire. The casing is made of …………… and this material is a good electrical …………… so the user is protected from electric shock.

2 In many countries, such as France, there are only two pins (connectors) on plugs instead of the three we have in the UK. Explain why there is a third pin on UK plugs.

3 Write a sales brochure explaining why everyone should have an RCCB in their home, and where it is best used.

… more at www.modularscience.co.uk

Fusing

Learning outcomes

After completing the work in this topic you will be able to:

- recall that a fuse is placed in the live conductor
- understand that a fuse protects the appliance, circuit and wires from overheating
- describe the action of a fuse and recall that a large current melts a length of wire, that the melting of a wire breaks the circuit, and that the correct choice of fuse depends on the current rating of an appliance

Did you know?

A man had done some electrical wiring on his house. In some places he had connected several appliances to the same piece of cable so the current through the cable was quite high. To save money, he had used thinner cable than he should have done. This meant that the cable became very hot as the current flowed through it. Worst of all, because he had become so annoyed with the fuse in the fuse box 'blowing' all the time, he had replaced it with ordinary copper wire.
As time went on, everything seemed to be working well. However, the cable wire became very hot every night when he switched things on.

Still the copper wire 'fuse' couldn't blow to prevent things overheating. The thin cable was lying on top of a gas pipe. Slowly it melted a small hole in the gas pipe.

Continued

Designed to self-destruct…

Fuses are designed to self-destruct. They have a thin piece of wire in the capsule, which can easily carry the normal current in the circuit. However, if the current is too high, because there is a fault on the device for example, then the fuse gets so hot it melts (sometimes called 'blowing'). This immediately breaks the circuit so no more current can flow. The fuse protects the appliance. It prevents the wires and the appliance from overheating and causing a fire (Figure 5.24).

Figure 5.24 Fuses have different ratings. A low current fuse has a very thin wire inside which will easily melt if the current increases slightly.

On the live side…

The fuse in a plug should be connected in the live conductor. The fuse in the supply to the circuit and the fuse in the supply to the house are all in the live wire. In this way, a major fault can blow the fuses in sequence as they are all on the same side of the device.

Getting it right…

Every appliance is marked with the information you need to select the right fuse (Figure 5.25). The power rating is the crucial fact. Low power appliances, such as table lamps and computers, have a power rating of less then 250 W. They only take a small current so they require the smallest fuse of 3 A.

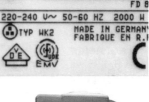

Figure 5.25 Low power appliances take only a small current so they require low rating fuses.

High power appliances, such as kettles or irons, have a power rating of perhaps 2500 W (2.5 kW). They require high currents so they need the largest fuse of 13 A. A mid-range appliance, such as a microwave oven, may be rated 750 W. It will need a 10 A fuse.

Getting it wrong…

If you choose the wrong fuse for your appliance, it may keep 'blowing'. This happens when the appliance uses a higher current than the fuse can tolerate. The high current will easily melt the fuse.

Choosing a fuse that can tolerate a higher current than the appliance is even worse. Everything will work perfectly, perhaps for years. However, if there is a fault, the current may get too high for the appliance. The fuse easily carries this high current but the wires and the appliance cannot (Figure 5.26). The appliance may be damaged or even catch fire. In a way, the appliance has protected the fuse!

The gas ignited and the house burnt down) Figure 5.27. This is a true story!

Figure 5.27 Getting it wrong!

Figure 5.26 a) Fuse refuses to allow sufficient current to the appliance and melts as soon as it is switched on.

Figure 5.26 b) High-rating fuse fails to protect the appliance from overheating.

Key Facts

- The fuse, in the live conductor, melts (blows) if the current through it gets too high. It therefore breaks the circuit and prevents the wires from overheating.
- If the wrong fuse is chosen for an appliance, it will fail to protect the user.

Questions

1 Copy and complete:

The fuse is designed to protect an appliance. It prevents the wires and appliance from …………… The fuse wire will …………… when a high current is passed through it. This is called 'blowing'. When a fuse blows, the circuit is broken so the current …………… flowing. A high power appliance takes a …………… current so it needs a …………… fuse. A low power device only needs a …………… current so it requires a …………… rating fuse. If a high-rating fuse is used instead of a low-rating fuse, we risk the appliance ……………

2 Produce a safety poster which shows the need to have the correct fuse in a plug.

Energy and electricity 179

Learning outcomes

After completing the work in this topic you will be able to:

- understand that when an electric current flows through a resistor, energy is transferred and the resistor is heated

- describe how the heating effect is used in a variety of appliances, such as electric bar heaters, immersion heaters, kettles, cookers and irons

- understand that energy from the mains supply is measured in kilowatt hours

- calculate the cost of energy from mains electricity by using the equation:
  cost = power (kW) × time (h) × cost of 1 kWh

If you can't stand the heat...

Whenever an electric current flows through a conductor, it transfers energy to the conductor and the conductor heats up. Many household appliances work because of this effect, for example electric bar heaters, immersion heaters, kettles, electric cookers and irons (Figure 5.28).

Wind up the current...

To generate heat requires a high current. A kettle may require 13 A to heat the water effectively (Figure 5.29). An immersion heater or cooker will be wired directly into the fuse box with its own 30 A fuse, as the current it requires is much higher.

Evaluating the energy...

Electricity in the home is supplied by electricity companies. They charge you for the amount of energy you use. The energy is worked out in kilowatt hours (kWh). This is simply calculated as the power of the device (in kilowatts) multiplied by the time of use in hours

kilowatt hours = kilowatts × hours

Counting the cost...

To generate a high temperature, the appliance has to have a lot of energy transferred to it, usually using a high current. This makes them expensive to run.

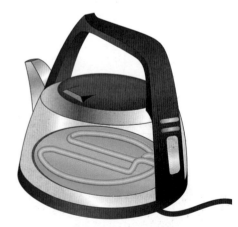

Figure 5.29 The thick metal element in a traditional kettle can carry a high current and can therefore get very hot to boil the water.

To work out how much it costs to operate an appliance:
- read off the power rating of the appliance in kilowatts (kW)
- find out how long the appliance is switched on for in hours (h)
- work out the cost using the equation:
  cost = power (kW) × time (h) × cost for 1 kWh

Figure 5.28 Electricity is particularly useful for heating in the home.

Example 1
To work out how much it costs to use an electric oven to cook a turkey at Christmas.
• power rating of the oven = 2.6 kW
• turkey takes 5 hours to cook = 5 h
• work out the cost using the equation:
cost = power (kW) × time (h) × cost for 1 kWh

cost = 2.6 kW × 5 h × 6 p
cost = 78 p

Example 2
To work out how much it costs to play a CD player for 6 hours.
• power rating of CD player = 12 W = 0.012 kW
• CD player used for 6 hours in the evening = 6 h
• work out cost using the equation:
cost = power (kW) × time (h) × cost for 1 kWh

cost = 0.012 kW × 6 h × 6 p
cost = 0.43 p

Example 3
To work out how much it costs to use a vacuum cleaner for 30 minutes.
• power rating of vacuum cleaner = 1500 W = 1.5 kW
• vacuum cleaner used for 30 minutes = 0.5 h
• work out cost using the equation:
cost = power (kW) × time (h) × cost for 1 kWh

cost = 1.5 kW × 0.5 h × 6 p
cost = 4.5 p

Did you know?

Leaving a television on standby still uses electricity. Switching it off completely can save several pounds per year.

Key Facts

• Current passing through a resistor makes it heat up. Electric fires, kettles and cookers rely on this heating effect to work.
• We pay for the energy supplied by electricity companies. The energy supplied is measured in kilowatt hours (kWh).

Questions

1 Copy and complete:
Electricity is often used for heating in the home. This works because a .... current flowing through a .... will generate heat. Examples of appliances that use this heating effect are .... and .... The energy used from the mains supply is measured in .... (kWh).

2 Work out how much it costs to operate a range of appliances in your home.

3 Design and produce a short flyer to be sent from an electricity company to its customers explaining how to calculate the cost of running the appliances in their homes. This should be on a piece of A4 paper folded into 3. There should be text and images to explain the ideas clearly.

4 Work out for how much time you can operate a CD player for 20p using the information in the text.

5 If a device costs 12p to operate for 8 hours what is its power rating?

6 Which wastes most money, leaving a 100 W light on all day or leaving a 1.2 kW heater on for 2 hours?

Energy and electricity 181

Learning outcome

After completing the work in this topic you will be able to:

* explain how an electric current is generated on a small scale by a magnet rotating inside a coil, as in a bicycle dynamo, and on a large scale, as in the generation of electricity

It started with a flick...

A simple observation by a Danish physicist led to our present-day use of electricity. Hans Christian Oersted noticed that a compass needle flicked every time he switched on a simple battery-powered circuit he was building. Michael Faraday in England heard about this and managed to build the first electric motor. Ten years later, Faraday started working on electricity again and this time built the first ever electricity generator.

Magnetism...

Electricity and magnetism are always linked. Moving a magnet near to a wire will make a current flow in the wire (Figure 5.30). Faster movement, a more powerful magnet or more coils of wire give a bigger current. And it doesn't matter whether it's a tiny dynamo or a giant generator, they both work in exactly the same way (Figure 5.31).

Figure 5.30 The movement of the magnet inside the coil causes an electric current to flow in the coil.

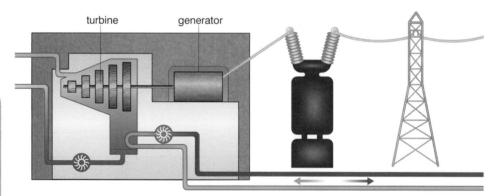

Figure 5.31 The giant generators in a power station generate electricity in the same way as a simple bicycle dynamo by rotating a magnet inside a coil of wire.

Transformers...

Many appliances now have **transformers** as part of their plugs, for example laptop computers and mobile phone chargers. Transformers are amazing devices. They create an electric current in a coil just because there is an electric current in another coil nearby. The two coils are not connected by wires in any way, and the power supply is only connected to one coil. Yet the second coil produces an electric current (Figure 5.33). The only thing the coils need is a thick iron core through their centres, which intensifies the magnetic field they experience.

Figure 5.33 The primary coil is fed by an alternating current and it produces a magnetic field around itself. The secondary coil feels this magnetic field and the result is an alternating current in the secondary coil.

The clever bit...

An amazing thing about transformers is that you can control exactly what voltage you want to get out of the secondary coil, and you can choose to have a much higher voltage than you put into the **primary coil** (Figure 5.34). Simply having 10 times as many coils of wire on the **secondary coil** will ensure that you get 10 times the voltage out compared with the voltage you put in ie. For a laptop computer, or charging a mobile phone the input may be 230 V but the output to the device may be only a few volts (Figure 5.35).

Key Facts

- Electricity is generated in power stations or bicycle dynamos by a magnet rotating inside a coil of wire.
- Transformers can change one voltage to another, for charging mobile phones for example.

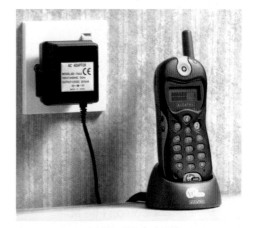

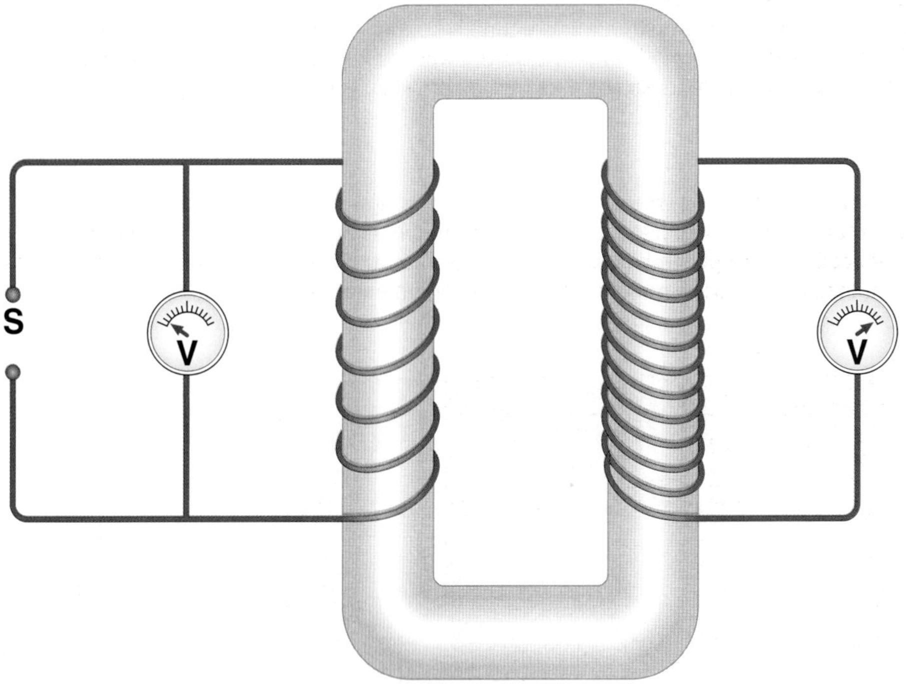

Figure 5.34 Ten times as many turns on the secondary coil gives you ten times the voltage you started with.

Figure 5.35 Charging a mobile phone only requires a very low voltage, but the transformer allows it to get what it needs direct from the mains.

Questions

1 Copy and complete:
An electric current is generated when a .... rotates inside a .... of wire. All electricity generating stations have enormous generators which generate electricity by rotating a .... inside a .... A small scale example of this idea is found in a bicycle ....

2 Explain briefly the difference between a dynamo and a transformer.

3 If a laptop neesds 20 V, what is the ratio of turns on the coils of its transformer?

biology   chemistry   **5.10**
physics

National Grid's problem...

The National Grid Company is responsible for transmitting electricity to the whole of the UK, and it's no simple job. Whenever an electric current flows through a conductor, the conductor gets hot and energy is wasted. This could mean that homes would never get enough electrical energy to run more than a couple of light bulbs as the rest would be lost as heat in the cables on the way to our houses. Luckily, scientists have worked out how to use transformers to solve this problem.

The solution...

Transformers can give us enormous increases in voltage. But of course you can't get something for nothing. You may get a massive increase in the voltage but you automatically get a massive decrease in the current. If the voltage is 10 times as big, then the current is 10 times smaller than when you started (Figure 5.36). Although this sounds like a drawback, in fact it is the big benefit of transformers.

Did you know?

If Thomas Edison had succeeded in persuading everyone to stick with d.c. electricity instead of a.c., we would all need a generator in our backyards and the enormous skyscrapers we see today could not exist as the electric current wouldn't be able to flow through the long lengths of wire without running out of energy.

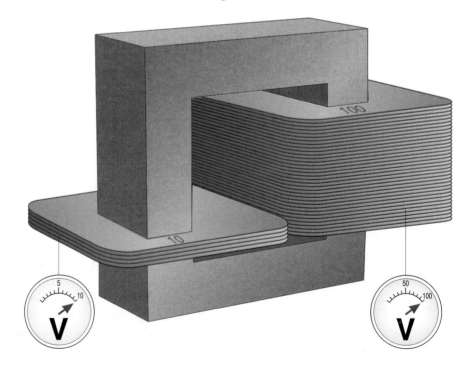

Figure 5.36 Ten times as many turns on the secondary coil gives you 10 times the voltage you started with but only $\frac{1}{10}$ of the current.

The transformation...

In our homes we use electricity at 230 V. Yet overhead cables carry up to 400 000 V. If this came into our houses it would be lethal.

Using a transformer to raise (**step up**) the transmission voltage to these extremely high values means that the transmission current is tiny. A tiny current creates a tiny amount of heat. By keeping the transmission voltage so high, National Grid makes sure that only a small amount of energy is wasted. In the end, this keeps our electricity bills down as well as making sure we receive enough power for our whole house (Figure 5.37). A stepdown transformer lowers the voltage to a safe 230 V before it is transmitted into our homes.

Tricks of the trade...

It is essential to know one thing about transformers – they only work with alternating current (a.c.). By changing the direction of the current, you get a changing magnetic field which affects the secondary coil. This is what sets the charged particles moving in the secondary coil. You get a.c. out.

Figure 5.37 Electricity is transmitted at very high voltages to save energy. Transforming to high voltages gives much smaller currents. The cables do not heat up so much and less energy is lost.

Key Facts

- Electricity is transmitted to our homes at very high voltages.
- It is 'stepped up' to high voltages using transformers because this makes the current very small and so makes sure that very little energy is lost as heat in the cables.
- Overhead cables are cheaper and easier to maintain than underground cables.
- Overhead cables cause less damage to the environment, although most people prefer not to see them in the countryside.

Questions

1   Copy and complete:

    When a transformer is used to give a massive increase in voltage, the current in the circuit is much .... It is important to have low currents flowing through the National Grid because this ....
    the amount of energy lost as
    ....

2   Explain why we would have very different lifestyles if transformers hadn't been invented

3   Read the interview with Simon Sutton (p.186) and then make a leaflet that explains the pros and cons of underground and overhead cables.

4   A transformer for a laptop takes the voltage down from

240 V to 20 V. If the current into the transformer is 0.2 A, what is the current fed to the laptop?

5   A power station will generate at around 32 kV and given a current of 20,000 A into the stepdown transformer. The overhead cables transmit at 400 kV. What do the cables carry?

Overground ...
Underground
Science Today

An interview with Simon Sutton at National Grid

Most people would prefer all overhead electricity power lines to be buried out of sight rather than straddling the countryside on large grey pylons. But as Simon Sutton of National Grid explains, the alternative – undergrounding – has its own environmental and technical problems.

"To most people, the big advantage of underground cables is that you cannot see them. The big disadvantage is that they cost a lot more to make and to lay underground, they are much more difficult to repair when things go wrong, and they can adversely affect the environment.

"Our network consists mainly of high voltage overhead lines (275 kV and 400 kV), but these only represent a fraction of all the overhead lines you see. The vast majority belong to the Regional Electricity Companies which supply electricity directly to your homes.

"Overhead lines have bare conductors as the air around them insulates them perfectly at no cost. In contrast, underground cables need substantial electrical insulation from the earth. Cables have to be buried 1 m deep to protect them from accidental damage, such as being dug up. This also means that the heat generated by the electrical current flowing through the cable cannot escape easily. To stop the ground around the cables becoming too warm, we have to space the cables a long way apart. On the other hand, overhead lines are cooled efficiently by the air around them (Figure 5.38).

Figure 5.38 Underground cables have to be insulated from the earth, while the air around overhead cables is a natural insulator.

"In order to bury cables that carry the same power as an overhead line, we usually need to dig four separate trenches each containing three cables. This can be as much space as the width of a dual carriageway and means moving 30 times as much soil as for overhead lines (Figure 5.39). All the extra work needed to lay the cables, and their more complicated design, means that overall, 1 km of underground cable route costs £10 million whereas the total cost of pylons and other equipment for 1 km of overhead route (including construction costs) is £500 000.

"There's also the problem of maintenance. Although our equipment is very reliable, we all know that things break down from time to time. With overhead lines, many of the faults are easy to see (you just look up!), and most can be repaired within a few hours. To locate and repair a fault in an underground cable can often take days or even weeks.

Figure 5.39 Overhead cables have a big visual impact.

Figure 5.40 Underground cables make a big impact on the landscape during construction and they also restrict land use.

"Most people would argue that overhead cables look ugly and therefore have a negative impact on the environment. But laying underground cables can disturb sensitive habitats and archaeological sites, and unfortunately the effects are sometimes irreversible. Nevertheless, in some areas of scenic beauty, we consider that underground cables are preferable and the extra cost is justified.

"Once overhead cables have been built, the land can be brought back into use quickly, and crops can be grown again, for example. On the other hand, underground cables prevent farmers from ploughing deeper than 45 cm, and trees and hedges cannot be allowed to grow because of the damage caused by their roots. It's also important that we are able to reach the cables in case we need to make a repair, so this further limits what can be planted above the cables.

"We try to avoid inhabited areas when choosing a route for pylons. In densely populated urban areas like London, overhead lines are impractical so we have to use underground cables. Of course the 230 V supply into most homes is by underground cable, but compared to National Grid's cables, these cables are a lot smaller, are easier to lay and are so much cheaper.

"At National Grid we have a duty to maintain an efficient and economical system for electricity transmission so we are always looking for improvements, such as assessing the benefits of new technology and maximising our use of the existing equipment."

Simon Sutton is a Cables Engineer at National Grid. He studied Physics and obtained a PhD from the University of Reading before getting his present job.

Energy for life

Learning outcome

After completing the work in this topic you will be able to:

- understand a range of energy transfer chains showing the environmental implications of generating electricity, including fossil fuel reserves and their use in generating electricity, the use of wind and waves in generating electricity, and solar heating systems and solar cells to produce electricity

The big dilemma…

Electricity is the cleanest, most convenient fuel we use. It can heat, cook, light and drive machines. It runs computers. It is instantaneous and completely controllable. It is the perfect fuel. Except… it creates pollution at the power station and is quickly using up all of the world's fossil fuel reserves – coal, oil and especially gas (Figure 5.41). Some people believe we should not be allowed to continue to use electricity so carelessly. Others point out that there are a number of alternative ways of generating electricity which should be developed further.

Fossil fuels

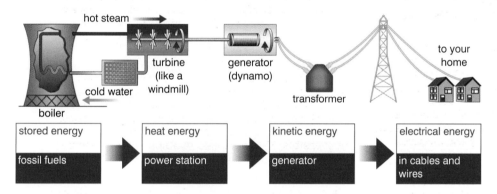

Figure 5.41 Fossil fuels are easily burnt to heat water in a power station. The steam produced turns the turbines. The magnet rotating inside the coil of wire generates electricity, which is delivered instantly to our homes through the National Grid. The drawback is that burning fossil fuels creates pollution and uses up our non-renewable fuel reserves.

Did you know?

Electricity has to be generated and transmitted to us as soon as we turn on an appliance. A major national event on television, such as a football final, can cause terrible problems for the electricity generating companies. If everyone switches on their kettle during half time, the generating stations will suddenly have to increase production, perhaps by starting up additional turbines!

Wind and waves…

People have used water and wind power for generations, but windmills and watermills were replaced by the more modern form of power – electricity generated from fossil fuels. We now find ourselves in trouble as pollution increases and fossil fuel reserves run out. Wind and wave power may soon be the best way forward, and the UK has excellent supplies of both (Figures 5.42 and 5.43).

Wave power

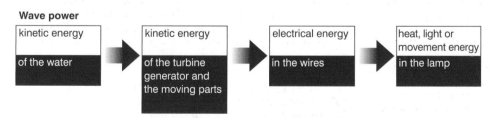

Figure 5.42 Movement energy from the wind or water rotates a turbine and generates electricity. This is fed into the National Grid and transmitted to any user in the country.

Energy and electricity (187)

Key Facts

- Fossil fuels are burnt to generate electricity but they are running out and they cause pollution.
- Renewable energy sources, such as wind, wave, water and solar power, are being developed to take over, gradually, from fossil fuels.

Did you know?

The latest way that scientists are using the sun is to electrolyse water to form hydrogen, which can then generate electricity in a fuel cell. Fuel cells will allow us to use solar energy to drive our cars and heat our homes, even when it is dark!

Hydroelectric power

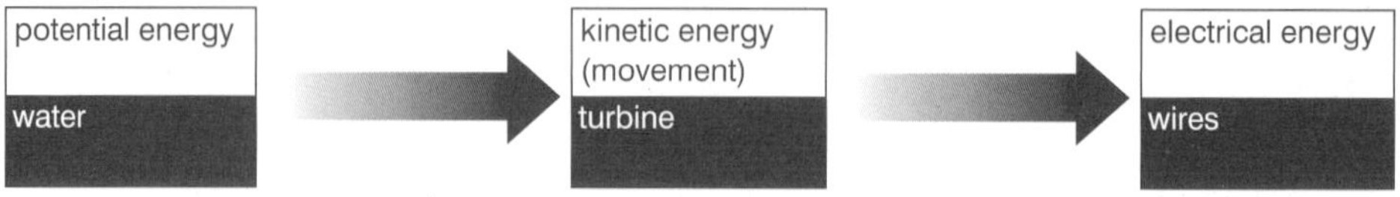

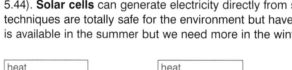

Figure 5.43 The potential energy of the water at the top is converted to movement energy of the water. This turns the turbine and generates electricity. The electricity is transmitted via the National Grid.

Solar power...

The UK does not have a good sunshine record. Yet scientists have succeeded in making solar heating systems and generating electricity from solar power even here.

Solar panels on the roof of a house can be used to heat up water for washing (Figure 5.44). **Solar cells** can generate electricity directly from sunlight (Figure 5.45). Both techniques are totally safe for the environment but have the drawback that most energy is available in the summer but we need more in the winter.

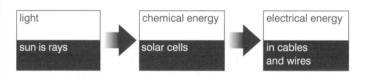

Figure 5.44 Solar panels are full of water. They absorb heat energy from the sun to warm the water directly.

Figure 5.45 Solar cells generate electricity directly from the energy in sunlight.

Questions

1 Copy and complete:
Fossil fuels such as .... and .... can be burnt in power stations to generate electricity. When fossil fuels are burnt in the power station, they heat .... which produces steam. The steam turns the .... to generate electricity. There are two main problems with using fossil fuels to generate electricity: .... and ....

2 Explain why electricity can be described as the perfect fuel.

3 Fossil fuels are described as non-renewable forms of energy. Explain what non-renewable means.

4 What are renewable energy resources?

... more at www.modularscience.co.uk

Learning outcome

After completing the work in this topic you will be able to:

* describe the advantages and disadvantages of methods of large-scale electricity production using a variety of renewable and non-renewable resources

Is there an answer?

Coal, oil, gas, solar, wind, wave or hydrogen? It is very difficult to identify the best method for generating electricity. People are still debating the pros and cons. There is no doubt that science will provide a solution.

Ann MacGarry works as an Education Officer at the Centre for Alternative Technology in Wales. The centre is dedicated to showing how sustainable technology can be used in everyday life and it welcomes visitors to see how they generate electricity, build energy-efficient houses, grow organic produce and recycle materials.

Ann has looked into the advantages and disadvantages of a range of methods of large-scale electricity production using a variety of renewable resources. In this interview, Ann explains what she has found out.

Q: "What is your interest in looking at renewable resources?"
Ann: "There is a desperate urgency to reduce our use of fossil fuels. This is most important because of the amount of carbon dioxide we are putting into the atmosphere and the effect it may be having on the world's climate."

Q: "So which method of electricity generation from renewable resources do you think has the most potential in the UK?"
Ann: "Wind power is our biggest resource. It is relatively cheap, relatively easy to construct and maintain and there is a good energy payback. Most wind farms are built on land that is not needed for other things. For example, on the coast at Blyth, in old docks in Liverpool, out at sea, or on upland hill sites. In fact, a farmer with a hill farm in Wales would make 90 p per year grazing his sheep on the land occupied by a wind turbine. He could get £1000 rent for having a wind turbine there instead, so farmers are usually very happy to have a wind farm on their land."

Q: "But there are people who say that wind turbines take up a lot of space, and that they are noisy and unattractive."
Ann: "The only real disadvantage of wind power is that it is visible. I personally think that wind turbines are beautiful. When I look at them I think they are providing clean energy so they've got to be better than power stations. And wind power isn't really noisy. It's no noisier than other ways of generating electricity. Traditional power stations and hydroelectric installations are noisy too. Finally, it's worth pointing out that conventional power stations take up a lot of space, and it's space that could be used for other things, such as housing or farmland."

Q: "Is wind power the only sensible option in your opinion?"
Ann: "Tidal power is another option. We can build large barrages across estuaries to generate electricity as the tide goes in and out. They have to be designed so that ships can still pass in and out of the estuaries. The big disadvantage is that the barrages affect wildlife habitats in the estuary. My concern is what will happen to these habitats anyway if we don't do something about pollution and climate change."

Did you know?

Did you know?

There are already several companies and private households using hydrogen fuel cells, especially in Canada, the USA and Germany. Some people even predict a time when there will be no National Grid and each house or group of houses will have a hydrogen fuel cell in their back yard. This will mean an end to power cuts.

Key Facts

- Renewable resources contribute less than 3% of the electricity used in the UK.
- We need to develop a mix of renewable resources.

Q: "Some people mention wave power. Do you think that is an option?"

Ann: "Wave power is another way of using wind power. It's very interesting. There are many devices being invented to use wave power. It needs a lot more research and development to get them built cheaply enough and robustly enough. It is possible that wave power may become cheaper than wind power."

Q: "And what about hydroelectric power?"

Ann: "Hydro is great in a way. It lasts a long time and becomes very cheap to produce. In fact, it's the cheapest electricity we produce in the UK at the moment. But, at the very most, we could only produce about 5% of our electricity this way and we don't have the scope for building more hydroelectric power stations. The 5% would include a number of small-scale installations but at any scale there is some physical change to the environment. There is always a legal requirement to consider the impact on local habitats, even though there is no requirement to consider the long-term global effect of what we are doing already."

Q: "Then there's solar power. Is that viable in the UK?"

Ann: "Solar power for generating electricity is too expensive at the moment for large-scale generation and the UK doesn't get much sun when we use most energy. But solar power for heating domestic water is certainly viable now."

Q: "So which way do you think we should go?"

Ann: "It shouldn't be seen as either–or. We need a mix of resources. The big advantage of wind and wave power is that they match our consumption – it's windier in the winter when we demand most electricity. Unfortunately, wind is a very variable resource and we are limited by what the National Grid can cope with from a variable resource. I understand that the grid could cope with 20% of our electricity generated by variable resources such as wind power without changing the way electricity is distributed. At the moment, renewable resources contribute less than 3% of the electricity used in the UK. I think, as a general point, we should look critically at the advantages and disadvantages of all the methods of generating electricity. Saying that the visual impact of a wind farm is comparable with the effect on the environment of the pollution produced by a coal-burning power station is not a realistic analysis, in my opinion."

Questions

1. Make a table that lists all the renewable and non-renewable energy resources. For each energy resource, list all the advantages and disadvantages.

2. Write a magazine article explaining what renewable energy resources are and why we need to research into them.

3. Use secondary sources to research the proportions of electricity provided by each source and display it as a pie chart.

... more at www.modularscience.co.uk

Insulation

Whether global warming is true or not, in northern Europe we spend much of our time trying to keep warm. From an early age, we are taught to 'wrap up warm', and to 'draw the curtains to keep the heat in'. Automatically, we are using the science of insulation to make ourselves comfortable. Heat naturally tries to flow from a warmer area to a cooler area. Good insulators prevent heat passing through them. We select good insulators of heat to prevent the heat energy from conducting away so that we can keep warm. Wherever we use them, they have one thing in common – lots of air pockets. Trapped air is a poor conductor and therefore it is a good insulator. If the air is not trapped, warm air will rise in convection currents and its heat will be taken to cooler areas and lost (Figure 5.46).

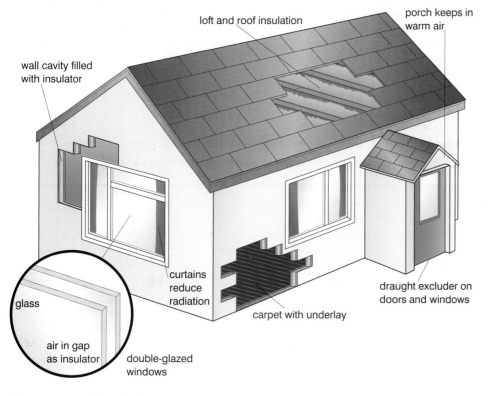

loft and roof insulation

porch keeps in warm air

wall cavity filled with insulator

glass

air in gap as insulator

double-glazed windows

curtains reduce radiation

carpet with underlay

draught excluder on doors and windows

Figure 5.46 A well-insulated house saves energy.

Did you know?

Insulators only work against conduction of heat. They cannot prevent heat from radiating away. If you need to stop radiant heat, the best way is to reflect it back where it came from using something shiny. Many people put aluminium foil on the wall behind their radiator to reflect heat into the room that would otherwise simply warm up the wall.

The future…

More recent developments for conserving heat include energy-efficient windows with a thin film coating, which reflects heat back into the room, and 'smart' windows, which can grow dark or can reflect light in hot weather to keep us cool.

A new material called aerogel has been developed, which is so good at insulating that 2.5 cm of it insulates as well as 25 cm of fibreglass or a window with 10 double panes of glass.

Saving money…

The big advantage of conserving heat using insulation is that you need to produce less heat. This is obviously cheaper and it means that there is less impact on the environment from generating the energy. There are other ways we can keep costs down and do our bit for the environment. All appliances are now graded A–E on how energy-efficient they are. Buying **energy-efficient** appliances, everything from dishwashers and fridges to light bulbs, makes a difference (Figure 5.47).

Figure 5.47 Appliances now have to be labelled with their energy efficiency rating so that customers can see how much the appliance costs to run.

Questions

1 Copy and complete:

Heat naturally flows from a .... place to a .... place. Good insulators of heat prevent heat from .... This is because they have pockets of trapped .... in them. Warm air rises and is lost in .... currents.

2 Conduct a survey of the class to see what forms of insulation students' homes have. See if there is any link between the insulation used and the age of the home. Find out why older homes typically have less insulation than more modern homes.

3 Explain why energy-efficient devices make a difference to our quality of life.

1.   The current in a wire was measured at different voltages.
      The table shows the results.

Current in amperes (A)	0.20	0.35	0.55	0.70	0.85
Voltage in volts (V)	0.8	1.4	2.2	2.8	3.4

(a)   Use the data to draw a graph of current against voltage.   (3)

(b)   Describe how the current in the wire changes when the voltage is increased.   (2)

                                                                                    (Total 5 marks)

Edexcel June 2003 (Specimen Paper), Paper 1P no. 5

2.   The diagram shows a circuit for emergency lighting.

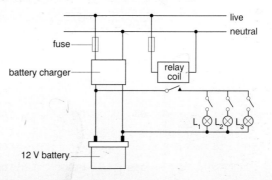

If the mains supply fails the relay switch closes and the lamps operate from the 12 V
battery.

(a)   Write down ONE reason for connecting the lamps in parallel.   (1)

(b)   When switched on, the current in each lamp is 5 A.

(i)   Calculate the current in the battery when all three lamps are switched on.   (1)

(ii)   Calculate the power of each lamp.   (3)

(c)   Lamps in emergency lighting circuits are connected to the battery using thick wires. Mains
       lamps of the same power are connected using thinner wires. Explain why.   (2)

                                                                                    (Total 7 marks)

Edexcel no. 11

3.   The diagram shows a circuit which contains a light dependent resistor (LDR).

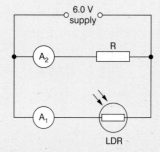

(a) On the circuit diagram, draw a voltmeter labelled V to measure the potential difference across the LDR. (1)

(b) (i) State the equation that shows the relationship between voltage (V), current (I) and resistance (R). (1)

(ii) Use this relationship to help you explain how the current in A_1 changes but the current in A_2 stays the same when the intensity of the light shining on the LDR increases. (4)

(Total 6 marks)

Edexcel June 1999, Paper 1H no. 15

4. The table below gives information about some of the energy sources that are used to generate electricity in the United Kingdom

Energy	Renewable	Combustion products	Known world reserves	Efficiency of electricity production
coal	no	carbon dioxide water sulphur dioxide	200 years	40%
oil	no	carbon dioxide water sulphur dioxide	40 years	35%
gas	no	carbon dioxide water	65 years	50%
wind	yes	none	none	40%

(a) (i) Which of these energy sources are fossil fuels? (2)

(ii) Why is wind described as being renewable?

(b) In recent years, gas-burning power stations have replaced many coal-burning ones.
(i) Give TWO advantages of burning gas rather than coal in power stations. (2)

(ii) Give ONE advantage of burning gas rather than coal in power stations. (1)

(c) Suggest TWO reasons why only a small proportion of our electricity is generated from wind. (2)

(d) Explain why it is important to develop renewable energy sources. (2)

(Total 10 marks)

Edexcel June 2003 (Specimen Paper), Paper 1P no. 3

5.   The diagram shows the energy flow from an uninsulated house.

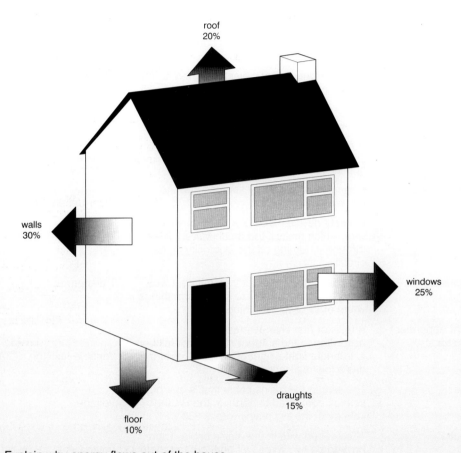

(a)   Explain why energy flows out of the house.   (1)

(b)   Where does the greatest energy loss occur?   (1)

    (Total 2 marks)

(c)   Suggest THREE ways of insulating the house.   (3)

(d)   Explain the advantages of insulating a house.   (2)

    (Total 7 marks)

Glossary 5

Alternating current	Current that flows alternately one way, then the opposite way, around a circuit. Mains current in the UK changes back and forth 50 times a second.
Ammeter	An instrument for measuring current, or the flow of charge in a circuit.
Diode	A device which allows electric current to flow in only one direction through it.
Direct current	Current that flows in only one direction around a circuit.
Earth	A safety wire to protect you from electrocution if the case of an electrical appliance accidentally becomes live.
Fossel fuels	Non-renewable energy sources burnt to release energy.
Fuse	A safety device made of a piece of very thin wire, which melts if too much current flows through it, turning off the electricity in the circuit.
Insulation	A material that does not transmit heat well. Insulation can be used to keep warm things warm or to keep cool things cool.
Light dependent resistor	A resistor that changes resistance according to the amount of light that falls on it. In bright light a light dependent resistor has a low resistance.
Live	The wire in the mains cable that is at a high voltage compared to earth. In the UK the voltage of the live mains wire is 230 V.
Neutral	The second wire in the mains cable. There have to be two wires ('in' and 'out') or there could not be a complete circuit.
Primary coil	The first coil in a transformer, that the input voltage is connected to.

Renewable energy	Energy resource which does not run out. Examples include solar, wind or water power.
Residual current circuit breaker	A safety device that measures the current in the live wire and the neutral wire and turns off the power if they are different, for instance if any current is flowing through you!
Resistance	A measure of how hard it is for electric current to pass through a component. A high resistance causes a low current.
Secondary coil	The second coil in a transformer. The output of the transformer is connected to the secondary coil.
Solar cells	Cells that use the energy in sunlight to generate electricity.
Solar panels	Panels that use the energy in sunlight to heat water.
Thermistor	A resistor that changes resistance according to its temperature. At a high temperature the thermistor has a low resistance.
Transformer	A device for changing the voltage. Transformers are commonly used in computers, mobile phone and electric toys, as well as to step up the voltage for transmission across the country.
Variable resistor	A resistor that can be changed to make it easier or harder for current to flow through. A dimmer switch is a variable resistor.
Voltage	A measure of the energy of the electric charge around a circuit. Increasing the voltage increases the current.
Voltmeter	An instrument for measuring the voltage in a circuit.

In this module you will learn about some of the most exciting parts of physics. Everyone is curious about where we came from, whether there is extraterrestrial life somewhere in the universe and what will happen when the Sun dies or the universe comes to an end. In this module you will find out more about the Big Bang, which began it all, what we know about the universe so far and whether it will all end in a Big Crunch.

We are living in a communications explosion. It seems that everyone has a mobile phone and the number of digital television channels grows every month. This module looks at how this has suddenly become possible.

But communications only use a small part of the electromagnetic spectrum. Physics can control all parts of the spectrum for everything from cooking and household security to advanced medical procedures.

You will be able to see just how useful the spectrum has become, and also the dangers it still holds.

Over half the population has been the subject of an ultrasound scan. Sound seems simple but has far more uses than most people realise. Observing unborn babies and locating obstacles at sea are two uses for sound that we consider.

We have evolved to live in a world where background radiation from the Earth and from outer space is normal. We are now making radioactive materials deliberately. Some are useful for medical treatments or form the heart of a smoke detector. Others are a by-product of nuclear power. How we dispose of the radioactive waste from these activities is a cause for concern. This module looks at the various options and how science is keeping us safe from contamination.

6

Waves

After completing the work in this topic you will be able to:

* describe transverse waves in terms of frequency, wavelength and amplitude
* recall that all electromagnetic waves travel at the same speed in a vacuum

Radio ga-ga…

BBC Radio 1: 97.6–99.8 FM
BBC Radio 5 Live: 693–909 MW
Virgin Radio: 1197, 1215, 1233, 1242 MW

These numbers identify exactly where to tune your radio to pick up each station. But they are actually giving out very different information.

FM stands for frequency modulated. The number is the **frequency** of the radio wave that travels from the transmitter to the radio. Your radio has to be tuned to recognise the particular frequency of the radio station you want. BBC Radio 1 transmits at 97.6 kHz (kilohertz). This means that there are 97 600 radio waves per second arriving at your radio (Figure 6.1). Hertz means 'waves per second'.

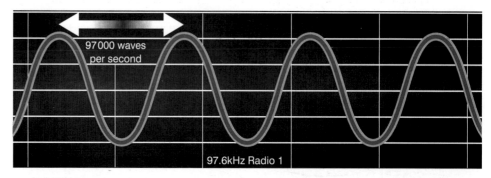

Figure 6.1 BBC Radio 1 transmits on a frequency of 97.6 kHz. It sends 97 600 radio waves per second to your radio.

MW stands for medium wave. The number is the **wavelength** of the radio wave. Virgin Radio transmits radio waves that have a wavelength of 1197 m – over 1 km! (Figure 6.2). Your radio has to be switched to medium wave and tuned to receive waves with this wavelength.

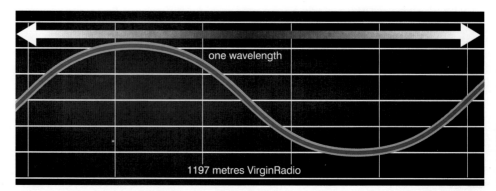

Figure 6.2 Virgin Radio transmits on a wavelength of 1197 m – the radio waves are 1197 m long.

The speed of light…

All radio waves have one thing in common – they all travel at the same speed across space (where there is a vacuum). They travel at the amazing speed of 300 000 000 m/s. Nothing can travel faster than this.

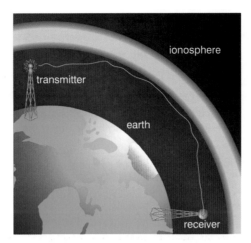

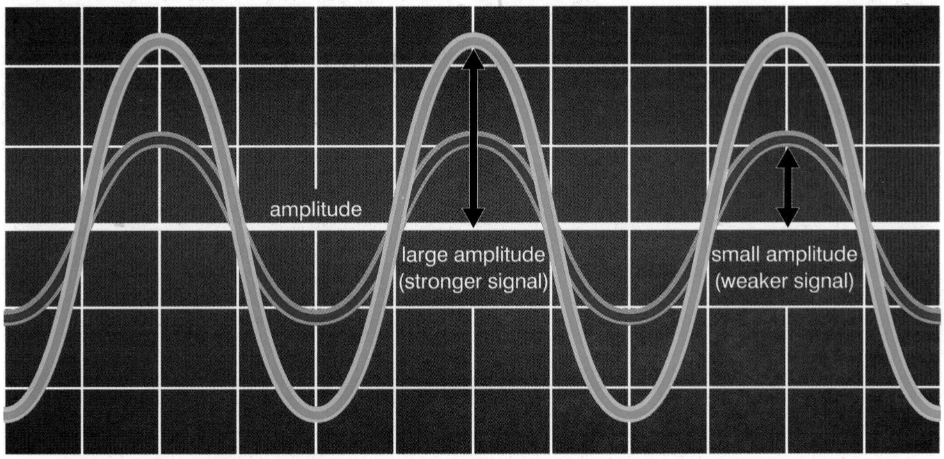

Figure 6.3 Short-wave radio waves can go round the Earth by bouncing off the atmosphere.

Getting mobile…

Mobile phones also use electromagnetic waves but they have much shorter wavelengths than radio waves. They are called microwaves and have a frequency of between 900 MHz and 1800 MHz. The transmitters you see along the motorway receive the signal from your phone and send them to another phone when you ring someone. If you are too far from a transmitter, your phone will indicate that you are getting a low-strength signal. What this means is that the **amplitude** of the signal is too small so it is carrying too little energy for your phone to be able to decode it (Figure 6.4).

Figure 6.4 A smaller amplitude wave carries less energy.

Did you know?

All electromagnetic waves travel in straight lines but short wavelength radio waves can bounce off a layer in the atmosphere and this is how they go round the curve of the Earth (Figure 6.3).

Key Facts

- **The wave frequency is the number of waves per second, measured in Hertz.**
- **The wavelength is the length of one wave (including a peak and trough) measured in metres.**
- **The wave amplitude is the maximum displacement of a particle from its normal position.**

Questions

1 Copy and complete:
The length of one complete wave (a peak and a trough) is called the .... It is measured in .... The number of waves formed per second is called the .... It is measured in .... All .... waves travel at the same speed (300 000 000 m/s) in a ....

2 Explain why the amplitude of a radio wave is important.

3 Draw an illustration which will help someone remember the difference between wavelength, amplitude and frequency.

Keep waving

Learning outcomes

After completing the work in this topic you will be able to:

- recall that the electromagnetic spectrum includes radio waves, microwaves, infra-red (IR) radiation, visible light, ultraviolet (UV) radiation, X-rays and gamma rays

- recall the order of the electromagnetic spectrum in increasing frequency and decreasing wavelength, including the colours of the visible spectrum

- recall that energy is associated with electromagnetic waves, and thus their potential danger increases with frequency

- describe transverse and longitudinal waves in terms of frequency, wavelength and amplitude

Spectrum...

In fact radio waves and microwaves are only part of a whole family of waves that can travel through the vacuum of space at the speed of light. They are called **electromagnetic waves** and they make up the **electromagnetic spectrum**. It includes:
- radio waves – for communication
- microwaves – for cooking and mobile phones
- infrared waves (IR) – for cooking and night vision
- visible light – for seeing
- ultraviolet (UV) – for suntans
- X-rays – for seeing broken bones
- gamma rays – for treating cancer

As you go down this list, the wavelength gets shorter (Figure 6.5). Gamma rays have a wavelength about the size of a single atom!

short wavelength

wavelength (in metres) 10^{-12}m 10^{-11}m 10^{-10}m 10^{-9}m 10^{-8}m 10^{-7}m 10^{-6}m

1nm   1μm

gamma rays   X-rays   ultra-violet   V R

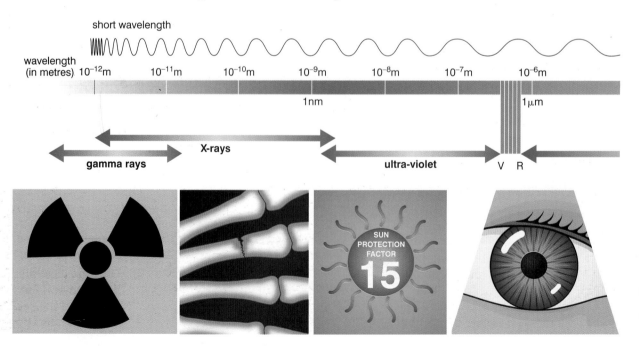

Figure 6.5 The electromagnetic spectrum.

Warning…

As you go down the list, the frequency of the waves gets higher. High-frequency waves carry a lot more energy than low-frequency ones so they are potentially a lot more dangerous. That's why it's perfectly safe to have radio waves in your house but ultraviolet (UV) can cause skin cancer, while X-rays and gamma rays can kill people when they occur in high doses, such as in atomic bombs.

Transverse…

All of these electromagnetic waves are called **transverse waves**. The ripples on a pond are also transverse waves because the water goes up and down while the wave travels across the pond. Scientists say that transverse waves occur when the disturbance is at right angles to the direction the wave is travelling (Figure 6.6). The amplitude of a transverse wave is how far the particles are moved from their normal position.

Did you know?

A student was asked to name two types of waves. He could remember the answer longitudinal waves, but struggled to remember the other – until he had a bright idea and wrote down… latitudinal waves!

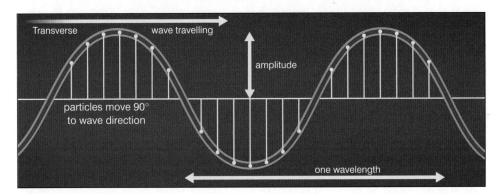

Figure 6.6 In a transverse wave, the disturbance is at right angles to the direction the wave is moving.

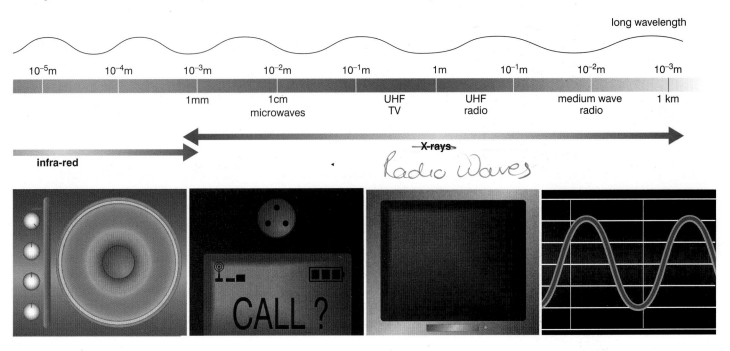

Key Facts

- Electromagnetic waves include radio waves, microwaves, infrared radiation, visible light, ultraviolet light, X-rays and gamma rays (in order of increasing frequency).

- Higher frequency waves carry more energy so are more dangerous. All electromagnetic waves travel at the same speed in a vacuum.

- Transverse waves are waves where the disturbance is at right angles to the direction the wave is travelling. Examples are ripples on water, waves on a string and all electromagnetic waves.

- Longitudinal waves are waves where the disturbance is along the direction the wave is travelling. Examples include sound waves and shock (seismic) waves.

Longitudinal…

Shock waves such as the thump, thump up your spine when you go to sit on a chair, miss and land on the floor, are called **longitudinal waves**. A longitudinal wave has a disturbance in the same direction as the direction the wave is moving (Figure 6.7). Sound is a longitudinal wave and the pulse that travels down a slinky spring is longitudinal too.

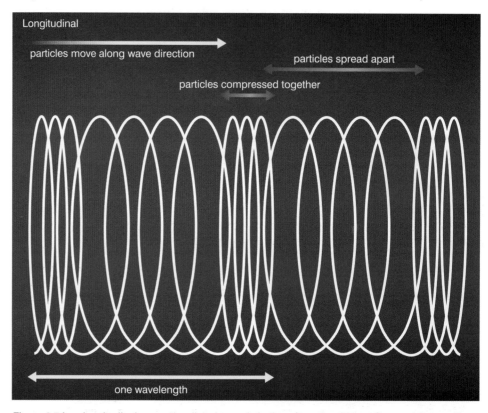

Figure 6.7 In a longitudinal wave, the disturbance is in the same direction as the wave is travelling.

Questions

1 Copy and complete:

In order of decreasing wavelength, the electromagnetic spectrum consists of
……………, …………… ,
…………… , …………… ,
…………… , …………… and
…………… The danger from electromagnetic waves
…………… as the frequency increases. All electromagnetic waves travel at the speed of light in a ……………

2 Write a revision guide for a student to explain the differences between transverse waves and longitudinal waves and also explain how the words frequency, wavelength, amplitude and speed can be used for both types of wave.

3 Class activity: make a decorative wallchart of a wave with varying frequency, wavelength and amplitude. Indicate short-wavelength/high-frequency areas compared with long-wavelength/low-frequency areas. Also mark the large and small amplitude regions.

… more at www.modularscience.co.uk

After completing the work in this topic you will be able to:

- explain that radio waves are used for broadcasting and communication
- explain that microwaves are used for cooking and satellite communication
- explain that infrared radiation is used for grills, night vision, remote controls, security systems and treatment of muscular problems
- explain that visible light is used for vision and photography
- explain that ultraviolet light is used for sun beds, security marking, fluorescent lamps and detecting forged bank notes
- explain that X-rays are used for observing the internal structure of objects or bodies
- explain that gamma rays are used for sterilising food and medical equipment, and treating cancers

The e.m. revolution…

Over millions of years of evolution the human animal has developed into a highly effective detector of electromagnetic waves (Figure 6.8).

  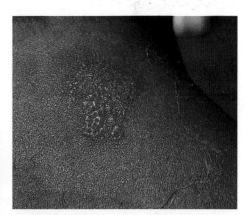

Figure 6.8 Humans have evolved to detect electromagnetic waves, seeing visible light, feeling heat from a fire or suffering sunburn from the ultraviolet rays of the sun.

- The human eye can sense exactly what frequency of visible light is hitting the retina and we see colour.
- Human skin can feel the warmth from the sun and from fires. It is reacting to the infrared waves.
- Human skin also senses the ultraviolet part of the spectrum and either suffers sunburn or develops a tan to protect itself from further damage.

Only in the last 100 years have humans worked out how to make use of the rest of the electromagnetic spectrum.

Figure 6.9 Some of the uses of radio waves.

Figure 6.10 Some of the uses of microwaves.

Figure 6.11 Some of the uses of infrared waves.

Radio waves…

To the Victorians, the telegraph system was their equivalent of the Internet, allowing immediate communication across the world. Now we use radio waves to receive a whole range of communications and we don't just restrict ourselves to terrestrial signals (Figure 6.9). Signals from satellites in orbit around the equator send us TV and radio programmes, allow us to phone relatives in the USA or Australia with perfect sound quality, or provide GPS (global positioning system) information on boats and in our cars, so we don't get lost.

Microwaves…

Some people claim that the most significant development in recent times has been the mobile phone. Tiny, pocket-sized devices can receive faxes, access the Internet and have the computing power of a desktop PC, as well as being used for conventional phone calls. Without microwaves this couldn't happen (Figure 6.10). Microwave transmitters are appearing everywhere to satisfy our demand to communicate. They are often disguised as trees so that they do not ruin the landscape!

Infrared…

For a long time, nature had the upper hand at night. The ability of humans to see in the dark is very limited, so we have evolved to sleep at night. Other animals have much better night vision and some don't need light at all. They sense infrared waves (the body heat) of their prey. Now humans are catching up (Figure 6.11). Infrared cameras allow victims of earthquakes buried under rubble to be seen. The camera senses the infrared from their body heat. The same cameras allow criminals to be tracked by police helicopters at night. Closer to home, TV remote controls rely on an infrared beam sent to the TV to change the channel, and many household alarm systems use infrared to sense an intruder. Athletes benefit from infrared when they receive heat treatment for muscular problems, while anyone who has ever used a grill or a toaster has relied on infrared to cook their food.

Visible…

For a long time, talented painters were highly regarded for their ability to paint realistic copies of scenes from nature. Then, with the invention of basic photography – the realisation that visible light could affect chemicals on a photographic plate – came the beginning of a complete change of attitude. Suddenly anyone could copy a scene from nature, perfectly, at the push of a button. It was from that time on that artists began to look for more original ways to portray a scene (Figure 6.12). This led to the Impressionists, the Surrealists, the Cubists and others who used their talent and imagination to do things a mere machine could never achieve.

Figure 6.12 An artist can portray a scene so that we perceive it differently.

Ultraviolet…

'Mad dogs and Englishmen go out in the midday sun'… so the saying goes. Certainly no self-respecting lady from Egyptian times to the Edwardian era would risk being tanned by the ultraviolet rays from the sun. A pale skin was always a sign of respectability, proving you didn't have to work out of doors like the lower classes. Now that we are all confined to offices, shops, factories and schools, a tanned skin is a sign of a good holiday. For those who prefer to cheat, sun beds can give out enough ultraviolet radiation for a deep tan in just a few hours (Figure 6.13).

Many animals can see ultraviolet light. Bees, for example, can sense ultraviolet light reflected from some flowers and see them as 'bee purple'. Ultraviolet light reflects off certain inks so that forged bank notes can be detected. Signatures on building society savings books or identification marks written on personal possessions can be kept secret from potential thieves as the writing is invisible until ultraviolet light is reflected off it (Figure 6.14). Washing powders often contain brighteners, which stick to clothes and reflect ultraviolet light to make the clothes seem 'bright white'.

Figure 6.13 The effects of ultraviolet light on skin.

Figure 6.14 Some of the uses of ultraviolet waves.

Energy and electricity 205

X-rays...

Henri Becquerel experimented on his wife when he first worked out how to use X-rays to see the internal structure of the body. The X-ray he took of her hand, showing the bones and her wedding ring on her 4th finger, is now quite famous. X-rays were soon used for everything from seeing inside Egyptian mummies to checking that people's shoes didn't squash their feet. Nowadays, X-rays are used more carefully but have many more uses. Medical physicists in hospitals and archaeologists still use X-rays, but now industrial plants also use them to check for cracks in metals or see how well a weld has formed (Figure 6.15).

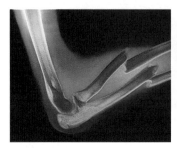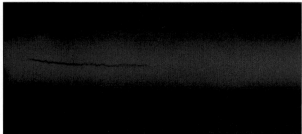

Figure 6.15 Some of the uses of X-rays.

Gamma rays...

Gamma rays come from radioactive materials or as cosmic rays from outer space. They have always been around as part of the 'background radiation'. Science fiction writers have enjoyed telling stories about the terrible effects of gamma rays on people, all of them untrue! It has been discovered that gamma rays can sterilise food or an item of medical equipment by destroying the bacteria on its surface without taking it out of its container. More significantly, gamma rays can destroy cancer cells and cure people of this terrible disease (Figure 6.16).

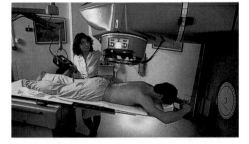

Figure 6.16 Some of the uses of gamma rays.

Questions

1 Make a large table to list all the waves in the electromagnetic spectrum and the uses of each type of wave.

2 Class exercise: make a 'wave-line' around the room to show the entire electromagnetic spectrum in order and illustrate (both images and written explanations) the uses of each part of the spectrum. Different teams can be responsible for different parts of the spectrum.

Radiation risks

Mobile phones under test...

There's a story that a lady bathed her poodle and put it into her microwave oven to dry. Whether this is true or not, any animal would die quite quickly if put into a microwave oven. The microwave part of the electromagnetic spectrum heats body tissue very effectively, which is why microwave ovens cook food so quickly. Some people know this fact and assume that the microwaves from mobile phone transmitters are equally dangerous. They forget that the amount of microwave energy from a transmitter is tiny compared with a microwave oven, and it is of a different frequency. However, tests are still being done to find out whether this new technology might have detrimental effects on people's health (Figure 6.17).

Figure 6.17 Mobile phones are tested for the possible harmful effects of microwaves.

Infrared burns...

Even infrared radiation has its risks. High intensity infrared will cause skin burns. Lasers give out ultraviolet, infrared or visible light but it is so concentrated that they too can cause damage to eyes, and more powerful ones can burn skin. The highest intensity lasers are able to burn through sheet metal (Figure 6.18).

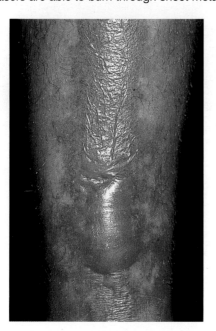

Figure 6.18 Some of the effects of infrared radiation.

Waves, atoms and space   207

Key Facts

- Some electromagnetic waves cause damage.
- Microwaves can cause excessive heating of body tissue.
- Infrared radiation causes skin burns.
- Ultraviolet light damages cells and may increase the risk of skin cancer.
- X-rays damage internal cells.

Increasing cancer risk...

Ultraviolet light is responsible for the recent epidemic in skin cancer in Australia. All exposure to sunlight causes damage to the surface cells of the skin. At first this is not noticeable. After a few years, the skin shows signs of ageing – wrinkling, leathery appearance, loss of elasticity. Worse than this is the increased chance of skin cancer. Treatment might require a large area of flesh to be removed, but in some cases the cancer proves to be fatal. Even using the highest protection suncreams is no guarantee of avoiding skin cancer (Figure 6.19).

X-rays...

Medical uses of radiation contribute by far the largest part of our exposure to man-made radiation. Even though this is far less than the radiation we receive from natural sources, hospitals are very careful to monitor the amount each patient receives, as too high a dose of X-rays will damage a patient's cells. This may make the affected organ work less effectively and could leave the patient quite ill. Everyone who works in the radiation area of a hospital has to wear a radiation badge to make sure they do not receive a high dose of X-rays (Figure 6.20).

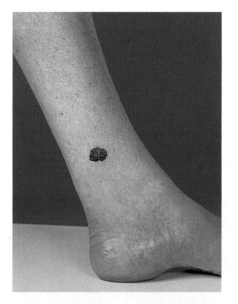

Figure 6.19 High exposure to ultraviolet light can increase the risk of skin cancer.

Figure 6.20 Medical workers are checked to make sure they don't receive high doses of X-rays.

Questions

1 Extend the table of uses for the electromagnetic spectrum that you made previously and include the dangers from each part of the spectrum.

2 Class exercise: extend the 'wave-line' you prepared previously to include the dangers from each part of the electromagnetic spectrum.

3 Write a sales brochure that tells the customer all the benefits of the electromagnetic spectrum.

... more at www.modularscience.co.uk

6.05
physics

Bending light

Visible light travels at the same speed as all the other waves of the electromagnetic spectrum when going through a vacuum – 300 000 000 m/s. At all other times, it travels slower than this. For example, visible light only travels at about 200 000 000 m/s through glass.

Did you know?

Television signals from satellites orbiting the Earth travel at 300 000 000 m/s. If you have a TV showing BBC1 from a terrestrial transmitter and another TV showing BBC1 from a satellite, you will notice that there is a split second delay between what you see and hear on the two televisions. The satellite is some 36 000 km above the Earth's surface. Even travelling at such a high speed, the TV signal takes longer to arrive from the satellite (Figure 6.21).

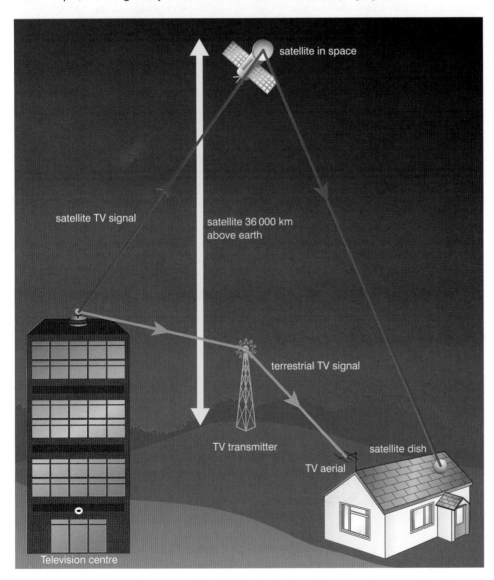

Figure 6.21 Even though it travels at 300 000 000 m/s, the television signal from a satellite takes noticeably longer to reach the television than one from a terrestrial transmitter.

Going off course...

Slowing down the light as it goes through glass obviously has an effect. It can make it change direction or "bend". Imagine a troop of majorettes or soldiers marching along in formation. If the group on the inside edge takes shorter steps they will slow down, while the rest carry on as before. The overall effect will be to swing the whole troop around. They end up going in a different direction from before (Figure 6.22).

Figure 6.22 By taking shorter steps (slowing down), the inner group will travel a shorter distance, so the whole troop will turn.

The opposite happens if the inside group speeds up again and the rest take shorter steps. They will return to their original direction (Figure 6.23).

Figure 6.23 The troop changes direction again as the inner side takes larger strides and speeds up before the others.

Key Facts

- Light can be made to change direction by sending it, at an angle, through a more dense material such as water or glass.
- This is called refraction and is caused by the light slowing down in the more dense material.

Refraction...

When light changes direction by slowing down or speeding up like this, it is called refraction. It only happens when a beam of light hits the glass at an angle (Figure 6.24). If the light beam hits the glass straight on, it still slows down but it all slows down at the same time, so there is no change of direction (Figure 6.25).

Figure 6.24 Light slows down as it passes through the glass. Hitting the glass at an angle will make the light beam change direction.

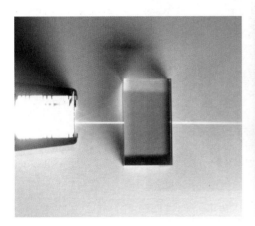

Figure 6.25 If the light hits the glass straight on then it is all slowed down at the same time. There is nothing to cause it to change direction.

Figure 6.26 Old window glass is often not completely flat. This makes light refract as it travels through the glass and makes the images appear distorted.

Did you know?

Looking through old windows often gives you a very distorted image. This is because the glass surface is not flat and the light beams are refracted in many different directions as they go through (Figure 6.26).

Questions

1 Copy and complete:

   When a beam of light enters water or glass it immediately .... down. When it leaves the glass or water it immediately .... up. If a light beam enters water or glass at an angle, it will change direction. This is called .... When light leaves water or glass at an angle, it changes direction again. This is because it is .... up.

2 Explain why someone may look deformed when seen through an old window. Draw a diagram to help your explanation.

3 Look at old windows in churches and other buildings. Write a tourist leaflet to explain how a visitor can tell that the window is old.

4 When light enters the Earth's atmosphere, it is refracted. Some people say that this means you never see a star exactly where it is. Explain how this could be true.

Light in bundles

Learning outcomes

After completing the work in this topic you will be able to:

- recall that light and infrared radiation pass through optical fibres with very little energy loss

- understand the difference between analogue and digital signals

Did you know?

There are more miles of optical fibres buried underground in the UK than in any other country (Figure 6.28).

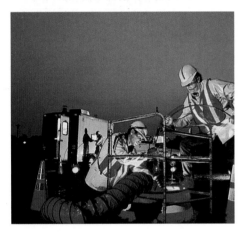

Figure 6.28 Cables containing bundles of optical fibres are being buried under roads to provide us with faster and more reliable telephone, fax, Internet and television connections.

Illuminating stuff...

An optical fibre is made of a special type of glass with a plastic coating. A beam of visible light or infrared radiation will pass along the fibre, bouncing back and forth from the sides.

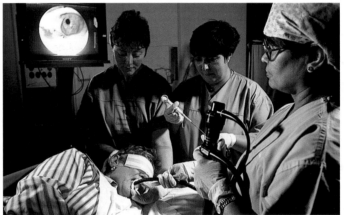

Figure 6.27 The bundle of optical fibres takes light into the patient and sends back images onto a television screen to guide the surgeon.

Optical fibres are extremely thin and are flexible enough to be pushed down a patient's throat. An endoscope contains a bundle of optical fibres to carry light into a patient's stomach and another bundle that sends an image back to the doctor so that any problem inside the patient may be seen without opening the patient up. Recently, keyhole surgery has used optical fibres to allow surgeons to perform operations through a tiny incision in the patient. Optical fibres relay images of what the surgeon is doing onto a television screen so that she or he can see which bits to cut or sew up (Figure 6.27).

Down the line...

Optical fibres are now used to carry information from phones, faxes, computers and television sets. The information (sound or images) is turned into a digital code (modulated) and this is sent down the fibre as a series of flashes of light. If the fibres were made of normal glass, the flashes of light would become very dim very quickly as they travel down the fibre. The perfectly pure glass used to make optical fibres means that the flashes of light will travel long distances without losing much energy (Figure 6.29). The signal can be boosted (amplified) every few kilometres so that the information it is carrying reaches the receiver. When the signal arrives, it has to be decoded (demodulated) into sound or images so that it can be understood. This is how most terrestrial phone connections and cable television work. Even a modem on a computer gets its name from what it does – **modulate** and **demodulate** a signal.

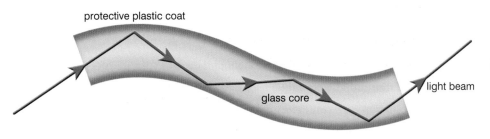

Figure 6.29 Light travels down the optical fibre with very little energy loss.

Going digital...

For a long time, TV and radio signals were analogue, which means they were sent as a wave. Recently, scientists have found a better way to send more accurate pictures and sound – digital signals. Digital signals are a binary code (Figure 6.30). The big advantage of digital signals is that interference in the radio station signal or TV picture is very unlikely to happen. Also, more information can be sent using digital technology so more television channels and more phone calls can travel down each optical fibre cable.

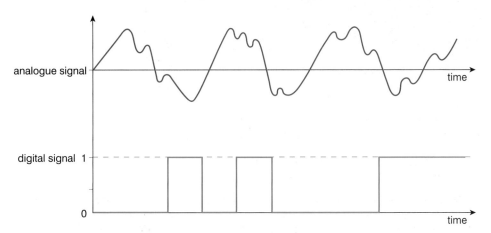

Figure 6.30 The analogue signal is a wave. The digital signal is a series of pulses. They both carry the same information.

Key Facts

- Infrared and visible light can easily pass through an optical fibre, which is made of a special type of glass.
- Optical fibres in communications such as phones and cable TV carry digital signals.
- Digital signals are a type of binary code that carries the information for the sounds or images.
- Digital signals are less likely to suffer from interference than analogue (wave) signals and more information can be sent, so more TV channels are possible.

Questions

1 Copy and complete:
Optical fibres are made of .... Light and .... waves can pass down optical fibres very easily. Optical fibres carry information in digital signals (a sort of .... code). The advantage of using digital signals is that there is less ....

2 Write about a day in the life of a message from a phone or fax to the receiver. Where is it encoded? Does it travel down a fibre or across the world as an electromagnetic signal? Where is it decoded before it is received?

3 Produce a leaflet to sell optical fibres to businesses. It should explain how useful optical fibres are and why they are good at their job.

Noise or sound?

Learning outcomes

After completing the work in this topic you will be able to:

* recall that sound is transmitted as a longitudinal wave
* understand that sound with frequencies above 20 000 Hz is known as ultrasound
* recall that human ears can detect a limited range of frequencies
* describe the use of ultrasound in medical imaging and echo sounding

Did you know?

Scientists are working on loud speakers that will direct sound to only one person in a room. There will be no need to wear headphones to listen to your favourite music, and no one will complain to you about hearing a tinny 'tsch tsch tsch tsch' beat from your music!

Sound waves are shock waves in the air or any other material, for example water, bricks or wood. The cone in a loudspeaker in a hi-fi system pulses backwards and forwards, pushing the air in front of it. Air particles collide with each other and the shock wave is passed on until it reaches your ear (Figure 6.31). Without the air in the room, this could not happen, which is why – "in space no one can hear you scream"!

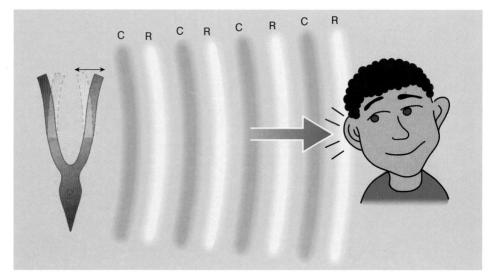

Figure 6.31 Air molecules collide with each other and pass on the disturbance. This is a longitudinal wave, which we call sound.
C = air is compressed
R = air is rarefied (thin)

Whale song...

Whale song can be heard over large distances. Sound travels much faster and further in water than in air. The whale expels air from its abdomen and the sound this makes is carried through the water to other whales (Figure 6.32). No one knows the purpose of these calls.

Hearing...

The human ear is very limited. At best it can hear sounds from about 20 000 Hz down to 20 Hz but even by the age of 15, the best many people can hear is about 15 000 Hz. The highest pitch you can hear gets lower as you get older and your hearing deteriorates, though for people who use personal stereos very loudly, hearing failure happens much more quickly. Health and safety laws require employers to provide workers in noisy environments with ear defenders to prevent deafness.

Figure 6.32 Whale song travels through the water faster than sound travels through air.

Ultrasound...

Many animals have a very different range of hearing. Cats have evolved to hear very high-pitched sounds, probably because mice have evolved to make very high-pitched squeaks (Figure 6.33). Sounds above the normal range of human hearing are called ultrasound.

Figure 6.33 Cats can hear much higher-pitched sounds than humans. This is how evolution has improved their chances of catching their prey.

Just checking...

Almost everyone under the age of 40 in the UK had an ultrasound scan before they were born. Using this clever technique, medical physics technicians use the ultrasound emitter-receiver to send a very high-pitched sound into the abdomen of a pregnant woman. A computer takes the echoes that bounce off the baby and uses the information to create an image. It is an easy way to check that the baby is developing normally and growing at the expected rate (Figure 6.34). Expectant mothers find it reassuring to see the baby and often want to know if it is a boy or girl. Ultrasound scans can give this information if the baby is facing the right way.

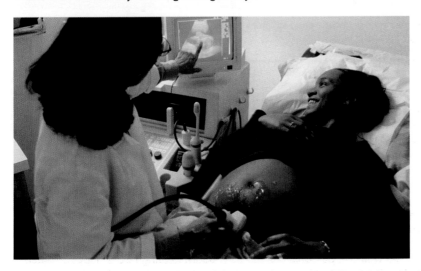

Figure 6.34 Ultrasound scans check that the baby is growing normally and that there are no disabilities or other problems visible.

Key Facts

- Sound is a longitudinal wave. Sound waves above human hearing (about 20 000 Hz) are called ultrasound. Most humans can only hear sounds above about 30 Hz and older people find they can no longer hear very high frequencies.
- Ultrasound is used to observe unborn babies and for echo-sounding to locate obstacles.

Waves, atoms and space

Going deeper...

Echo-sounding by ships can also use ultrasound. The time it takes the sound to reflect from the bottom of the sea will depend on how far down it is and how fast the sound travels. By timing the echoes, it is simple to work it out. The sound will also reflect off shoals of fish or other obstacles that the ship is trying to avoid (Figure 6.35).

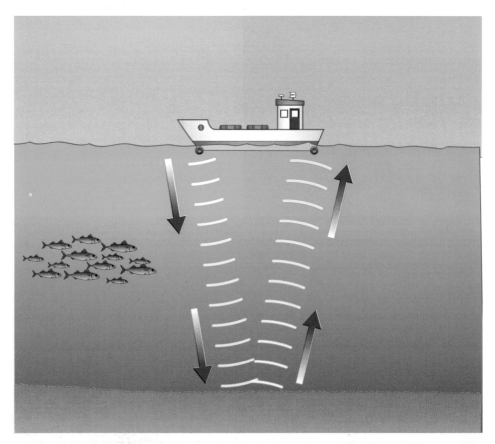

Figure 6.35 The time taken for the echo to return can be used to work out how deep the water is or how far away an obstacle is.

Questions

1 Copy and complete:

Sound is not an electromagnetic wave, it is a mechanical wave. Sound cannot travel through a .... and it travels much .... through air than it does through water. Sound is a .... wave while light is a transverse wave. Humans can hear sounds with frequencies up to about .... Sounds with higher frequencies are called .... Our ears cannot detect such high frequencies.

2 Write a guidance leaflet for someone explaining how ultrasound can be used.

3 Find out about the ultrasound scan of an unborn baby. Interview someone who has had an ultrasound scan (your mother perhaps).

Space

Learning outcomes

After completing the work in this topic you will be able to:

- recall that the Moon orbits the Earth and that other planets also have moons

- understand gravitational field strength g, and recall that g on other planets and on the Moon is different from g on Earth

- explain that gravitational force causes planets to orbit the Sun, and causes the Moon and artificial satellites to orbit the Earth, and comets to orbit the Sun

Event of a lifetime…

Date: Wednesday 11 August 1999
Place: Cornwall, England
Event: a total eclipse of the Sun (Figure 6.36)

Only planets with a moon can experience an eclipse. All planets orbit a star (our star is the Sun). A moon is a 'natural satellite' and always orbits a planet. Some planets have more than one moon, others have none at all. When a moon's orbit takes it between the Sun and the planet, the Sun's rays cannot penetrate and there is an eclipse of the Sun (Figure 6.37).

Figure 6.36 The total eclipse of the sun visible from the UK mainland, August 1999.

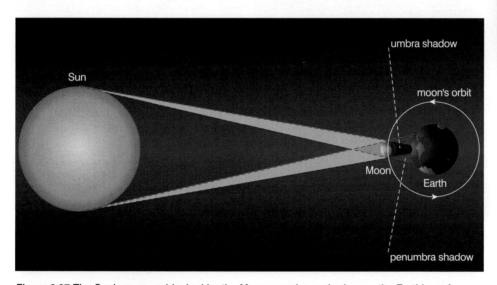

Figure 6.37 The Sun's rays are blocked by the Moon, causing a shadow on the Earth's surface – an eclipse.

During an eclipse, astronomers have the opportunity to make observations that are impossible under normal circumstances. Einstein's General Theory of Relativity was confirmed by observations made during an eclipse when the astronomers saw evidence that the Sun's gravity caused light to bend very slightly.

Keeping it together…

All stars, planets and moons have their own gravitational field. It is gravity that:
- keeps planets in orbit around their stars
- keeps moons and artificial satellites in orbit around their planets
- keeps things down on the surface of a planet or a moon

Did you know?

The Earth's Moon is moving away from the Earth at the rate of a few centimetres per year. This may affect the area over which a total eclipse can be observed in the future.

Waves, atoms and space   217

Key Facts

- Moons are natural satellites that orbit planets, though not all planets have moons and some planets have several.

- Gravity is the force that keeps moons in orbit around planets and the planets in orbit around the Sun.

Gravity is a force which attracts all objects to all other objects. The heavier the object, the more gravitational attraction it has. The Sun's gravity is strong enough to keep the nine planets of our Solar System in orbit (Figure 6.38). The Sun's gravity gets weaker as you get further away from it, so objects beyond Pluto (the furthest planet) are hardly attracted to the Sun at all. The closer planets orbit much faster than the outer ones because the Sun's gravity is much stronger nearer to the Sun.

Without gravity, the planets would simply fly off into space in a straight line, as there would be nothing to keep them going round in their orbit. If the Earth's gravity suddenly switched off (which is impossible!), everyone would simply fly off into space!

The force of gravity on the Earth is 9.8 N per kilogram. Our Moon's gravity is only 1/6 of the gravity on Earth. This means that the high-jump record would be nearer 15 m on the Moon than the 2.5 m it is on Earth (Figure 6.39).

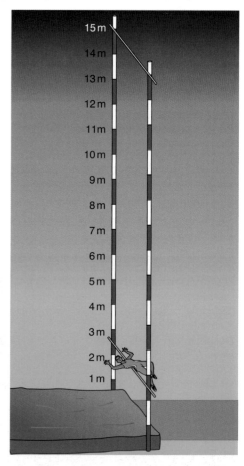

Figure 6.38 The outer planets orbit slowly because the Sun's gravity is much weaker further away.

Figure 6.39 The weak gravity on the Moon makes it easy to jump much higher than on Earth.

Questions

1 Copy and complete:

Some planets, such as Jupiter and ...., have moons (natural satellites). A moon orbits a planet because the force of .... stops it flying off into space. The strength of gravity on the Earth is 9.8 N per kilogram. Bigger planets have a .... force of gravity than the Earth. Our Moon has a .... force of gravity than the Earth because it is ....

2 If a pole-vaulter on Earth clears 5 m, what might he clear on the Moon if his space suit didn't restrict his movements?

Spies in space

After completing the work in this topic you will be able to:

*   explain that gravitational force causes comets to orbit the Sun
*   describe how the orbit of a comet differs from that of a planet

Twinkle twinkle little satellite…

Some of the artificial satellites orbiting the Earth are only a few kilograms in mass and are about the size of a football. The Surrey Space Centre at The University of Suirrey, Guildford builds and launches these so-called nanosatellites for governments around the world (Figure 6.40). They are used for weather forecasting, monitoring rainforests and land use, checking on the ozone hole or counting cosmic rays!

Gravity keeps these artificial satellites in orbit. Polar satellites orbit at high speed as they are closer to the Earth where gravity is stronger. They complete one orbit in about 100 minutes and can photograph the whole surface of the Earth in a day, segment by segment, as it spins beneath them (Figure 6.41).

Figure 6.40 Surrey's 6.5 kg nanosatellite launched into Low Earth orbit in June 2000.

Geostationary satellites are much further away from the Earth so they orbit much more slowly. They take 24 hours to complete one orbit above the equator, a complete Earth day. This is how they stay above the same point on the Earth's surface. They are used for satellite television and telephone communication (Figure 6.42).

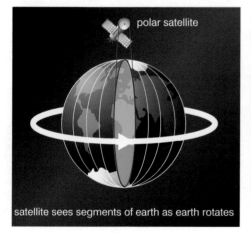

satellite sees segments of earth as earth rotates

Figure 6.41 Polar satellites are used for weather forecasting and spying. They can monitor the whole Earth, segment by segment, in a day.

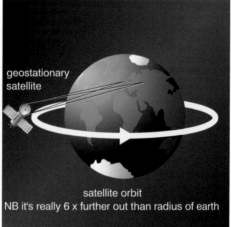

satellite orbit
NB it's really 6 x further out than radius of earth

Figure 6.42 Geostationary satellites orbit at the same rate as the Earth is rotating so they remain above the same spot at all times.

Did you know?

Heavier celestial objects have bigger gravitational fields – their gravity is much stronger. A black hole has such strong gravity that you would be crushed to the tiniest microdot if you fell in.

Key Facts

- The Earth's gravity keeps artificial satellites in orbit.
- Satellites have many uses, including telecommunications and weather forecasting.
- Comets orbit stars due to gravity but they have very elliptical orbits so are infrequent visitors.

Genuine exam howler

Question: Explain why a comet travels slowest when it is furthest from the Sun.

Answer: Because this is where it is cornering!

Comets...

"As I looked across to Philae Temple, I saw the comet Hale-Bopp and I couldn't help thinking that the last time anyone saw this comet here was when they were building the temple almost 3000 years ago" (Figure 6.43). *Alun Vaughan, physicist.*

Comets are the oddest members of solar systems. They orbit a star. The star's gravity keeps the comet in orbit but the orbit is such an exaggerated elliptical shape that the comet takes thousands of years to complete one orbit (Figure 6.44). A comet streaks away from the star at high speed but, in the same way as a ball thrown upwards will be slowed down, stopped and finally pulled back down to Earth by gravity, the comet will be slowed down and drawn back towards its star, speeding up as it gets closer. Some scientists consider that collision with a comet may have caused the extinction of the dinosaurs.

Figure 6.43 Comets are the occasional visitors to solar systems.

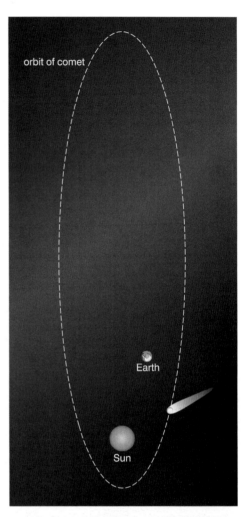

Figure 6.44 A comet's orbit is an exaggerated ellipse. It speeds away from the Sun slows down and then is drawn back by gravity, speeds up and flies past at great speed.

Questions

1 Copy and complete:
   Geostationary satellites orbit above the .... They take .... to orbit the Earth once. From the Earth it seems that they stay .... Polar satellites orbit much faster than geostationary satellites. They can monitor the whole of the Earth's surface in ....

2 Write a brief description of why comets are such odd members of a solar system. What do comets orbit? What makes them stay in orbit? Why do they take so long to complete one orbit?

3 Why don't satellites fly off into space?

4 Why do comets slow down as they get further from the sun?

One in a billion...

Our Sun is one of about 200 million stars that make up the Milky Way galaxy (Figure 6.45). In ancient times, people saw the Milky Way as a bright, misty band of light stretching across the night sky. Some civilisations thought it was the road to heaven. Today it is still there but the light pollution from towns makes it almost impossible to see.

Figure 6.45 The Milky Way galaxy seen from Earth.

Where am I?

Our Milky Way galaxy is like many other spiral galaxies in the universe. It is a large collection of millions of stars with a bulge in the middle surrounded by a roughly circular disc. The circular disc has spiral arms, and our Sun is on the inner edge of the Orion arm, about half way out from the centre of the galaxy. The whole thing is spiralling, and our Sun takes about 200 million years to make its journey around the galaxy (Figure 6.46).

Did you know?

Scientists have detected a hot fountain of gas at the centre of the Milky Way, which may show that our galaxy is revolving around a black hole.

6.10 Infinity and beyond

Key Facts

- The Solar System is part of a huge collection of stars called the Milky Way galaxy. The universe is populated by galaxies like this.
- There are a number of missions seeking to find extraterrestrial life, such as the Viking Lander mission to Mars.
- People also listen to radio waves from deep space for evidence of extraterrestrial life.

Did you know?

Scientists are now finding that distant stars also having have planets obiting them. This increases their chance of their being extra terrestrial life.

Is anybody there?...

Our Milky Way galaxy is only one of the enormous number of galaxies that make up the universe. Scientists have found evidence that some distant stars have planets orbiting around them but the search goes on for extraterrestrial life. Some astronomers listen every day to the radio signals coming from space to see if there is any evidence of life in other parts of the universe.

Figure 6.46 A spiral galaxy like the Milky Way.

Is there life on Mars?...

In our own Solar System, the most likely place to find extraterrestrial life is the planet Mars. The Viking Lander is seeking evidence of microbial life forms in the soil, but we certainly don't expect to find little green men! (Figure 6.47).

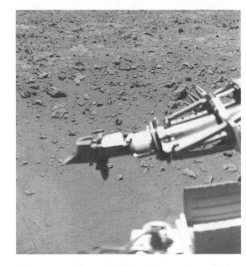

Figure 6.47 Searching for life on other planets.

Questions

1 Write your complete address, including town, country, continent, planet, solar system and location within the galaxy, so that extraterrestrial life can find your exact position.

2 Do you think it is likely that there is intelligent life elsewhere in the universe?

... more at www.modularscience.co.uk

Star life

Learning outcomes

After completing the work in this topic you will be able to:

* describe evolution of small stars like the Sun through the stages from nebula, to main sequence, to red giant, white dwarf and black dwarf

* understand that gravitational force causes a nebula to collapse to form a star

A star is born...

Around 5 billion years ago there was a great cloud of gas and dust called a **nebula**. The gas was mainly hydrogen and helium left over from the beginning of the universe, while the dust was made of heavier elements left over from an earlier generation of stars. The gas and dust began to collapse in on itself because of the force of gravity between all of the particles. Slowly, as the cloud contracted, it began to spin and flatten out into a disc shape. The centre became hotter and hotter as the gases and dust collided. Eventually, nuclear reactions started in the hot centre and our Sun was born. The rest of the cloud went on to form the planets, moons, asteroids and other debris we call our Solar System.

Living like a star...

All stars are born the same way. The nebula contracts because of its own gravity pulling the gas particles together, and it gets so hot that nuclear reactions begin to fuse hydrogen into helium. Our Sun is a small star born about 4.5 billion years ago. By the time it is about 10 billion years old it will have used up all its hydrogen and will start using its helium as fuel. Slowly it will form heavier elements like carbon and all the time it will be cooling down and expanding to form a **red giant**. The inner planets, Mercury and Venus, will be engulfed and life on Earth will end.

When all its fuel is used up, the Sun will collapse suddenly into a very hot, dense **white dwarf**. With no more fuel, it will cool until, at the end of its life, it will become a **black dwarf** (Figure 6.48).

Figure 6.48 The life expectancy of small stars like our Sun.

Did you know?

If Jupiter had been just a little larger it would have turned into a star and our solar system would have had two suns.

Key Facts

* Stars have a definite life history. They are formed from a nebula – a cloud of dust and gas – which collapses because of gravity.
* When a star runs out of hydrogen fuel, it begins to turn helium into heavier elements and at the same time expands and cools into a red giant.
* Finally it collapses into an extremely hot white dwarf, then cools into a black dwarf when it has no fuel left at all.

Questions

1   Write the complete recipe for producing a star such as our Sun. Then explain how the juvenile star is likely to change as it matures and grows old.

2   Explain how life on Earth will end if we don't destroy ourselves first.

Learning outcomes

After completing the work in this topic you will be able to:

- describe the Big Bang theory of the origin of the universe and consider other theories such as the Steady State theory

- outline evidence in support of the Big Bang theory about the origin of the universe; red shift gives evidence that the universe is expanding; microwaves give evidence of the original explosion

- explain how the future of the universe depends on the amount of mass present

Dr Jim Al-Khalili is a physicist who works at Surrey University in Guildford (Figure 6.49). He is famous for writing a popular science book called *Blackholes, Worm Holes and Time Machines* and he often appears on television to explain scientific ideas. In this interview, Jim tells us what the Big Bang is all about.

Q: "The Big Bang is something we've all heard about but how did the idea start?"
Jim: "The Standard Model of the Big Bang was originally developed to explain Edwin Hubble's observation that distant galaxies are all moving away from us at a rate that increases the further away from us they are. Hubble noticed that distant stars give out light that is redder than he expected. He called this the 'red shift' and proved that it was caused by the galaxies moving away from us. This provided evidence that the universe is expanding. The idea was then suggested that, by working backwards in time to roughly 15 billion years ago, all matter would have been originally squeezed together. This marks the birth of the universe".

Q: "So the Big Bang was a sort of explosion?"
Jim: "It is wrong to think of the Big Bang as an explosion within empty space and at some moment in time. According to theory, space and time themselves, which are part of the very fabric of the universe, were also created at the instant of the Big Bang. Everything started with what is called a 'singularity' – a point of zero size and infinite density, which exploded, creating matter, energy and the space and time for it to exist in. After the universe had expanded and cooled sufficiently, atoms formed and clumped together to make up the stars and galaxies."

Q: "And now we see other galaxies moving away from us?"
Jim: "The expansion is that of space itself rather than stars and galaxies moving through it".

Q: "And do scientists have any other evidence for the Big Bang?"
Jim: "Yes we do. Firstly, we are able to detect the background microwave radiation permeating space that is the afterglow of the intense heat of the Big Bang itself. Another clue is the relative abundance of atomic elements. The fact that roughly three-quarters of matter in the universe is hydrogen, with most of the rest as helium – the two lightest elements – requires a universe that was initially hot and dense but which cooled rapidly as it expanded."

Figure 6.49 Jim Al-Khalili, physicist and author.

Key Facts

- Scientists now believe that the universe began with the Big Bang and that this has caused all the galaxies to be rushing away from each other.
- We can see the movement of the galaxies as the light from them is redder than expected – the 'red shift'.
- The universe may continue expanding forever as it seems unlikely that there is enough matter in the universe for gravity to stop the expansion.

Q: "Will the universe just keep on expanding?"
Jim: "Until recently, the issue of the fate of the universe was very much an open question. If it contained sufficient matter then it would one day, in the distant future, re-collapse under its own gravity. If not, it would continue to expand forever. Current observations suggest that the latter of these two scenarios is correct. Indeed, it appears that the rate of expansion is increasing rather than slowing down (Figure 6.50)."

Figure 6.50 An image of a galaxy taken from the Hubble Space Telescope.

Questions

1 Explain why it is wrong to describe the Big Bang as an explosion in space.

2 What was the clever idea that led scientists to the theory of a Big Bang?

3 Explain how the evidence supports the idea of a Big Bang.

4 What would make the universe collapse in on itself – the so-called Big Crunch? Why is this unlikely to happen?

... more at www.modularscience.co.uk

Recipe for life…

Everything in this universe is made up of combinations of just over 100 different types of atoms. It is the **protons** that are the key to these atoms. The only difference between one atom and the atom of a different element is how many protons it has in its nucleus (Figure 6.51).

hydrogen	1 proton
helium	2 protons
lithium	3 protons
beryllium	4 protons
boron	5 protons
carbon	6 protons
nitrogen	7 protons
oxygen	8 protons
…………	
uranium	92 protons
…………	

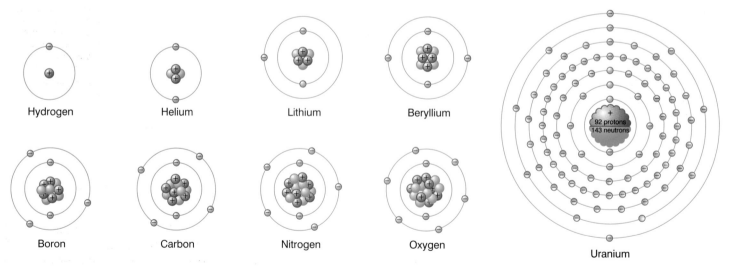

Figure 6.51 Each of the 100 or so elements has a different number of protons.

There are no gaps in this sequence. For any number of protons between 1 and 100 there is a known element. The number of protons for any element is its **atomic number**, also called its **proton number**. Scientists are now creating atoms with more and more protons – up to 120 at the last count! Unfortunately these man-made elements fall apart in a fraction of a second but this doesn't stop the scientists giving them a name and taking the credit for discovering a new element!

Getting it wrong…

Initially scientists thought that an atom's nucleus only contained protons and they decided that the atom's mass would tell them how many protons there were. They then created a table listing the atoms in order of atomic masses. Unfortunately this all went horribly wrong by the time they got to chlorine, which seemed to have 35.5 protons. They needed a new theory. The idea of another particle in the nucleus was suggested. It would weigh the same as a proton but would have no electrical charge (the proton has a positive electrical charge). They named it the **neutron** but it was several years before they managed to detect a real **neutron** and prove that the initial idea was right.

Sorted…

We now know that, apart from hydrogen, every atom has protons and neutrons in its nucleus. The total mass of the atoms depends on the total number of protons plus neutrons – its **mass number** or **nucleon number**. Any atom is completely identified by listing its atomic number and mass number, for example $^{12}_{6}C$ (Figure 6.52).

Variety is the spice of life…

The number of neutrons in an atom's nucleus can vary. This explains why chlorine didn't fit into the original scheme. All atoms of chlorine have 17 protons (atomic number 17). Some have 18 neutrons (mass number 35); some have 20 neutrons (mass number 37). Finding the mass of a sample of chlorine will give an average mass number of 35.5. Atoms with different numbers of neutrons are called **isotopes** (Figure 6.53).

Carbon

Figure 6.52 $^{12}_{6}C$ means that carbon has an atomic number of 6 (6 protons) and a mass number of 12 (6 protons plus 6 neutrons).

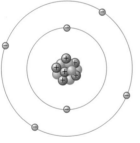

Carbon 12

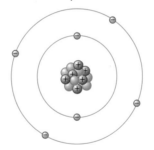

Carbon 13 isotope

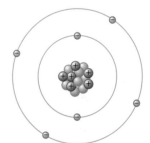

Carbon 14 isotope

Figure 6.53 Carbon always has 6 protons but may have 6, 7 or even 8 neutrons; these are called the isotopes of carbon. Many elements have isotopes.

Questions

1 Copy and complete:
Atoms have ………… and ………… in their nuclei, except hydrogen which only has ………… The atomic number of an atom tells you its ………… number. The mass number of an atom tells you the number of ………… plus ………… Isotopes of an element have the same number of ………… in their nucleus but a different number of ………… This means their ………… number is the same but their ………… number is different.

2 The word atom was used to describe things that were indivisible. Why is it the wrong word to use?

Radioactivity

Falling apart...

Medical physicists in hospitals administer special isotopes of certain elements to patients as part of their treatment for cancer or to look at the activity of their heart or kidneys (Figure 6.54). The isotopes they use often have more neutrons than normal, making them likely to break apart. These are **radioactive isotopes**. They are **unstable** because their nuclei are too heavy or they have very different numbers of protons and neutrons.

Figure 6.54 Medical physicists work in hospitals administering radioactive treatments to patients. This could be to cure cancer or to monitor how well an organ is working.

Losing weight...

When an atom's nucleus is too heavy it will throw out a small part of itself – two protons and two neutrons together. This group is called an **alpha particle** (Figure 6.55). The atom is now lighter and has changed into a different element because it has fewer protons.
Compared with an electron, an alpha particle is heavy and moves slowly but hits things very hard. It can easily knock an electron off the outside of another atom. This is called ionisation because the alpha particle has made the target atom into an ion (Figures 6.56 and 6.57).

$^{226}_{88}$Radium

α – particle

$^{4}_{2}$He

(parent nucleus)

$^{222}_{86}$Radon

(daughter nucleus)

Figure 6.55 By throwing out an alpha particle from its nucleus, the atom has become lighter and has changed into a different element so it is no longer radioactive.

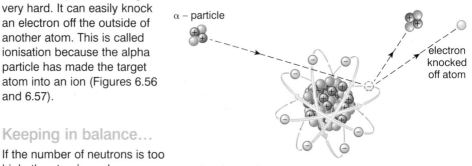

α – particle

electron knocked off atom

Figure 6.56 The alpha particle easily knocks electrons off the outside of other atoms and turns them into ions. This is called ionisation.

Keeping in balance...

If the number of neutrons is too high, the atom's nucleus can change a neutron into a proton as it tries to become more balanced. To do this, it has to get rid of a small negative charge (neutrons are neutral, protons are positive). A tiny electron comes out of the nucleus, called a **beta particle** (Figure 6.58). Some people wrongly think that this electron has come from the collection of electrons that orbit the nucleus!
A beta particle is an electron from the nucleus so it is tiny, light and moves very fast. It can **ionise** other atoms but gets slowed down every time it hits another atom until, eventually, it runs out of energy and stops (Figures 6.59 and 6.60).

Figure 6.57 The cloud chamber shows a trail made by an alpha particle as it ionises the atoms it collides with.

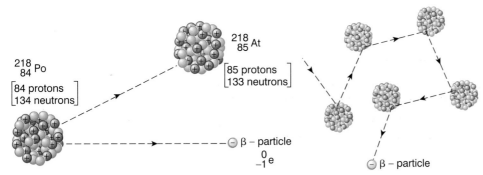

Figure 6.58 As a neutron changes into a proton, the leftover negatively-charged beta particle (electron) is thrown out.

Figure 6.59 The beta particle collides with atoms but it is so light it gets knocked off course with each collision. This is why it zig-zags until it runs out of energy.

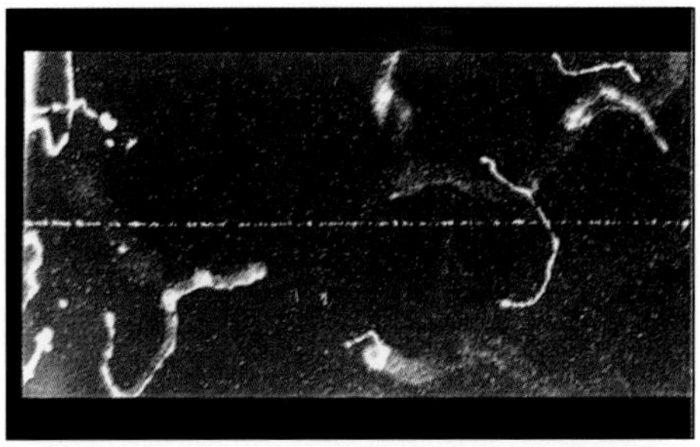

Figure 6.60 The cloud chamber shows a trail made by a beta particle as it zig-zags along, ionising the atoms it collides with.

Gone in a flash...

Sometimes an atom's nucleus has too much energy, possibly because it has just emitted an alpha particle or a beta particle. It needs to get rid of this energy so it emits a pulse of very high-energy electromagnetic radiation, called a gamma ray (Figure 6.61). A gamma ray is not like an alpha or a beta particle. It is not a particle. It does not have any mass. It is a beam of radiation like light but it can travel straight through the human body. It travels at the same speed as light in a vacuum (300 000 000 m/s) but it is not very good at ionising atoms when it hits them.

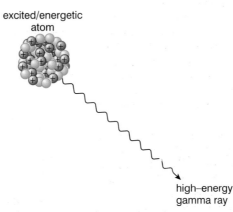

Figure 6.61 The high-energy gamma ray is a pulse of electromagnetic radiation which can pass through a human body.

Randomly does it...

One thing the three types of radiation have in common is that they all happen randomly. There is no way to predict which atom in a group will emit radiation or when. There is no way to make an atom emit radiation more quickly or to prevent it from happening.

Key Facts

- Alpha, beta and gamma radiation are emitted from radioactive sources.
- Alpha particles are comparatively large and slow but they are capable of ionising atoms by knocking electrons off them.
- Beta particles are comparatively light and quick.
- Gamma rays are high-energy electromagnetic radiation so are very penetrating.
- They are all emitted from unstable atoms and the whole process is completely random.

Questions

1 Why is alpha radiation sometimes called 'ionising radiation'?

2 What makes gamma entirely different from alpha and beta radiation?

3 Draw a spider diagram of properties which shows how the three types of radioactivity (alpha, beta and gamma) are different from each other.

4 Explain how an atom changes into a completely different element when it emits

a) an alpha particle

b) a beta particle.

Radiation

Learning outcomes

After completing the work in this topic you will be able to:

* describe the properties of alpha, beta and gamma radiation including their penetrating powers and their use in smoke alarms and for controlling the thickness of sheet material and sterilising medical equipment

* describe the dangers of ionising radiation including the risk of causing mutation in living organisms and the risk of damage to living cells and tissues

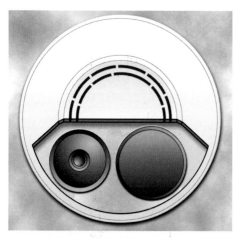

Figure 6.62 Alpha particles are going from the radiation source to the sensor through the air. In a fire, the alpha particles cannot get through the smoke. The detector senses that very few alpha particles are getting through and sets off the alarm. Wafting air into the alarm will turn it off as this drives away the smoke and the alpha particles can now get through.

A matter of penetration...

Radiation can be useful. It can be dangerous. The properties of alpha, beta and gamma radiation affect what they can do and how dangerous they can be (Table 6.1). The dictionary definition of a 'property' is a 'characteristic attribute or distinctive feature of something'. The fact that each type of radiation has different properties makes them very useful (Figures 6.62, 6.63 and 6.64).

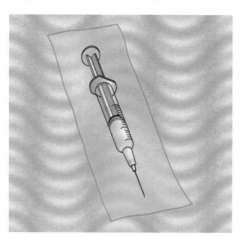

Figure 6.64 Gamma rays can penetrate the bag and are very high-energy so they kill any bacteria on the syringe. This sterilises the syringe, and the bag will prevent future contamination.

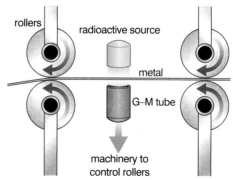

Figure 6.63 If the beta particles can just penetrate the metal it is the correct thickness. Too thick, and fewer beta particles will get through. Too thin, and too many beta particles will get through. The computer monitors the number of beta particles and provides feedback to ensure that the metal is always the same thickness.

Making the right choice...

Alpha particles are used in smoke alarms and beta particles are used for controlling the thickness of sheet metal. For medical use, alpha particles are too dangerous as they ionise and cause internal damage to the patient as well as being unable to be detected outside the body. Gamma rays can easily penetrate the body and be detected outside but they are very high-energy and also cause

	Mass	Charge	Speed	Penetration
alpha	heavy	positive	slow	poor
beta	light	negative	fast	quite good
gamma	zero	zero	speed of light in vacuum	highly penetrating

Table 6.1 The properties of alpha, beta and gamma radiation.

internal damage to the patient. Beta particles are just right. They can penetrate skin but are not strongly ionising and not very energetic so they cause the patient minimal harm (Figure 6.65).

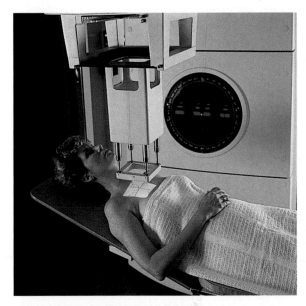

Figure 6.65 The radiation is aimed at the patient's body from many directions to avoid damaging healthy tissue.

Double-edged sword...

When medical physicists decide to use gamma radiation to treat a cancer patient they are treading a very fine line. A cancer patient has a tumour which is made up of cells that keep dividing out of control. The treatment must kill these cells without harming healthy cells. Gamma radiation kills cells. The medical physicist will aim the gamma rays at the tumour from every angle so that the tumour cells receive the full dose but the surrounding healthy cells receive very little and very few of them are affected (Figure 6.66).

The irony...

A large dose of gamma radiation can make you ill. On the skin it can cause a surface burn. Internally, the cells are damaged or killed so they cannot function properly. It may cause some cells to begin to divide uncontrollably, which can develop into a cancerous tumour.

Legacy...

A very high dose of radiation will cause cells to divide incorrectly. If the sperm or ova are affected then the genetic information they carry may be incorrect and the embryo may be malformed. This is called mutation and usually results in a miscarriage. Studies of people affected by the Hiroshima atomic bomb have shown that they now have no more chance of producing malformed babies than in the normal population.
Indeed, they seem to have a lower incidence of cancer than a typical population.

Did you know?

Medical physics is one of the fastest growing areas of medicine. All of the high-tech medical machinery relies on physics. Medical physicists can even use antimatter in PET scans (positron emission tomography) to monitor activity in the brain (Figure 6.67).

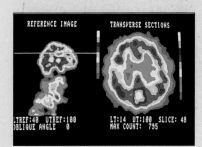

Figure 6.67 Positron Emission Tomography (PET) scans can monitor brain activity. Here the bright area of a baby's brain shows the possibility of epilepsy.

Waves, atoms and space 231

Key Facts

- Alpha particles are used in smoke alarms and for controlling the thickness of sheet metal.
- Beta particles are used in medical treatments.
- Gamma rays are used for sterilising medical equipment and treating cancer.

Did you know?

At the European Commission Joint Research Centre in Germany there is an Institute of Transuranium Elements. Scientists there work to prevent the trafficking of nuclear materials by terrorists. Trucks crossing borders between countries have to drive past detectors which can detect beta particles and gamma rays through the walls of the truck. Detecting alpha particles from uranium or plutonium is more difficult as alpha particles cannot pass through metals. They have to use specially designed detectors called 'neutron coincidence detectors'.

When they find a smuggled consignment the scientists have to work out exactly what is in it as this give clues about where it was made and what it was going to be used for.

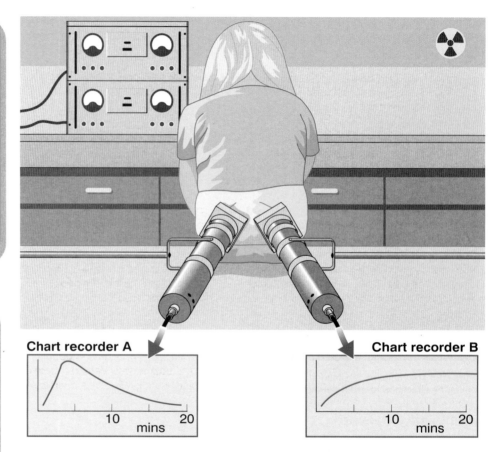

Chart recorder A

10   20
mins

Chart recorder B

10   20
mins

Figure 6.66 Beta particles can penetrate the patient's skin and can be detected outside the body to monitor how well the blood is circulating or how well an organ is functioning.

Question

1. Write a key or identification guide so that someone can work out the different types of radiation.

2. Produce a sales leaflet that explains the pros and cons of the different types of radiation and their potential uses.

… more at www.modularscience.co.uk

Learning outcomes

After completing the work in this topic you will be able to:

* recall the existence of background radiation from the Earth and from space, including regional variation in the UK, for example because of radon gas released from rocks

* describe problems associated with the safe disposal of radioactive waste

It's behind you...

Radiation is all around you every day. Since the very beginning, the human race has evolved to be surrounded by what we now call background radiation. The amount varies from place to place. For example, in Cornwall the rocks give out much higher levels of radiation than in Suffolk. Sleeping in the gutter may be a risk not because you will get run over but because the kerb stone is often made of granite which is naturally radioactive. Radon gas is given off by some rocks. Radon is also radioactive which means it gives out radioactive particles. If a house is built on these rocks, the radon gets into the house and the occupants will be exposed to higher levels of background radiation.

From outer space...

Cosmic rays from outer space are also part of background radiation. Pilots and people who fly across the Atlantic often will receive higher doses of cosmic rays because there is less atmosphere above them to absorb the rays. A pilot will be grounded if his cosmic ray dose gets too high.

Controversy...

People are always concerned about radiation yet medical radiation such as X-rays and other hospital procedures also contribute significantly to our background radiation without causing us any harm. Interestingly, the radiation from nuclear power contributes only a tiny amount to our background radiation, despite what is often reported in newspapers. Consequently, the disposal of radioactive waste has become a major safety issue in recent years as everyone becomes more concerned about the effects of pollution.

Risk...

The risk from all the radiation around us is tiny compared to the risk from smoking.

Did you know?

So far there have only been 20 known cases of smuggled nuclear materials - BUT there are over 30,000 missing radioactive sources in Europe alone!

Key Facts

* There is background radiation everywhere, from the rocks on Earth and from space.
* Nuclear power and medical treatments produce radioactive waste which can be stored underground until it is safe.
* Great care is taken to ensure that radioactive waste does not leak into underground water supplies.

Question

1   Class activity: Read about the Concensus Conference on page 234 then hold a debate on the pros and cons of burying nuclear waste compared with retaining it on the surface.

2   Write a magazine article to explain why people living near to a nuclear waste burial site can be reassured that they are safe. Include all of the scientific research to support your argument.

Consensus conference ...

Science Today

In 1999, the UK Government sponsored a Consensus Conference on the subject of the disposal of nuclear waste. A panel of ordinary people were chosen at random from the electoral role. None of them were scientists or knew much about radioactivity. They were asked to look at all of the evidence, talk to experts from all sides and produce a report for the Government on the most acceptable method of disposing of nuclear waste.

The vast majority of nuclear waste is low-level waste from medical and similar sources. The high-level waste from spent nuclear fuel forms a tiny proportion of the whole. It is important that all of this waste is kept away from people, the water supply and the food chain so that no one is affected by it.

The panel spent several weekends together in hotels learning all they needed to know to make an informed decision on the subject of nuclear waste disposal. They learnt about the effects of radiation on humans and how much radiation we are all exposed to in our everyday lives. They learnt about the geological studies to find places to bury the waste.

The panel quizzed experts from all over the country. They were convinced that the scientists had found places where there would be no subsidence and no danger of the containers of waste being damaged by earth movement or rock falls. They were convinced that the containers were robust enough to last a very long time and would not corrode.

They agreed that even if some of the waste material leaked out, there would be no danger of the water supply becoming contaminated as the disposal sites were far from water supplies. This meant that the waste would not be able to contaminate wildlife and enter the food chain. They were also satisfied that if the waste leaked out, the levels of background radiation in the area would not change much and would still be lower than the natural radiation in some parts of the world.

The panel was also impressed to find out that a lot of research is being done to find better ways to make the nuclear waste safe more quickly, such as by 'transmutation' or changing elements.

By the end of the conference, the panel was aware of the dangers of nuclear waste and the problems of disposing of it safely. The members realised it takes a very long time before the waste is safe and that it must be kept away from populations throughout that time.

Their final conclusion was that the waste could be disposed of safely by deep burial at specially chosen, geologically stable sites. They decided that the waste should be monitored and that it should be possible to retrieve the waste in the future when research has found new ways to treat it and make it safe.

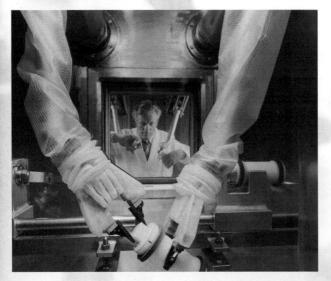

1.   The diagram shows the variation in background radiation in England, Scotland and Wales.

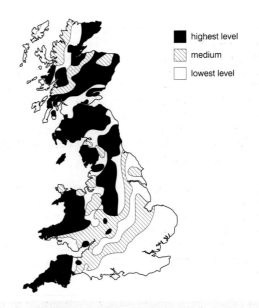

highest level

medium

lowest level

(a)   The background radiation is calculated by finding the average value of a large number of readings.
Suggest why this method is used.   (2)

(b)   The high levels of radiation in some parts of Britain are caused by radon gas escaping from underground rocks such as granite.

Radium-224 ($^{224}_{88}$ Ra) decays to form radon-220 ($^{220}_{86}$ Rn).

(i)   What particle is emitted when radium-224 decays?   (1)

(ii)   Radon-220 then decays to polonium by emitting an alpha particle.
Complete the decay equation for radon-220.

$$^{224}_{88} Rn \longrightarrow Po + He$$ (2)

(iii)   The half-lives of these isotopes are given in the table.

Isotope	Half-life
radium-224	3.6 days
radon-220	52 seconds

A sample of radium-224 decays at the rate of 360 nuclei per second.
The number of radon-220 nuclei is growing at less than 360 per second.
Suggest a reason for this.   (2)

(iv)   Radon-220 has a short half-life and it emits the least penetrative of the three main types of radioactive emission. Explain why the presence of radon gas in buildings is a health hazard.   (3)
(Total 10 marks)

Edexcel GCSE Double Award June 1999, Paper 6H no. 9

2.   The diagram shows the waves that make up the electromagnetic spectrum.

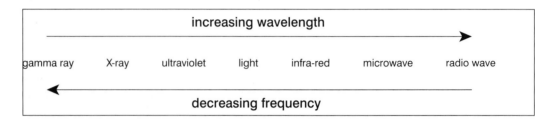

(a)   In going from light to radio waves, describe how:

(i)   the wavelength changes;

(ii) the frequency changes.   (2)

(b)   Which TWO waves in the spectrum are most harmful to humans?   (2)

(c)   Choose ONE of the waves shown in the diagram.
Name ONE use for the wave that you choose and describe how it is used.   (3)
                                                                                          (Total 7 marks)

Edexcel GCSE Double Award June 2000, Paper 3F no. 3

3. (a)   The table compares some properties of alpha, beta and gamma radiation.

Radiation	Nature	Absorbed by
alpha	2 protons and 2 neutrons	card
beta	electron	aluminium foil
gamma	electromagnetic radiation	partially by lead sheet

(i)   Which type of radiation carries a positive charge?   (1)

(ii) Which **two** types of radiation would not pass through a brick wall?   (1)

(iii) Which type of radiation could be used to sterilise medical instruments wrapped in
aluminium foil?   (1)

(b)   Carbon-14 ($^{14}_{6}C$) is a radioactive isotope of carbon.

Describe the difference between an atom of carbon-14 and an atom of carbon-12 ($^{12}_{6}C$) in
terms of the particles they contain.   (2)
                                                                                          (Total 5 marks)

Edexcel GCSE Single Award 1527 June 2000, Paper 6H no. 4

4.   In 1609, Galileo was one of the first scientists to use a telescope. He used it to look at the planet Jupiter. The diagrams show what he observed one night.

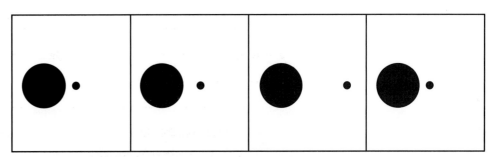

The small object close to Jupiter had not been seen before. It was later named Io.

(a)   Suggest a conclusion that Galileo could draw from his observations.   (1)

(b)   Explain how Galileo's observations went against the belief that all heavenly bodies revolve around the Earth.   (3)

(c)   Galileo published his findings in a book called *The Starry Messenger.*

Why did Galileo publish his findings?   (1)

Edexcel GCSE Single Award 1527 June 2000, Paper 6H no. 9

5.   The diagram shows the orbit of a comet.

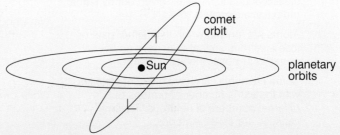

(a)   Describe TWO differences between the orbit of a comet and the orbits of the planets.   (2)

(b)   (i) Draw an arrow on the diagram to show the gravitational force on the comet when it is at its furthest distance from the sun.   (1)

(ii) Describe what happens to the size and direction of this force as the comet approaches the sun.   (2)

(c)   Comets consist of frozen water and gases.

Suggest why a comet can only be seen when it is close to the sun.

Edexcel GCSE Single Award 1527 June 2000, Paper 6H no. 10

Glossary 6

Alpha particle	A particle given out from the nucleus of some radioactive elements. It is a helium nucleus consisting of two protons and two neutrons.
Amplitude	This is a measure of how large each wave is. Amplitude tells us the volume of sound, the brightness of light, or the strength of a phone signal.
Atomic number	The number that shows how many protons an element contains.
Beta particle	A particle given out from the nucleus of some radioactive elements. It is an electron.
Black dwarf	A small, dense, cool star that has used most of its fuel, and has reached the end of its life cycle.
Demodulate	To turn digital code back into sound or images that can be understood.
Electromagnetic spectrum	This is the name given to the spectrum of waves shown in order of frequency or wavelength. It goes from radio waves at one end to gamma rays at the other.
Electromagnetic waves	These are a group of waves sharing many similar properties. They all travel through a vacuum and all travel at the speed of light.
Frequency	This is the number of complete cycles of a wave in each second. It is measured in Hertz (Hz)
Gamma ray	This is a pulse of very high energy electromagnetic radiation given out by some radioactive elements.
Ionise	Atoms are ionised when they either gain or lose electrons so that they have an overall negative or positive electric charge.
Isotopes	Some elements can have different varieties, with the same number of protons but different numbers of neutrons. These varieties are called isotopes.
Longitudinal waves	These are waves where the amplitude of the wave is in the same direction as the direction the wave travels in. Sound waves and shock waves when you hit something are longitudinal waves.
Mass number	This is the same as the nucleon number.
Modulate	To turn sound or images into a digital code that can be sent down optical fibres or as radio waves.
Nebula	A cloud of dust and gas in space.
Neutron	An electrically neutral particle found in the nucleus of all atoms except hydrogen. It has the same mass as a proton.
Nucleon number	The number of particles in the nucleus of an atom. The nucleon number is the sum of the proton number and the number of neutrons.
Proton	An electrically positively charged particle found in the nucleus of all elements.
Proton number	The number of protons that an element has. It is also called the atomic number.
Radioactive isotope	An isotope that gives out radioactivity, e.g., alpha or beta particles or gamma rays.
Red giant	A massive, cool star, further through its life cycle than our Sun.
Transverse waves	Waves where the amplitude of the wave is at right angles to the direction the wave travels in.
Ultrasound	Sound waves that are so high pitched (high frequency) that humans are unable to hear them.
Unstable	Nuclei that tend to break apart because they are too heavy or because they contain too many neutrons.
Wavelength	This is a measure of the length of each complete wave. 'Medium wave' radio waves have a wavelength of over 1km, light has a wavelength of less than one thousandth of a mm.
White dwarf	A small, extremely dense star, about the size of Earth, but with the mass of our Sun.

Why Is Coursework Important?

You have been studying science for a number of years, probably from when you first started at school. During those years, practical work in science has been an important feature of your studies. It will have helped you to understand some of the points your teachers have been making in the classroom.

Carrying out practical work is seen as an essential feature of any modern science course. Practical work allows all students an opportunity to put theory into practice. It is probably the aspect of science courses that students most clearly enjoy, and remember.

Over the years you will have spent many hours exploring and testing new ideas in science, and this is a big reason for science's status as a National Curriculum core subject.

Many of you will go on to study science at sixth form and maybe even at University. You will carry out practical work as part of your science studies wherever you go. Practical work adds enjoyment and makes the subject come alive. It makes all the theory real, and it helps people to see just how important science is to all of us in this modern world.

This is the reason why practical work features so heavily in the GCSE, and since such a lot of time is spent doing practical work in lessons, it should be assessed to see how well you can do it.

In science, practical work is assessed from a very early stage in your school career. When you get to prepare for the GCSE examination, practical work, which counts towards your examination grade is called 'coursework'.

Your marks for coursework will count for up to 20% of your final grade(s) in science.

If you are studying for a Double Award course, then your coursework will count for up to 25% (or 20%) of BOTH certificates. It doesn't matter which examination group sets your exam paper and it doesn't matter which syllabus your centre uses – the 25% (or 20%) rule still applies.

Many students do very well in the coursework component of the GCSE examination, but there is always room for improvement!

So, here are a few tips to help you do better. Remember, a good performance in coursework, could help YOU to get a better grade in your science examination.

Teachers and Examination Group Moderators will judge the standard of your work under four skill headings.

These are shown in the table below:

Skill area	What it is about
Skill P – Planning Experimental Procedures	Thinking about fair testing, using your scientific knowledge, and making a prediction. Fair testing means keeping everything the same, except for the one thing, which you choose to change. E.g. "I am planning to see how temperature affects the rate of a reaction between ...."
Skill O – Obtaining Evidence	Collecting the data, and presenting your results. The most usual way to present your data is in a results table. Don't forget correct headings and correct units in the table!
Skill A – Analysing Evidence and Drawing Conclusions	Doing calculations **OR** drawing graphs, and explaining the results scientifically. Anything more than averages counts as doing calculations. Graphs may be either bar charts, or line graphs. You should use some science in the conclusion.
Skill E – Evaluating the Evidence	Writing about the quality of your results and the method you used. Were there any anomalous reszod you used? Is your evidence sufficient? Are there any areas of your graph where you need more evidence?

It is very important that you know what is required of you in all four skill areas. This module aims to give you clear guidance on what is needed at each mark level in each skill area. There are also some examples of students' work, followed by questions, and a commentary on each piece of work.

GOOD LUCK WITH YOUR COURSEWORK!

Skill P: Planning

This is what to do	Mark	Grade
Write down something you plan to do, which is both simple and safe.	2 marks	**About Grade G**
Plan something to do, either in the laboratory, in the computer room, or outside. Make it a fair test. (See previous page). Choose the right equipment to carry out your task. (The equipment should be available for your use in school, and you should know how to use it safely). If you can, make a prediction. (Say what you think will happen).	4 marks	**About Grade E**
In addition to the above: Write about the science involved, showing how it applies to your task. Plan to control the variables which will affect your task, and to take account of those you cannot control. (Variables are things that can change and have an effect on your results). Say how many measurements/observations you plan to make, and say why you chose this number. Say what range you plan to take your measurements over. (Range means what starting point, and what finishing point, for your readings). Make a prediction, if you can, and give scientific reasons to support your prediction.	6 marks	**About Grade C**
In addition to the above : Use **detailed** scientific knowledge in your plan. (Detailed means about Grade A standard science). Say how you intend to use equipment to give **precise, accurate and reliable** results. Use either a 'trial run', your earlier work, a text book, a CD Rom, or the Internet, to help in the planning of your task. If you can, justify your prediction, using **detailed** scientific knowledge.	8 marks	**About Grade A**

The information in the table gives you a guide to what is needed to achieve different grades. However, these are only general statements that apply to all investigations. You must consider how each statement can be satisfied within the particular investigation that you are planning.

Write out a plan either to:

Investigate which orange juice contains the most vitamin C, or,

Investigate how changing the concentration of sodium thiosulphate solution affects the rate of reaction with hydrochloric acid, or,

Investigate the effects of different concentrations of sugar solution on pieces of potato.

In writing out your plan use the following as a guide.

For 2 marks – you simply need to state what you plan to do

- Write down a single sentence stating what you are planning to do; e.g. I am going to find out which orange juice contains the most vitamin C.

- Are you certain that what you are planning is simple and safe to carry out?

For 4 marks – you need to give more details

- Where are you going to carry out the investigation? Will you carry it out in the laboratory? Does it involve a simulation that you may need to run in the computer room? Is it a field study that involves gathering data from outside?

- What apparatus are you likely to need and is it available?

- How are you going to make the investigation a fair test? You must keep everything the same except the one thing you are investigating. For example, if you are planning to investigate the effects of the concentration of sodium thiosulphate on the rate of reaction with hydrochloric acid you must keep the concentration of the hydrochloric acid the same and the temperature the same since both of these will also affect the rate of this reaction.

- Is it possible to make a sensible prediction about what you think will happen? This may not be possible for all investigations.

For 6 marks – you need to discuss the science involved in your investigation

- How are you going to keep everything the same apart from what you are investigating?

- Could there be some things that you can't keep exactly the same? What are they? Are they likely to affect your results in a significant way?

- Over what range of values will you take measurements? For example, if you are going to investigate the effects of different concentrations of sugar solution on pieces of potato, what will be the lowest and highest concentrations of sugar solution you will use?

- How many measurements or observations will you need to make in order to get meaningful results? You need enough results to see any pattern or trend but there is no advantage in taking an excessive number of measurements. For example, in the above investigation you may decide to use sugar solutions of 0.0, 0.2, 0.4, 0.6, 0.8, 1.0 mol/dm^3. This would give you sufficient measurements to show any trend or pattern. Taking only 0.0 and 1.0 mol/dm^3 would give insufficient information while taking measurements from 0.0 to 1.0 mol/dm^3 in steps of 0.1 mol/dm^3 produces more information than is really needed.

- At this stage can you make any further sensible prediction about what you think will happen?

For 8 marks – you need to give a detailed account of the science involved in your investigation.

- What are you going to do to ensure your results are precise, accurate and reliable? Are you going to take more than one set of measurements? Are you going to repeat measurements that don't appear to fit the general pattern or trend? Is the apparatus you are using sufficiently accurate; e.g. should you be measuring volume of liquid with a pipette rather than a measuring cylinder?

- Have you been able to obtain any information say from books, the Internet, a CD Rom simulation, some earlier work or perhaps a small–scale trial run that has helped you in your planning?

- What are the scientific principles behind this investigation? For example: if you are going to investigate the effects of the concentration of sodium thiosulphate on the rate of reaction with hydrochloric acid you could discuss how chemical reactions occur in terms of particles colliding together.

- Can you use these scientific principles to support your earlier predictions? For example, in the above investigation changes in the rate of a reaction are related to the numbers of reacting particles so an increase in concentration of sodium thiosulphate might be expected to bring about an increase in the rate of reaction.

In the remaining pages of this section you will find four plans. Read through each of them carefully and then look at the Principal Moderator's comment. This explains why the work has been given the mark it has.

When you have examined this work look back on the plan you have prepared. What mark would you give your plan? Are there any particular problems with your plan? Can you now see ways of improving it?

Here is Steven's plan to investigate the energy change in a reaction.

Energy changes in neutralisation

1. Introduction

I am trying to investigate what factors are relevant to the heat change involved in neutralisation reactions. In this experiment I have decided to change the concentration of the different chemicals that I use and then I will measure the temperature of the liquid before and after.

2. List of apparatus

A glass beaker
Polystyrene cup
Thermometer
Hydrochloric acid
Sodium hydroxide
Measuring cylinder
Tap water

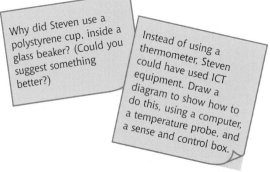

Why did Steven use a polystyrene cup, inside a glass beaker? (Could you suggest something better?)

Instead of using a thermometer, Steven could have used ICT equipment. Draw a diagram to show how to do this, using a computer, a temperature probe, and a sense and control box.

3. Method

We took a glass beaker and placed a polystyrene cup inside it. Then we measured out 25 ml of both acid and alkali first and poured one into the cup and took the temperature. We then poured 25 ml of the other in and took the temperature again to see how much the temperature had risen.

We then repeated the experiment first keeping the strength of the acid the same. We varied the concentration of the alkali by adding water and reducing the amount of sodium hydroxide. We did this in equal steps e.g. 20 acid and 5 water, 15 acid and 10 water, 10 acid and 15 water. I am going to record my results in a table for each test and then put them in a graph.

Tip

When measuring the temperature change that occurs during neutralisation it is important to mix the acid and alkali by stirring with the thermometer and to take the maximum temperature of the mixture.

4. Making the tests fair

I will make sure that I am accurate with all my measurements. If I think that the results are not right, I will do them again and check they are right. Each time I lowered the amount of acid by 5 ml.

Look at Steven's prediction in section 5. Do the results show that Stephen changed the amount and strength of the acid?

5. Prediction

I am trying to find out if the change of amount and strength of the acid effects the temperature. I think that the less acid there is the less the temperature will rise.

Look at sections 4 and 6 of Steven's work. Do the results match what Steven said he planned to do?

6. Results

What is missing from the headings in the table of results?

Sodium hydroxide ml	Hydrochloric acid (ml)	Water	Start temp	Finish temp	Temperature raised
25	25	–	18	29	11
20	25	5	17	28	11
15	25	10	17	28	8
10	25	15	17	21	4
5	25	20	17	19	2

Do you think that the absolute concentrations of the hydrochloric acid and sodium hydroxide solution are important? Explain your answer.

If Steven used sulphuric acid (a dibasic acid) in place of hydrochloric acid would he get the same results?

Steven's energy change plan

Teacher's mark	Principal Moderator's Comments
4	There is a fair test with a simple prediction. Suitable equipment has been chosen. However, there is no explanation of neutralisation. For anything more than 4 marks Steven should have included something about the science involved in neutralisation. Whilst the range of readings planned is fair enough, (5–25 ml) the total number of readings planned is not sufficient to consider the award of 6 marks. He could have planned to take more than 5 readings.

Kate was asked to investigate a 'murky' problem. She was told that on certain days there was a problem with the local river because the nearest chemical company discharged waste chemicals (including sodium thiosulphate and hydrochloric acid) into the river. It was noted that the problems seemed worse in the summer. This is her task:

A murky problem

1. Introduction

A chemical company on the banks of the River Lagan routinely discharges waste chemicals into the river. On certain days, when waste products include sodium thiosulphate, hydrochloric acid and sodium chloride, the river water in the vicinity becomes cloudy and the stones and sand at the bottom can no longer be seen. Observers have noticed that this problem is worse in the summer – INVESTIGATE.

Temperature.....

2. Hypothesis

I think that the higher the temperature, the quicker the reaction will be.

3. Apparatus

Bunsen burner	Burette
Thermometer	Hydrochloric acid
Test tube	Sodium thiosulphate
Beakers	Paper with drawing on it
Clock	

4. Plan

I will place a piece of paper underneath the beaker as I cannot conduct the tests in the river. I will heat the hydrochloric acid at different levels and take the temperature of it. I will then pour this into thiosulphate and take the temperature of the mixture. I will take the time that the mixture takes to go cloudy enough so that the paper underneath disappears. I will then put these results in a table and then draw a graph.

> What does the chemical reaction between sodium thiosulphate and hydrochloric acid produce, and why might the problem seem worse in the summer?

> In her plan Kate uses the terms 'dependent variable' and 'independent variable'. What do these terms mean?

Before doing this experiment, I conducted some experiments of my own and found that temperature would show better results than concentration of sodium thiosulphate and also the effect of sodium chloride (salt).

My dependant variable for this experiment will be the time and rate of the reaction. My independent variable will be the temperature of the mixture and my controlled variable will be the amount of acid I use to heat up and the amount of thiosulphate.

> What previous work do you think Kate actually did? (Principal Moderator's note: It is always a good idea to give details about what previous work you carry out **and show how the results from the previous work have been of use in deciding what to do in the main task.**)

> Look at Kate's hypothesis. What is missing from her statement?

5. Method

I used exactly the same apparatus as I said in the plan. The only thing I changed was I heated up the hydrochloric acid instead of the sodium thiosulphate as I thought that this would give me better results. I used 40 cm^3 of each solution which I poured in a large beaker.

> This task could be done as an ICT task. How would you use a light sensor and other equipment to do this? Draw a diagram.

6. Safety

During this experiment you must take a number of safety precautions in order to carry the experiment out safely. First of all, because you are using acid you must wear safety goggles in order to protect your eyes and because you are going to heat something up you must not run in the classroom and not leave stools or bags out for anyone to trip on.

In this experiment I used a piece of paper with a drawing of a fish on it. I used this because I could not conduct the experiment in the river and so I used something you would normally see in a river. You must use the same drawing for the whole experiment to keep it a fair test. Results from the experiments...

> Do you think it was a good idea to heat the acid, but not the water? What would you do?

Kate's 'murky problem'

Teacher's mark	Principal Moderator's Comments
5	Kate has satisfied the 4 mark descriptions. However, there is no indication that Kate knows anything about the science of the reaction. She doesn't say anything about how the speed of particles increases as the temperature rises, resulting in a larger number of effective collisions, which in turn would produce more sulphur, so obscuring the drawing of the fish quicker. Kate doesn't say in her plan what the number and range of readings is to be, but the results table (not shown in the extract) does show that she planned to take readings at 7 different temperatures between room temperature and 80 degrees Celsius. The mark descriptions for 6 marks are partly achieved, so Kate gets 5 marks.

Sam carried out an investigation into how temperature changes affect the Vitamin C content of some orange juice. Here is his plan.

To investigate the factors influencing vitamin C

This investigation is all about investigating all the possible factors such as concentration, temperature etc. which influence the rate at which vitamin C is made in orange juice or any other kind of juice. My investigation is about determining whether different kinds of temperature – e.g. cold, hot, warm etc. – affect the rate at which vitamin C is made.

I will use the same amount of orange juice in 4 flasks and place them in 4 different temperature conditions such as at room temperature, in a fridge, in a water bath and on a windowsill. This experiment will be left there for a week and I will test how much vitamin C there is in the juices using a dye called DC Pip which will be added to the orange juice.

This experiment is important because we need to know what conditions are best for preserving the vitamin C as it is a very important vitamin for the body. By carrying out this experiment we can find out all such factors which maintain a good level of vitamin C in orange juice.

My experiment is quite safe, as I am not dealing with very dangerous chemicals. Care has been taken with the DC Pip, so I will wash my hands using it and I will try not to get it into my mouth. I should wear overalls in case the dye falls.

I will try to make my experiment fair, so I will have to keep all the important factors in my experiment the same such as concentration of the orange juice, the size of the conical flasks and the type of orange juice. I will have to use the same type and amount of orange juice in the same container to keep all my measurements fair. If I put cling film on one of the tops of the flask I have to do the same for the others. The only factor I will have to change is the temperature surroundings.

In the fourth and fifth paragraphs, Sam talks about controlling the variables. Which important variable does he not mention? How does Sam try to ensure that his method is a fair test?

What simple mistake did Sam make in his first paragraph?

I will also have to take precise and accurate readings. This means I will have to use a measuring cylinder to measure the orange juice. I will have to keep my eye level with the level of the orange juice to take precise readings. I will also have to do this when measuring the amount of DC Pip. I will have to come at the same time each day in order to take readings so that the experiment is fair. When I add the orange juice to the DC Pip I have to make sure that I shake the mixture carefully after each drop so I know when it turns orange. I have to make sure each drop is equal and that the mixture will have to turn completely orange before I stop adding drops of orange juice to the DC Pip.

I think the range of my readings should be taken 3 times a day for one week. This will give me accurate results and tell me when there is a decay in the vitamin C during a whole week. I will take these readings at the following times: 8.30am, 1.00pm, and either 3.30pm or 4.00pm depending on when we finish school.

Draw a diagram to show how this task could have been set up to observe the colour change of the DC Pip using ICT equipment.

1. Scientific knowledge

Re-read Sam's paragraph on 'scientific knowledge'. Do you think it is all relevant? What would you do to improve on it?

A disease caused by lack of vitamin C is scurvy. Another name for vitamin C is ascorbic acid. This vitamin keeps our epithelia in a healthy state. It is abundant in green vegetables such as spinach and citrus fruits, e.g. oranges and lemons. If people eat these kind of foods they will not get scurvy, i.e. maintains healthy skin and strong capillaries.

Vitamin C is destroyed by heating. As a result a lot of it can be lost during cooking and while food is being kept hot afterwards. In restaurants where food is kept hot for a long time, over 90% of vitamin C may be lost.

DC Pip is short for 2,6 dichlorophenolindophenol.

Vitamins are required in very small quantities, but they are a group of complicated compounds. Chemicals in this group show a wide variety of molecular size and shape.

2. Predictions

I predict that the most vitamin C present will be in the orange juice react in the fridge. This means there will be less drops of orange juice needed to change the colour of the DC Pip to an orange colour. I think this because the temperature will be colder so the vitamin C has a better chance of surviving. Vitamin C is destroyed by heating so this means the orange juice kept in the water bath (where the temperature is high) will lose all of its vitamin C faster than the orange juice kept at room temperature or in the fridge. This is because if it is not exposed to high or low temperatures so it will be in the middle, which means it will gradually lose its vitamin C. At the end of the week I think the juice will lose its vitamin C because over time vitamin C can only decay.

3. Aim

To investigate the factors influencing the rate of vitamin C.

4. Apparatus

Orange juice (Marks and Spencer Jaffa Juice)
4 conicle flasks
cling film
perpette
beaker
DC Pip
measuring cylinder.

What piece of apparatus might Sam have used, instead of a pipette, to add the orange juice to the DC Pip with greater accuracy and precision?

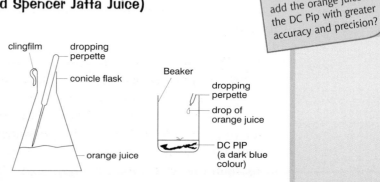

Sam's Vitamin C plan.

Teacher's mark	Principal Moderator's Comments
6	Sam gets credit for his diagram, which is good enough, and can be given instead of a list of equipment. Note that no marks are deducted here for his incorrect spelling of 'perpette' [pipette] and 'conicle' [conical]. Sam's scientific knowledge is good enough for 6 marks, but not 8. There is no indication as to how DC Pip reacts chemically with orange juice, or what happens to Vitamin C when it is heated, other than 'it is destroyed by heating'. Sam did not use any secondary source to help him plan the task, nor did he carry out a 'trial run' to help in the planning. These are features of the 8 mark criteria.

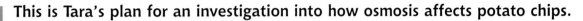

This is Tara's plan for an investigation into how osmosis affects potato chips.

An experiment to Investigate the effect of Sucrose Concentration on Osmosis in potato chips.

1. The key Factor that I plan to Investigate and what I will do to Make My Experimental Work a Fair Test

The key factor that I plan to investigate is sucrose concentration, and I will vary the sucrose concentration, and calculate the effects of this factor on osmosis in the potato chips by recording the mass before (before the chip is placed into the solution), the mass after (after the chip has been placed into the solution for certain length of time of 1 hour), the difference between these masses, and then the percentage weight changes at each concentration. Also, at each concentration I will take two readings (one being an average), and then I will calculate the required averages.

> Tara has chosen to investigate how the mass of the potato chips changes in different sucrose solution concentrations. What other variable could she have chosen?

Because I am measuring osmosis, I will try to keep constant the other factors that effect osmosis, those other than the concentration of sucrose (and water). I will be using potato chips from the same variety of potato (assuming that the genetic make-up and therefore partially permeable membranes will be more similar in make-up). I will use the same volume of solution at each concentration of sucrose solution (that being 25ml). I will leave the potato chips in solution for the same time at each solution concentration. I will use the same method at each concentration, and for each potato chip individually, in that I will dry the excess water off the chips in a similar manner, and use the same accuracy of the weighing scales, prepare the chips for use in the same way and other aspects. I will keep the surface area of the chips as constant as possible, this being that I will use chips of the same cross sectional area and length. I found in my preliminary work that the chips in the higher concentrations of sucrose solution tended to float thus excluding a certain part of their cross-sectional area from the solution, I do not know how to remedy this. I will carry out all of my experimental work at room temperature and thus temperature will not affect my experiment. The time will not affect my results because I plan to leave my chips in solution for 1 hour at each concentration, I discovered that significantly enough results were obtained after this length of time in my preliminary work.

Obviously I will vary the sucrose concentration, using concentrations of 0.0 mol/litre (de-ionised water purely), 0.2 mol/litre, 0.4 mol/litre, 0.6 mol/litre, 0.8 mol/litre and 1.0 mol/litre. Apart from the concentration of 0.0 mol/litre the solutions have been made up beforehand.

Tara refers to 'preliminary work' for this task. What preliminary work should she have done?

Tara's preliminary work identifies a problem with floating potato chips. How could she have solved this problem, and why is important?

2. What I predict Will be the effect of Changing the Key factor that I Plan to Investigate and the Scientific Reasoning why I am Making This Prediction

I predict that the effect of changing the sucrose concentration will be that as the concentration of the sucrose solution increases, first the mass of the chip will increase, and then the change in mass will gradually decrease until mass is lost and this mass loss will gradually increase in amount.

I think that the reason for this prediction is that when the sucrose concentration is low, the concentration of water outside the cells of the potato chips will be greater than that inside, and therefore water will osmose into the cells of the chip which will gain mass. As the concentration of sucrose increases, the concentration of water outside the cell will eventually become less than inside the cells of the chip, and thus the water will osmose out of the chip and mass will be lost. Here are diagrams to show how water osmoses across the partially permeable membranes of the chips, and in which direction in both high concentrations of sucrose solutions and low concentrations of sucrose solutions.

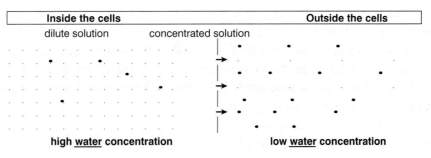

Key:
- • = Sucrose particle
- · = water molecule
- → = osmosis
- | = partially permeable membrane

Tara uses the words 'plasmolysed' and 'turgid' when describing the potato cells. What do these words mean?

In the higher sucrose concentrated solution, the net movement of water (osmosis) is to the outside of the cell, and the chip will lose mass, the cells will become plasmolysed.

The chip in a low concentration of sucrose solution, is the opposite of the diagram above, in that the water osmoses into the cells of the chip, mass is gained, through osmosis of water into the plant cells, the cells will become turgid.

3. What I plan to do

I plan to cut out 12 potato chips (cylinders) of uniform diameter, using a cork borer, and 20 mm length each time.

I will place 2 of each of these chips into each concentration of sucrose solution (0.0, 0.2, 0.4, 0.6, 0.8 and 1.0 mol/litre), leave them in there for 1 hour.

I will have weighed them before putting them into the solution, and I will weigh them when they come out (after lightly drying off the excess water). I will then calculate the percentage change in mass.

$$\frac{\text{Change in mass (g)}}{\text{original mass (g)}} \times 100$$

The apparatus that I will use are; a whiteboard, a scalpel, a pair of tweezers, 6 small beakers, a set of scales accurate to $\frac{1}{100}$ of a gram

I plan to take 12 results over a range of 1.0 mol/litre. I will then average these results down to 6, then make various calculations and plot a graph.

My results should be fairly accurate apart from the error that I have already identified.

At the end of the plan, Tara intends to draw a graph. How should the axes be labelled?

Tara could plan to plot the graph using a computer. Describe, step by step, how this is done.

Tara's Osmosis Task

Teacher's mark	Principal Moderator's Comments
8	Tara's scientific knowledge and understanding is sufficiently detailed (i.e. about grade A standard) to support the prediction and the plan. She realises that repetition of measurements will increase the reliability of the data obtained. Tara carries out preliminary work to establish a suitable time for immersion of the chips. [Note: she really ought to have given details of the results of the preliminary tests]. There is no direct reference to any secondary source used in the production of her plan. Using (and acknowledging) such material may have strengthened her plan. Tara has just about satisfied the requirements for 8 marks in skill P.

Skill O: Obtaining Evidence

This is what to do	Mark	Grade
Collect some evidence, in a safe way, using simple equipment (e.g. beakers, hand lenses, thermometers, heating equipment etc).	2 marks	About Grade G
Collect sensible evidence, (using appropriate equipment) for your task. Record your evidence in the most appropriate way. (Usually this means just writing down your results).	4 marks	About Grade E
In addition to the above: Collect sufficient evidence in an orderly, and systematic way. Repeat readings where you can, and make sure you repeat any measurement, which looks out of place with the others. (Such readings are called anomalous). Make a sensible number of observations or measurements, (over a suitable range), and write them down. The number of readings needs to be enough to be sure you have properly tested the relationship between the variables. If you present your results in a table, don't forget to use correct names **and** units for **each** column.	6 marks	About Grade C
In addition to the above: Show how you obtained results which are **accurate** (think about **which** equipment to use), **precise** (think about **how** to carry out the task, in order to get accurate readings, using the best equipment available to you), and **reliable** (could someone repeat your method, and get very similar results?) Reliability is a key feature of 8 marks. Results need to be repeated, and there should be consistency between the sets of readings.	8 marks	About Grade A

This skill is about obtaining evidence and demonstrating that this evidence is reliable and meaningful. You can use the information in the table to get a general idea of what is needed to achieve different grades. However, you must consider how each of the statements in the table can be satisfied with the particular results that you have obtained.

Level 2 – you only need to collect some evidence.

- Can you collect some evidence using simple equipment? For example, you might use a thermometer to measure the temperature of a liquid and write this temperature down, or you might use a balance to measure a change in mass.

Level 4 – You need to be a bit more organised in collecting and recording your evidence.

- Is the evidence you are planning to collect sensible and relevant to the investigation you have planned?

- Is the equipment you are going to use appropriate? For example, if you need to measure volumes of liquids accurately you should be using a measuring cylinder and not relying on the scale given on the side of a beaker.

- How are you going to record your evidence? Wherever possible record your evidence in the form of a table or in some other logical way, such as a list or a flow diagram, so that it is easy to see and understand.

Level 6 – you need to collect evidence in a systematic way, taking an appropriate number of readings.

- How much evidence do you need to obtain in order to make your investigation reliable and useful?

- Have you thought of the most systematic way of obtaining evidence? Investigations in which evidence is obtained haphazardly generally take much longer than they should and the evidence collected often contains errors. Devise a strategy and then stick to it.

- Does your investigation involve taking readings? Over what range are you going to work? How many readings will you need to take to make your results meaningful?

- Look out for anomalous readings – these are readings that don't seem to fit the general trend or pattern (which you will be able to see if you enter your results into a table as you collect them). Repeat these readings to be sure they are correct. You may have made an error, such as misreading a thermometer, or you may have discovered something very interesting!

- Have you written the title and given the unit in each column of your table?

Level 8 – you need to be able to show that your method is reliable and your results are accurate, and that the method used could be repeated to give similar results.

- How accurate are your results? To some extent this is going to be limited by the equipment used. For example, the width of a wire cannot be measured accurately with a ruler; a micrometer must be used.

- What steps have you taken to ensure that your method of measuring is precise? Do you know that, when reading a mercury-filled thermometer, you should take your reading from the top of the meniscus? Are you planning to use ICT equipment to obtain readings? Do you know how to use it properly? If not, find out from your teacher before you waste time obtaining results that may not be reliable.

- It is often useful to repeat a procedure in order to obtain a second or even third set of readings. Obtaining sets of readings that are similar helps to demonstrate that your method is sound and reliable.

- Could I come along tomorrow and repeat the procedure using only your notes and get a similar set of results? If the answer to this question is no you have not satisfied this level.

In the remaining pages of this section you will find five investigations in which evidence was obtained. Read through each of them carefully and then look at the Principal Moderator's comment. This explains why the work has been given the mark it has.

When you have examined this work think about the ways in which you obtained your evidence in a recent investigation. What mark would you give yourself for obtaining evidence? Was everything really as good as it could have been; or can you now see better, more accurate and reliable ways of obtaining evidence that will get you up to a higher level?

Leon carried out a rate of reaction task. He varied the temperature of the acid, before adding marble chips. He kept the mass and surface area of his marble chips constant, and he measured the total volume of carbon dioxide gas produced.

Leon said: "I will make the experiment fair by using the same size chips, and the same amount of acid. I will repeat the experiments three times, and then get an average."

Leon used 25cm³ of acid and 6 sized 6–9 chips in his experiments.

> Leon does not say which acid he used for this task. Which would you have used?

Rate of Reaction Task

1. Results

> What happens to the mass of the marble chips when they react with acid? How could Leon have used this to follow this reaction? What ICT equipment could he use?

> Leon uses 6 sized 6–9 marble chips for each test. What would have been a better idea?

Temperature in °C	Volume of water displaced (cm³)			
	1	2	3	Average
Room temp	2	1	1	1.33
30°C	2	3	3	2.66
40°C	4	7	6	7.33
50°C	20	15	18	17.66
60°C	15	15	20	16.66

> What should Leon have recorded instead of 'Room temp'?

> Do you think it likely that Leon's recorded temperatures of 30, 40, 50, and 60°C were measured accurately? What would have been a better ICT solution?

> Look carefully at Leon's results for 50°C and 60°C. Are the recorded averages of 17.66 and 16.66 meaningful? What should he have done about it?

Leon's Marble Chips

Tip

Dilute sulphuric acid should not be used with marble chips because the product formed when they react, calcium sulphate, is not very soluble. After a short time a layer of calcium sulphate will cover the marble chips and no further reaction is possible so the results obtained will not be accurate.

Teacher's mark	Principal Moderator's Comments
6	Leon has used a range of 5 temperatures, which is just about sufficient for this task. He has said how much acid was used, what strength the acid was, and what sized marble chips were used. However, Leon doesn't say how he measured the very small volumes of gas evolved. The results table is correctly headed, though 'volume of water displaced' should have been replaced with 'volume of gas produced'. There are three sets of readings, but the measurements at 50 and 60°C lack some consistency. The 'room temperature' reading should have been given in °C. Notice that Leon doesn't say what mass of marble chips were used. Just to say that 6 chips sized 6–9 were used, is not particularly precise.

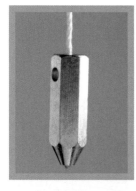

The table below shows Jim's results for a pendulum task. He kept the mass of the pendulum bob constant, varied the length of the string, and measured the time taken for 20 complete swings. He did each measurement three times.

Pendulum Task

Results

Length of string	weight	1	2	3	average	time
10	96.5g	14.12	14.22	14.33	14.22	0.71
20	96.5g	19.09	19.15	19.28	19.17	0.96
30	96.5g	23.06	23.13	23.15	23.11	1.16
40	96.5g	26.88	26.81	26.81	26.83	1.34
50	96.5g	29.75	29.69	29.65	29.70	1.49
60	96.5g	32.75	32.63	32.63	32.67	1.63
70	96.5g	35.00	34.85	34.08	34.98	1.75
80	96.5g	37.37	37.34	37.50	37.40	1.87
90	96.5g	39.22	39.63	39.66	39.50	1.98
100	96.5g	41.78	42.65	42.00	42.01	2.10

Jim did each measurement three times. Do you think he would have got a significant improvement in accuracy if he had repeated each measurement five times – or would it have been a waste of time?

How could you improve the column headings in the table?

Jim has included units for 'weight', but what has he missed out from his table?

💡 Tip

Averaging out results in the way Jim has for each length of string is a good way of improving accuracy. We are assuming that the three measurements are around the correct value with at least one value being a bit above and one value a bit below so when they are averaged any error is made as small as possible. However, this should only be done if the values of the measurements are very similar. Where one value is significantly different from the others it should be taken to be incorrect and ignored.

Jim's Pendulum Task

Teacher's mark	Principal Moderator's Comments
5	The measurements were taken systematically, and they were repeated. The repeat readings are reasonably consistent [i.e. there is little variation between the repeat readings]. A wide number and range of readings was used, (10–100 cm in 10cm intervals) but the table does not give units for length or time, and the term 'weight' has been used instead of 'mass'. Jim would have been awarded 6 marks had he corrected these two simple errors.

When Wasim carried out his electrolysis task, he made a number of observations of what he saw happening at each current value. He then produced the table of results below.

Electrolysis Task

1.2A

Current drops to 1A in first minute, then rises to 1.2A by 2 mins, 1.25A at 5 mins.

Anode visibly worn away at edges.

Anode thinner. Some flakes of copper break off anode and fall to bottom of beaker.

Larger clumps of copper deposit at edge of cathode. Cathode is thicker.

Beige coating on cathode. Solution is warmer. Solution does not change colour.

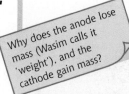

Why does the anode lose mass (Wasim calls it 'weight'), and the cathode gain mass?

1.4A

Current drops to 1.2A in first minute, then rises to 1.3A by 2 mins, 1.46A at 5 mins.

Anode visibly worn at edges. Anode much thinner.

Flakes of copper break off anode, forming a small pile at bottom of beaker.

Larger clumps of copper deposit at edge of cathode. Cathode much thicker. Beige coating on cathode. Solution is much warmer. Solution does not change colour.

At 1.4A and 1.6A Wasim reports that flakes of copper appeared in the beaker. What should Wasim have done in order to make his measurements accurate?

1.6A

Current drops to 1.2A in first minute and gradually rises back up to 1.6A by 5 mins.

Anode is worn away with holes. Anode very thin.

Flakes of copper break off anode, forming a large pile at the bottom of the beaker.

Large lumps of copper deposit at the edge of cathode. Cathode is very thick.

Solution is very warm. Solution does not change colour.

RESULTS

Current (A)	Set 1 – Change of weight after 5 min (g)		Set 2 – Change of weight after 5 min (g)		Average of 2 sets – Change of weight after 5 mins (g)	
	Anode	Cathode	Anode	Cathode	Anode	Cathode
0.8	–0.07	+0.09	–0.06	+0.09	–0.065	+0.090
1.0	–0.10	+0.10	–0.13	+0.11	–0.120	+0.105
1.2	–0.15	+0.16	–0.13	+0.12	–0.140	+0.140
1.4	–0.20	+0.16	–0.14	+0.15	–0.170	+0.155
1.6	–0.12	+0.14	–0.16	+0.18	–0.140	+0.160

Does any one set of Wasim's results appear to be anomalous (out of order with the others)?

What should Wasim do about the anomalous set of results?

Consider the range of current values used. How could Wasim have obtained more data in order to make his results more reliable?

Wasim's Electrolysis Investigation

Teacher's mark	Principal Moderator's Comments
7	The readings have been repeated, and there is not much variation between them. This suggests that the measurements are reliable. The results are clearly and accurately presented, with correct column headings and correct units. They appear to have been made with precision and skill. This is a difficult task, requiring precision and accuracy in measurement. There is a range of 5 readings, which is just sufficient for this task, but the last set of readings do not fit the pattern, so there is some inaccuracy here. Wasim has only 4 sets of reliable data, and this is not sufficient to achieve full marks. Wasim has made some very detailed observation notes at three different current values.

Coursework

Skill: Osmosis

Here are Susan's results for her work on osmosis. Susan used 25 cm³ in total for each concentration, and she used potato cylinders of the same cross sectional area, and length.

Osmosis Investigation

Here is a table of results to show the masses of potato chips before and after they have been placed in varying concentrations of sucrose solutions. I will also show the percentage changes in mass for each chip.

Results

Concentration (mol/litre)	Mass before (g)	Mass after (g)	Percentage change in mass
0.0	1.73	1.87	8.1
0.0	1.61	1.70	5.6
0.2	1.82	1.92	5.5
0.2	1.70	1.81	6.5
0.4	1.73	1.70	-1.7
0.4	1.63	1.61	-1.2
0.6	1.69	1.52	-10.1
0.6	1.63	1.50	-8.0
0.8	1.52	1.30	-14.5
0.8	1.66	1.45	-12.7
1.0	1.66	1.65	1.42
1.0	1.65	1.41	–14.5

> In the first table, why do you think Susan took two readings at each concentration?

I then decided to make good use of the repeats that I made to gain average masses and percentage changes in mass which I calculated with the formula

$$\frac{\text{change in mass (g)}}{\text{original mass(g)}} \times (100)$$

How did Susan calculate the percentage change in mass for the chips?

Concentration (mol/litre)	Average mass before (grams)	Average mass after (grams)	Average percentage change in mass (%)
0.0	1.67	1.79	6.90
0.2	1.76	1.87	6.00
0.4	1.68	1.66	–1.50
0.6	1.66	1.51	–9.10
0.8	1.59	1.38	–13.6
1.0	1.66	1.42	–14.5

Given that living matter shows some variation (i.e. from one piece of potato to the next), do you think these results are reasonably consistent?

Look at the final column in the second results table. Does Susan have sufficient results to produce a really accurate graph? Where on the graph would you advise her to take further readings?

In this second table I have calculated the average masses before and after being in solution (to 3 S.F.) for 1 hour, and I also calculated the average percentage change in mass (to 3 S.F. also).

Susan's Osmosis Task

Teacher's mark	Principal Moderator's Comments
8	The results are clearly and accurately recorded, (i.e. correct table headings and units). The readings have been repeated, and for this task, they are very close together, which suggests that the data is reliable. Note that the masses of the potato chips have been measured to two decimal places, and that a range of 6 concentrations has been used. This is a demanding task, and Susan has done very well to obtain sufficiently precise and accurate results.

Alec investigated the effect of varying the length of Constantan wire on the values of current and voltage in a circuit. He used lengths of between 60 and 200 cm, taking readings at 20 cm intervals, and he switched off the power pack between readings.
He then repeated each reading at a different current value, so that he could compare average resistances. Alec then repeated all of this for four different values of Constantan wire.

Resistance Task

Results

Constantan wire, diameter 0.234 mm, area = πr^2 = 0.043 mm^2
I had to use 0.3A, instead of 0.5A as a repeat reading because I was unable to reach 0.5A on this thickness of wire.

Why did Alec switch off the power pack between readings, and how would that have improved the quality of his results?

length/cm	Current at 0.4A		Current at 0.3A		Average
	Voltage/V	Resistance/Ω	Voltage/V	Resistance/Ω	Resistance/Ω
200.0	9.80	24.50	7.30	24.30	24.40
180.0	8.75	21.88	6.56	21.87	21.88
160.0	7.82	19.55	5.90	19.60	19.58
140.0	6.79	16.98	5.09	16.97	16.98
120.0	5.80	14.50	4.42	14.73	14.62
100.0	4.86	12.15	3.63	12.10	12.30
80.0	3.93	9.83	2.94	9.80	9.82
60.0	2.96	7.40	2.21	7.37	7.39

Did Alec use a satisfactory number, and range, of readings to test the relationship between length and resistance? Do you think the data is reliable?

SWG32

Constantan wire, diameter 0.274mm, area = πr^2 = 0.059 mm^2 (3dp)

What instrument could Alec have used to accurately measure the wire diameter?

length/cm	Current at 0.4A		Current at 0.5A		Average
	Voltage/V	Resistance/Ω	Voltage/V	Resistance/Ω	Resistance/Ω
200.0	6.95	17.38	8.71	17.42	17.40
180.0	6.25	15.63	7.79	15.58	15.60
160.0	5.60	14.00	6.97	13.94	13.97
140.0	4.82	12.05	6.02	12.04	12.05
120.0	4.19	10.48	5.19	10.38	10.43
100.0	3.46	8.65	4.29	8.58	8.62
80.0	2.84	7.10	3.55	7.10	7.10
60.0	2.31	5.33	2.68	5.36	5.35

In general, the resistance values at the higher current for each wire are a little less than those for the lower current. Can you suggest a reason, which could possibly explain why this is?

SWG30

Constantan wire, diameter 0.315 mm, area = πr^2 = 0.078 mm^2

length/cm	Current at 0.4A		Current at 0.5A		Average
	Voltage/V	Resistance/Ω	Voltage/V	Resistance/Ω	Resistance/Ω
200.0	5.38	13.45	6.71	13.42	13.40
180.0	4.84	12.10	6.07	12.44	12.12
160.0	4.35	10.88	5.37	10.74	10.87
140.0	3.76	9.40	4.71	9.42	9.41
120.0	3.22	8.05	4.00	8.00	8.03
100.0	2.71	6.78	3.36	6.72	6.70
80.0	2.18	5.45	2.75	5.50	5.50
60.0	1.64	4.10	2.05	4.10	4.10

What information should Alec tap into the computer in order for it to produce graphs in the next stage of his investigation?

SWG28

Constantan wire, diameter 0.376 mm, area = πr^2 = 0.11 mm^2

length/cm	Current at 0.4A		Current at 0.5A		Average
	Voltage/V	Resistance/Ω	Voltage/V	Resistance/Ω	Resistance/Ω
200.0	3.60	9.00	4.49	8.98	8.99
180.0	3.22	8.05	4.08	8.16	8.12
160.0	2.86	7.16	3.58	7.16	7.16
140.0	2.51	6.28	3.16	6.32	6.30
120.0	2.15.	5.38	2.71	5.42	5.40
100.0	1.80	4.50	2.27	4.54	4.52
80.0	1.45	3.63	1.79	3.58	3.60
60.0	1.11	2.78	1.36	2.72	2.75

SWG26

Constantan wire, diameter 0.457 mm, area = πr^2 = 0.16mm^2

length/cm	Current at 0.4A		Current at 0.5A		Average
	Voltage/V	Resistance/Ω	Voltage/V	Resistance/Ω	Resistance/Ω
200.0	2.50	6.25	3.09	6.18	6.22
180.0	2.26	5.65	2.79	5.58	5.62
160.0	1.99	4.98	2.47	4.94	4.96
140.0	1.75	4.38	2.17	4.34	4.36
120.0	1.47	3.68	1.86	3.72	3.70
100.0	1.24	3.10	1.54	3.08	3.09
80.0	1.00	2.50	1.25	2.50	2.50
60.0	0.76	1.90	0.94	1.88	1.89

Alec's Resistance Task

Teacher's mark	Principal Moderator's Comments
8	Alec has made his measurements in a systematic manner. There are eight measurements taken at lengths of wire varying from 0.6 to 2.0 metres. This is a good number and range of readings. The values for each of the calculated resistances are very close which implies that his measurements were accurate. There are repeat readings for each of five different wires, which are recorded clearly in a results table containing correct column headings and correct units. Note that Alec has quoted the different wire diameters [perhaps measured with a micrometer?] and also he has calculated the cross sectional area for each wire.

Skill A: Analysing and Considering Evidence

This is what to do	Mark Awarded	Grade
Say (in a few words) what you have found out in your task.	2 marks	About Grade G
Present your results in a simple bar chart, or some other type of chart. Use your results to identify a pattern, or trend in the results.	4 marks	About Grade E
Process your results by **EITHER**: a) doing some calculations, such as substituting into a formula (but **not** just averaging some data) **OR**: b) drawing a graph with a line of best fit (if this is appropriate), either by hand, or with the aid of a computer. (If using a computer, you will need to check that it draws the line of best fit. If it doesn't, make sure that you draw in the correct line on the graph.) Use your calculations, or the information shown by your graph to come to a conclusion, and explain the results using your scientific knowledge. (You don't need to write out again any scientific knowledge, which is in your plan, but you may want to refer to it. E.g. "see page 1, paragraph 3", which gives the scientific explanation…)	6 marks	About Grade C
In addition to the above: Use detailed scientific knowledge and understanding (i.e. About Grade A standard) in your explanation of the results. You may wish to include some more difficult mathematical processing, such as obtaining gradients from graphs, or plotting rates of reaction. (Rate is proportional to the inverse of time). Refer back to your prediction, (if you made one) and explain how well your results match up. Use the information in your graph (or your numerical work) to do this.	8 marks	About Grade A

This skill is about presenting the results you have obtained in a meaningful way and then trying to identify a pattern or a trend in them. The information in the table gives you a guide to what is needed to achieve different grades. However, you must consider how each of these general statements can be satisfied with the particular results that you have obtained.

Level 2 – you simply need to simply state the result

● Write down a single sentence stating what you found out. This may simply be the question that you asked in the planning skill. For example, your planning statement might have been 'I am going to find out which fruit juice contains the most vitamin C' and your result might be 'Orange juice contained the most vitamin C'.

Level 4 – you need to display your results in a simple bar chart and identify a pattern or trend.

● Use your results to draw a bar chart. Are the heights of the bars in the same proportion as your results? Have you labelled each bar and the height axis?

● Can you see any pattern or trend in your results? Do they go up or come down? Can you write a statement like 'as .... increases so .... increases/decreases'?

Level 6 – again you need to display your results and identify a pattern or trend but for this level the treatment must be more sophisticated.

● Use your results to draw a line graph with a line of best fit. This line is unlikely to go through all of the points (and in exceptional circumstances may not go through any of them) but its shape should indicate the general trend shown by the points. It may be a straight or curved line. Have you chosen sensible scales so that most of the grid is being used? Have you labelled the axes? Is there a point that appears apart from the others? Don't put a kink into the line of best fit just because one reading is apart from the others. Accept that it is an anomalous result and ignore it.

● Instead of drawing a graph you can also satisfy this level of **Skill A** by doing some reasonably demanding calculations. These may involve substituting values into equations such as $R = V/I$ to find a resistance; $P = VI$ to find electrical power or $E = msT$ to find the energy released by burning a fuel. Write down the equation you are going to use in words. Are the values you are going to substitute into the equation in the correct units? In what unit is the answer?

● Look at the line graph your have drawn or the calculations you have carried out. Can you use your results to come to a conclusion about the investigation? Can you explain this conclusion using your scientific knowledge? For example, you may have drawn a graph showing how the rate of a reaction increases with temperature. You should be able to make a statement like 'as temperature increases the rate of reaction increases because particles are colliding more often'.

Level 8 – you need to show a higher level of scientific knowledge in your explanation

● Can you obtain any more results from your graph by finding the area under the line or the gradient. For example, if you have a graph of distance against time the area under the graph gives the total distance travelled and the gradient gives the velocity. Similarly, in a graph of velocity against time the gradient gives the acceleration.

● Can you plot another graph based on the same results? For example, if you have used data to plot a graph of concentration against time, what happens if you plot concentration against 1/time?

● Can you use scientific principles to explain your results? Your explanation needs to show understanding beyond level 6. For example, in explaining why the rate of a reaction increases with temperature, you might describe how the kinetic energy of the particles increases as the temperature increases and, because they are moving around more quickly, they are likely to collide more often, and when they do the collision is more likely to be effective. Try to correctly use terms like 'exothermic', 'endothermic' and 'activation energy'.

● Relate what you have found back to any predictions you made in your planning. Vague statements are no use at this level. You must use information specifically from your graph, or the results of calculations in your analysis.

In the remaining pages of this section you will find four attempts at analysing evidence. Read through each of them carefully and then look at the Principal Moderator's comment. This explains why the work has been given the mark it has.

When you have examined this work look back on any analysis you have carried out on a recent investigation. What mark would you give your analysis? Are there things you have forgotten to do? Can you now see ways of improving your analysis so pushing it to a higher level?

Here is James's conclusion to his osmosis task, in which he placed pieces of potato in four different solutions. He weighed the potato chips before and after doing the test.

Tip

The terms 'histogram' and 'bar chart' are often used as if they mean the same thing but this is not the case. In a histogram comparison is made on the basis of the area of each block; the blocks may not all be the same width. In a bar chart, which is what we would normally use to display simple data, the bars are all the same width and comparison is made on the basis of the height of each block.

Osmosis Task

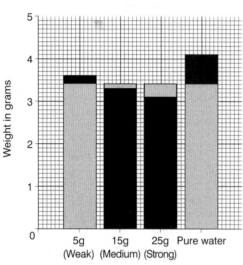

Key

■ Indicates final highest weight

▨ Previous highest weight

How could James have improved the way he presented the information in the bar chart?

What labels would you have chosen for the axes?

What evidence, missing from James's set of results, would have produced more convincing results for this task?

This graph clearly shows that the potato which was placed in 5g and pure water solutions increased in weight

Tip

When drawing a bar chart it is not necessary to leave a gap between the bars but it does improve the presentation and it is worth doing where space allows.

Conclusions

From carrying out the osmosis experiments I believe that the molecules inside a potato would escape if the potato was placed in high concentrated and medium concentrated solutions of sugars. This would and did result in reduction in size and weight of the potato. My results table proves this.

James's conclusion is not well written. How could he have expressed himself more clearly?

James's Osmosis Task

Teacher's mark	Principal Moderator's Comments
4	There is a simple bar chart showing initial and final weights of the potato chips. However, the 'pure water' column is in the wrong place. Putting it to the left of the 5 g column, would have made the pattern easier to see. There is an attempt at a scientific explanation, but a more detailed explanation is needed for 6 marks. James has attempted to find a pattern in his conclusion, though it is not expressed very clearly.

This is Kate's conclusion to her 'murky problem' practical (p.246).

Kate's 'Murky Problem'

1. Method

She was looking at the reaction between sodium thiosulphate and hydrochloric acid, which produced a yellow precipitate of sulphur.

She varied the temperatures and noted the time taken for a drawing of a fish to be covered by sulphur.

She calculated the rates at various points [Rate is proportional to 1/time], and then she produced the graph and conclusion below.

2. Results

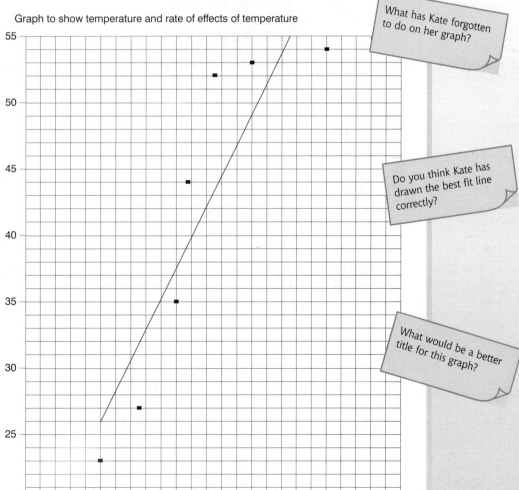

Graph to show temperature and rate of effects of temperature

What has Kate forgotten to do on her graph?

Do you think Kate has drawn the best fit line correctly?

What would be a better title for this graph?

Tip

When plotting a graph use most, or all of the grid and not just one corner of it. This allows you to space readings out and gives you greater accuracy if you need to read information off the graph.

Tip

When deciding on the scale for an axis, think in terms of blocks of one, two or four large squares but never three. Choosing blocks of three large squares leads to small squares being equivalent to awkward fractions such as thirds, and makes accurate plotting very difficult.

3. Conclusion

"Looking at my graph and results, I can see that I have proved my hypothesis that

Is Kate's conclusion consistent with the evidence she obtained?

rate increases with temperature because at low temperatures particles of reacting substances do not have much energy. However when the substances are heated, the particles take in more energy. This causes them to move faster and collide more often. The collisions have more energy so more of them are successful. Therefore the rate of the reaction increases."

Kate's 'Murky Problem'

Teacher's mark	Principal Moderator's Comments
5	Kate has attempted to draw a line graph, but there is no scale on the X axis, and neither axis is labelled. The line of best fit could be much better too! She hasn't used her data points in drawing the graph. Kate has only partly achieved this part of the assessment. The scientific explanation given by Kate is correct, (with sufficient detail at about grade C standard) so Kate can be awarded 5 marks.

Sarah carried out an investigation into the efficiency of an electric motor.

Efficiency of an electric motor

1. Method

She attached masses (ranging from 50 to 350 g) to a mass hanger, and recorded the time taken for an electric motor to raise the masses a certain distance. Sarah then performed some numerical calculations, drew a graph and wrote a conclusion.

She used these equations to do her numerical work:

$$\text{Efficiency} = \frac{\text{Output power}}{\text{Input power}} \qquad \text{Output power} = \frac{\text{Work Done}}{\text{Time taken}}$$

$$\text{Input power} = \text{Current (A)} \times \text{Voltage (V)}$$

$$\text{Work done} = \text{Force (N)} \times \text{Distance (m)}$$

> What would have been an accurate way to measure the time taken for the masses to rise by 1.48m?

> What is the scope for using ICT equipment in this task?

2. Results

> Look at Sarah's readings in the time taken column. Would you agree that they are sufficiently consistent, or would you have repeated any of them?

Mass (g)	Force (N)	Time taken (s)	Average time (s)	Voltage (V)	Current (A)	Distance "D" (M)
50	0.5	1.41 1.42 1.17	1.33	7	0.66	1.48
100	1	1.79 1.49 1.67	1.65	7	0.78	1.48
150	1.5	1.48 1.59 1.73	1.6	7	0.83	1.48
200	2	1.86 2.14 2.57	2.19	7	0.88	1.48
250	2.5	2.34 2.39 2.6	2.44	7	1.01	1.48
300	3	3.25 3.33 2.97	3.18	7	1.04	1.48
350	3.5	4.24 4.10 4.25	4.19	7	1.17	1.48

Work done by motor (J)	Power output of motor (W)	Power input of circuit (W)	Efficiency of motor (%)
0.74	0.56	4.62	12
1.48	0.9	5.46	16.4
2.22	1.39	5.81	23.9
2.96	1.35	6.16	21.9
3.7	1.51	7.07	21.4
4.44	1.4	7.28	19
5.18	1.24	8.19	15

How did Sarah convert masses in grams, to forces in Newtons?

Tip

When drawing curves freehand don't be tempted to simply join the plots one at a time. The result looks horrible and you will get no credit for it. Try to get a smooth line by drawing from what will be the inside of the curve so that you draw the line as you rotate your wrist.

Tip

Efficiency may be expressed as a number between 0 and 1 or as a percentage by multiplying the number by 100. However, in either form it has no units.

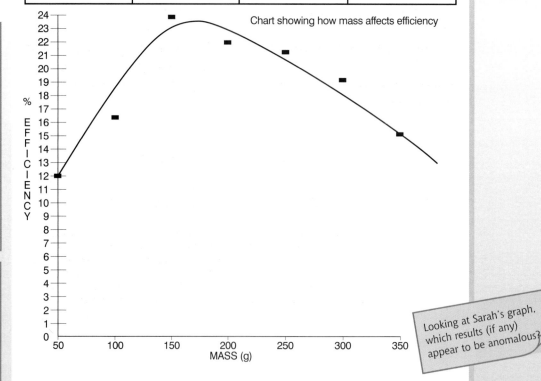

Chart showing how mass affects efficiency

Looking at Sarah's graph, which results (if any) appear to be anomalous?

3. Conclusion

Sarah wrote: "From my graph I can see that the efficiency peaks at a mass of 150g with a high of **23.9%**. My lowest value was 12% and was recorded when the 50g mass was attached. I would say that as the mass increased so did the efficiency up until a certain point was reached, after which the efficiency decreased. My prediction turned out to be correct to a certain extent in that I was correct in saying that heavier masses have a

Tip

Don't be afraid to identify anomalous results. It is better to ignore such results when drawing a graph than distorting the line by trying to include them.

smaller efficiency – I was incorrect in that I didn't predict that the lighter masses too would have a low efficiency. It did not occur to me that the efficiency would peak at a certain mass. I believe that the efficiency of the heavier masses was lower due to the fact that a larger current was required to lift the masses. I am aware that a larger current is responsible for a greater heat loss than that of a low current.

This comes from the equation $P = I^2R$

The above equation comes from $P = I \times V$ and $V = I \times R$, so $P = I^2R$

There may have also been some energy loss in the heavier masses due to sound and friction. The low efficiency of the lighter masses is harder to account for. It may be due to fact that the lighter weights were moving so fast it was hard to time it correctly or maybe more likely to the effect that friction was having on the experiment and since these were light weights this could easily have affected them. Even in the lighter weights there were energy changes and energy was lost in the form of sound and heat."

Sarah's Electric Motor

Teacher's mark	Principal Moderator's Comments
7	Sarah has done some numerical processing, and she has drawn a graph. She has attempted to explain her results using scientific knowledge but there is some confusion in her conclusion, (about frictional effects with the lighter masses), which means she doesn't quite deserve the top mark. Sarah has, however, made a good job of linking her results to her prediction, and she has clearly stated why her results do not match her prediction.

Here is Michael's graph and conclusion to his osmosis task.

The Effect of Sucrose Concentration on Osmosis in Potato Chips

1. Results

Michael could have improved his labelling of the X axis. How?

At what value does the graph's line cross the X axis?

Michael produced this graph on a computer. How would you have produced this graph using a computer?

What should you do if the computer produced line is 'dot-to-dot', i.e. not a smooth curve?

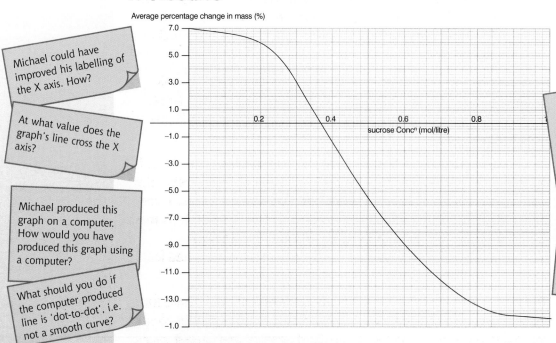

Where the graph line cuts the x axis, the solutions are said to be isotonic. What does isotonic mean in the context of this task?

If Michael had been asked to determine the 'isotonic point' exactly, what should he have done?

2. Conclusion

From the graph, you can see that as sucrose concentration increases, first (at a concentration of 0.0 mol/litre which is de-ionised water) the percentage mass change is a large gain of 6.90%. This falls to an increase of 6.00% at a concentration of 0.2 mol/litre. The mass change = 0.0 at a concentration of 0.38 mol/litre. The percentage change in mass continues to fall rapidly, and at a concentration of 0.4 mol/litre, the mass decreases by 1.50%, this decrease continues, and at a concentration of 0.6 mol/litre, the decrease in mass is 9.10%. When the concentration is 0.8 mol/litre, the decrease becomes slightly less rapid and the percentage mass lost is 13.6%.

Tip

Under some circumstances you might want to plot two graphs on the same grid. Take care not to get the plots mixed up or you will end up in a mess. Use different symbols for each set of plots and use different styles, such as full and broken, or colours when drawing lines of best fit.

The decrease further evens out, and at a concentration of 1.0 mol/litre the mass lost is 14.5%, and the curve evens out substantially.

The reason for these changes in mass is osmosis (see plan for definition), and the rate and direction of osmosis is different at varying concentrations. When the concentration of the sucrose is 0.0 mol/litre (no sucrose is present) the water concentration is higher outside the potato chip (and its cells). This concentration gradient therefore causes water molecules to osmose down the concentration gradient, across the partially permeable membrane and into the plant cells (those of the potato chips). This was the case at concentrations of 0.0 and 0.2 mol/litre, where mass was gained by the chips. This causes the cells to become turgid (the chips that gained mass were physically stiff, because their cells are filled with water).

At a concentration of 0.38 mol/litre, the concentration of water inside the chip (and its cells) and outside the chip are the same, because the net movement of water is 0.0, and no mass is gained or lost by the chip.

At concentrations of 0.4, 0.6, 0.8 and 1.0 mol/litre, mass is lost by the chips, this is because the concentration of water inside the cell is greater than that outside the cell, therefore water osmoses out of the cell. At the concentration of 0.4, 0.6, 0.8 and 1.0 mass is lost because of this, and the cells of the chips became plasmolysed (and the chips quite soft) because the cells had lost water.

The trend of my graph I have already explained, in that firstly the mass is gained, then the mass increase decreases until it becomes a mass decrease, it continues to rapidly decrease, and then it evens out at the end. This analogy is as the sucrose concentration increases.

The graph does support my original prediction (as I have explained) that I stated in my planning.

Michael's Osmosis Task

Teacher's mark	Principal Moderator's Comments
8	Michael has processed his results by calculating the percentage change in mass. He has drawn a graph with correctly labelled axes, and he has drawn the correct line of best fit. The conclusion is explained in sufficient detail (at about Grade A standard) to access the top mark, and is based on his processed evidence. Michael explains how his results are related to his prediction.

Skill E: Evaluating the Evidence

This is what to do	Mark Awarded	Grade
Make a simple, relevant, comment about the way you did your experiment or investigation. Alternatively, make a simple, relevant, comment on the results you obtained. Comments such as "I have got good results" don't count.	2 marks	About Grade F
Say something meaningful about the accuracy of your results. Think about what you actually did, and refer to your graph. If you have any anomalous results say which they are. (You could also show them on your graph by circling them). Think about the way you did your task, and say whether your method was good enough to do what you wanted to do at the start. If possible, suggest an improvement to your method, to make your results more accurate and reliable i.e. something to ensure that your method could be repeated and the same (or better) results obtained.	4 marks	About Grade C
Discuss by referring to your graph, (or your numerical data) whether you think your results were sufficiently reliable to achieve what you set out to do. If you have any anomalous results, make some reasonable suggestions to explain what you think may have caused them. Think about what you did. Suggest in some detail a way to improve the quality of your results, (i.e. was the method you used good enough or could you have improved some aspect of it? Was the range you used wide enough? Did you take enough readings in all areas of the range you used?).	6 marks	About Grade A

This skill is about evaluating what you have done. It involves you looking back through your investigation and giving some honest opinions about what was good and what was not so good, and how the procedure can be improved. The information in the table gives you a general idea of what is needed to achieve different grades. However, you must consider how each of these statements can be satisfied with the particular results that you have obtained.

Level 2 – You need to make a simple relevant comment about what you have done

- Are you able to make a simple relevant comment about how you carried out the investigation or on the results you obtained? The important thing here is *relevant*. Comments like "It was a very good experiment and I enjoyed doing it" may well be true but they are not relevant and will not get any marks. What is needed are comments like "If I was going to repeat this experiment I would take readings over a wider range so that it would be easier to see the pattern between ...".

Level 4 – You need to comment meaningfully on the accuracy of your results

- Did the apparatus you used allow you to obtain the necessary degree of accuracy? If not what other piece(s) of apparatus would you need and how would they allow you to get results that are more accurate? For example, you might have measured temperatures between 25 and 60°C using a thermometer of range 0 to 360°C with gradations every 2°C. A thermometer of range –10 to 110°C with gradations every 1°C would have allowed you to measure temperature with greater accuracy.

- Identify any anomalous results that don't seem to fit the general pattern or trend shown by the rest.

- Were there any problems with the procedures you used? How could you modify these procedures so that your results would be more accurate?

Level 6 – You need to talk about the reliability of what you did and give a detailed account of how procedures could be improved

- Look back at the plan of your investigation; this is what you set out to achieve. Are your results sufficiently accurate to answer the questions posed in the plan?

- What about the measurements you took? Did you take sufficient results to be able to plot a graph and draw a line of best fit with sufficient accuracy? Did you take readings over a wide enough range or could the range be meaningfully extended?

- What about the procedure you adopted? Was any of the apparatus particularly difficult to use? Was any apparatus or equipment unreliable? For example, did a burette leak from around the tap or did one of the leads used in an electric circuit appear to be faulty? Can you think of an alternative way of doing things that would be more reliable? Give all of the details.

- Did you get any anomalous results? Don't ignore them and hope that the moderators won't spot them when they come to look at your work. It is to your credit that you recognise results that are anomalous and if you can explain how they came about and what can be done to avoid this problem in repeating the investigation you will be rewarded for it.

The amount of detail needed to obtain a good level in this skill is often underestimated; even by the more able students. In the remaining pages of this section you will find five evaluations. Read through each of them carefully and then look at the Principal Moderator's comment. This explains why the work has been given the mark it has.

When you have examined this work look back at the last evaluation you carried out on an investigation. Did you really spend the amount of time on it that you should or did you just treat it as something of little value at the end of the investigation? What mark would you give your evaluation? Do you now appreciate the importance of evaluation? Can you now see things that you should have commented on and suggest how the reliability of the investigation can be improved?

Below is Andrew's evaluation of an osmosis task.

Osmosis Task

1. Method

He had placed potato chips in different strengths of sugar solution. In each case he measured both the change in mass and the change in length of the potato chips.

2. Evaluation

Andrew wrote "I believe if I was to do this experiment again I could improve by using more solutions like 0.01, 0.25 and so on, because this would give me more results to plot on a graph and I could get a better best line of fit".

What could Andrew have done to improve the quality of this evaluation?

Andrew's Osmosis Task

Teacher's mark	Principal Moderator's Comments
2	Andrew has made a simple relevant comment on the procedure he used, since he appreciates that more results should enable him to draw a better line of best fit.

Rosemary did an investigation using a pendulum. Here is her evaluation.

Pendulum Investigation
Evaluation
"I think that I went the right way about doing this investigation, and I don't think that there is anything that needs to be improved upon other than if I had repeated the results and taken averages I would have had more reliable results.

Using a light gate would improve the accuracy of my results and make it more reliable".

> Rosemary has produced a similar standard of evaluation, compared with Andrew's. It is, however, marginally better. In what way is it better?

> How would the use of light gates be likely to improve the reliability of the evidence?

> Draw a diagram to show how Rosemary could have set up the pendulum using light gates, a sense and control box, and a computer.

Rosemary's Pendulum Investigation

Teacher's mark	Principal Moderator's Comments
3	Rosemary has made similar comments to Andrew, but she has gone one stage further by suggesting the use of a light gate, which when connected to suitable computer equipment should produce more reliable data (in terms of measuring the time for the pendulum's swing). She has achieved part of the 4 mark description and so she can be awarded 3 marks.

This is John's evaluation for a rate of reaction task

Rate of Reaction Task

Evaluation

I thought that my experiment went well although I had to repeat a few of the temperatures because my results were a long way out, so I discarded the odd result and wrote in the fourth result. This gave me a better average. I thought that my measurements were quite accurate because I used the same amount of acid (25 ml) and I used the same size chips (size 6-9). I found that my results for 60°C was an odd result. This means that the gas must have escaped before I could get the bung in the top of the boiling tube. This happened a few times but I re-did some experiments because the bung wasn't in the boiling tube properly and it wasn't bubbling as much as it should. I think that at 60°C the reaction went so quickly that most of the gas escaped before I could put the bung in the top of the boiling tube. This means that the reaction slowed down and the hydrogen irons began to move around slower and the chips had been eaten away quite a bit by the acid.

I only got one bad odd result so the rest of my results were reliable. My results showed me that every 10°C that the temperature rises the reaction rate speeds up (it doubles). My experiment showed me that my prediction was right. It proved

Why does John feel his results are generally accurate (apart from one anomalous result)?

What gas is evolved in this reaction? Can you write the chemical equation?

The final sentence in the first paragraph does not make much sense. Rewrite it in your own words, so that it does make sense.

that the rate of reaction doubles every 10°C and that the hydrogen irons move around faster as the temperature is increased. I could improve my experiment by using different sized chips. If I used smaller chips the reaction would be more speeded up and I would have got better results and if I had used larger chips the reaction would slow down and the experiment would have gone too slowly. I could also have used other strengths of acid.

I used 0.5 molar so the reaction didn't go too quickly but if I used 1 molar acid it would have given me higher probably better results. To get better results and improve my experiments I could have repeated the same experiment about 5 times and then get an average.

I think that the experiment would be better if I could mix the acid and chips after I had put the bung in the top of the boiling tube.

In the second paragraph, John talks about "the reaction rate doubling every 10°C." What would you have done (in the analysis section) to show this?

In the final paragraph John says ..... "I could have repeated the experiment about five times and then got an average". He doesn't give a reason for this proposal. What might the reason be?

Draw a piece of apparatus, which John could have used in order to meet the improvement suggested in the final sentence.

John's Rate of Reaction Task

Teacher's mark	Principal Moderator's Comments
4	During the carrying out of the practical, John conducts three tests at each temperature. Where he discovered an anomalous result, he did a fourth test, and then discarded the incorrect result. He has clearly identified an anomalous result, at 60°C. There are comments on the procedure John used, and there is a suggestion that repeating the experiment "about five times to get an average", would improve the reliability of his results. Mixing the acid with the marble chips, after the bung is put on, would also improve the reliability of the evidence, though John does not give a reason for this suggestion. Note: John is not penalised for the use of the word 'irons' rather than 'ions'.

This is Alec's evaluation for his resistance task

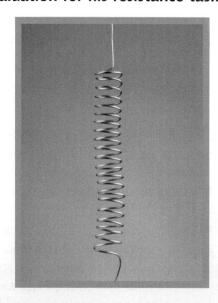

Resistance Task

Evaluation

"My results were very accurate as my repeat readings with 0.5A were very close to my first readings. There were only a few experimental errors, where points did not fit exactly on the straight line or curve. There were no anomalous results. The experimental errors could be due to a number of reasons; flickering of the voltmeter or ammeter, not measuring the wire accurately, and having kinks in the wire.

Due to experimental errors, reading voltmeters and ammeters and measuring the wires, my results are not that reliable.

If I take a typical value of voltage, e.g. 5.0V and the voltmeter flickered and was 0.01V out, the error would be:

$$\frac{0.01 \times 100}{5} = 0.2\% \text{ error}$$

If my ammeter reading was 0.01A out on my worst (lowest) reading of 0.4A the error would be

> Do you think that Alec has given reasonable ideas to explain his experimental errors?

$$\frac{0.1 \times 100}{0.40} = 2.5\% \text{ error}$$

If the length was not accurate due to kinks in the wire, or not measuring accurately, the error of my lowest length 60cm would be:

$$\frac{0.1cm \times 100}{60 \ cm} = 0.16\% \text{ error}$$

If the crocodile clips (2) did not grip the wire in the right place so that the wire was the exact length, the error would be:

$$\frac{0.4cm \times 100}{60cm} = 0.7\% \text{ error}$$

This means the total estimated error of my results would be 3.56%. My results are therefore not very reliable as this error may be due to more kinks or more inaccurate readings. If I was to repeat the experiment again, to reduce the experimental error I would stretch the wire out completely, free of kinks and sellotape it at more frequent intervals so it is kept straight.

To extend the enquiry I would investigate with different materials of wire.

The worst percentage errors were from the flickering of the voltmeter and ammeter. If possible I would repeat the experiment with more sensitive voltmeters and ammeters so the results would be more accurate".

Has Alec made suggestions to improve the reliability of his experimental data?

Alec's Resistance Task

Teacher's mark	Principal Moderator's Comments
5	Alec has made comments on the accuracy of his results. He has also made suggestions to improve the reliability (e.g. To stretch the wire out to avoid kinks.) Alec has also identified a number of sources of experimental error. His detailed mathematical analysis of percentage errors partly satisfies the 6 mark descriptions. The brief suggestions to extend the enquiry, are lacking in the detail needed to consider the award of 6 marks. He does not say what he would do with the different wires.

This is Wasim's evaluation for his electrolysis task (p.263).

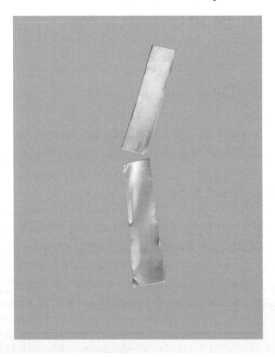

Electrolysis Task

Evaluation

On the whole, I think that this investigation went quite well and I believe I carried it out to the best of my abilities in the conditions provided. My range of 5 currents was adequate to plot a graph which supports my hypothesis, giving enough evidence to support a firm conclusion. The one point which did not follow the trend has been explained in the Discussion of Results. There is not a great difference between my first and second set of results, showing that they are reasonably accurate and reliable. The amount of copper lost from the anode and gained at the cathode was also fairly consistent, showing that the tests were carried out accurately.

Do you think a 'range of 5 currents' is sufficient for this task?

What range of current values would you use?

Do you think Wasim has 'enough evidence to support a firm conclusion'?

I chose this method of setting up my circuit because it is standard and also it is the simplest and easiest to set up. I used copper for my electrodes and not carbon so I would not have to change my solution each time to keep the concentration the same as the copper from the anode replaces that which has been lost from the solution because there was not enough copper sulphate solution.

Sources of error

1. The current fell initially, especially for the larger currents, and, in some test, did not rise back up to the first setting for 3-4 min. This is because, the bigger the current, the longer it takes for the flow of ions in the solution to reach the speed required for that current. Also, heating up of the solution causes the ions to move more, creating resistance and lowering the current. This affected the results because, in some test, electrolysis at the initial setting of the current was not truly reflected in the results as the electrolysis was run at a lower setting for part of the test.

2. Although care was taken to dry the electrodes carefully, some copper may have been blown or chip off before it was weighed, so the weight recorded may have been slightly less than the actual weight.

3. The heating up of the solutions at higher currents changed the temperature, which should have been controlled because a rise in temperature causes the ions to move more and increases the chances of collision with the electrodes.

4. The loss of copper from the anode was not exactly the same as the gain in weight of the cathode for every test, so the concentration of copper ions in the solution may have varied slightly, affecting the chance of collision with the electrodes.

5. The anode completely dissolved away for some tests, so the surface area for reaction was changed, affecting the speed of reaction.

6. The scale and ammeter were only to 2 decimal places, so there is a + or − of 0.005 for the readings.

Possible improvements

1. Running the tests for longer to reach a consistent current.

2. Adjusting the current during the tests to keep it constant.

3. Doing the test in a water bath to control the temperature.

4. Using carbon electrodes and changing the copper sulphate solution each time to keep the concentration consistent.

5. Change the copper electrodes each time, using electrodes with identical surface area to control the surface area for reaction.

6. Using more sensitive scales and ammeters that give readings to more decimal places.

Possible extensions

1. Investigating higher and lower currents to see if the directly proportional trend continues or if there are other limiting factors.

2. Investigating other variables, like temperature and concentration.

3. Investigating electrolysis with other solutions.

4. Further research into Faraday's Laws to explain my results in more depth.

Part of the criteria for the award of six marks in skill E is the discussion of plausible reasons (reasonable suggestions) to explain any anomalous results. Has Wasim done this adequately?

Wasim's graph looked like this:

The Y axis was labelled "increase in weight of cathode (g)". Was Wasim correct to draw a straight line, in the range 0–0.8A?

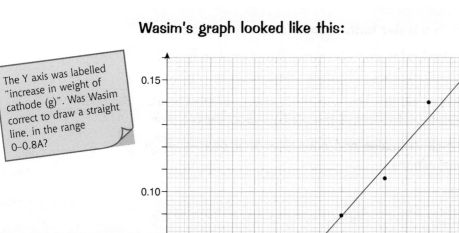

Is the plotted point at 1.6A just an anomalous result? Could there be a simple reason, which might explain this result?

Do you think Wasim should have extended his X axis, in order to take further readings at higher currents? What would be the point of doing this?

Wasim's Electrolysis Evaluation

Teacher's mark	Principal Moderator's Comments
6	Wasim comments on the accuracy of his results, and identifies an anomalous result (which he discusses in his analysis section, not shown in this extract). Wasim discusses his procedure and he makes some good suggestions for improvement to the technique. Wasim makes some detailed comments on the anomalous result and provides some possible explanations. There are a number of suggestions for making an improvement to the quality of the data, and for extending the enquiry. He has done just enough here to satisfy this part of the 6 mark descriptions.

Index

Index

Periodic Table

group numbers

1	2
Li 3 lithium	Be 4 beryllium
Na 11 sodium	Mg 12 magnesium
K 19 potassium	Ca 20 calcium
Rb 37 rubidium	Sr 38 strontium
Cs 55 caesium	Ba 56 barium

— the alkaline earth metals
— the alkali metals

H 1 hydrogen

Sc 21 scandium	Ti 22 titanium	V 23 vanadium	Cr 24 chromium	Mn 25 manganese	Fe 26 iron	Co 27 cobalt	Ni 28 nickel	Cu 29 copper	Zn 30 zinc
Y 39 yttrium	Zr 40 zirconium	Nb 41 niobium	Mo 42 molybdenum	Tc 43 technetium	Ru 44 ruthenium	Rh 45 rhodium	Pd 46 palladium	Ag 47 silver	Cd 48 cadmium
Lanthanides see below	Hf 72 tungsten	Ta 73 tantalum	W 74 tungsten	Re 75 rhenium	Os 76 osium	Ir 77 indium	Pt 78 platinum	Au 79 gold	Hg 80 mercury

— the transition metals

3	4	5	6	7	0 (or 8)
					He 2 helium
B 5 boron	C 6 carbon	N 7 nitrogen	O 8 oxygen	F 9 fluorine	Ne 10 hydrogen
Al 13 aluminium	Si 14 silicon	P 15 phosphorus	S 16 sulphur	Cl 17 chlorine	Ar 18 argon
Ga 31 gallium	Ge 32 germanium	As 33 arsenic	Se 34 selenium	Br 35 bromine	Kr 36 krypton
In 49 indium	Sn 50 tin	Sb 51 antimony	Te 52 tellurium	I 53 iodine	Xe 54 xenon
Tl 81 thallium	Pb 82 lead	Bi 83 bismuth	Po 84 polonium	At 85 astatine	Rn 86 radon

— the halogens
— the noble gases

Lanthanides

La 57 lanthanum	Ce 58 cerium	Pr 59 praseodymium	Nd 60 neodymium	Pm 61 promethium	Sm 62 samarium	Eu 63 europium	Gd 64 gadolinium	Tb 65 terbium	Dy 66 dysprosium	Ho 67 holmium	Er 68 erbium	Tm 69 thulium	Yb 70 ytterbium	Lu 71 luteium

Actinides

Ac 89 actinium	Th 90 thorium	Pa 91 tantalum	U 92 uranium	Np 93 neptunium	Pu 94 plutonium	Am 95 americium	Cm 96 curium	Bk 97 berkelium	Cf 98 californium	Es 99 einsteinium	Fm 100 fermium	Md 101 mendelevium	No 102 nobelium	Lr 103 lawrencium